MANAGING MANUFACTURING OPERATIONS: A CASEBOOK

T. A. J. Nicholson

M

© T. A. J. Nicholson 1978

First published 1978
Reprinted 1981

Published by
THE MACMILLAN PRESS LTD
London and Basingstoke
Companies and representatives throughout the world

Printed in Great Britain by
BILLING AND SONS LTD
Guildford, Worcester and London

British Library Cataloguing in Publication Data

Nicholson, T A J
  Managing manufacturing operations
  1. Factory management — Great Britain — Case
  studies
  I. Title
  658'.007'22 TS155

ISBN 0-333-22617-8
ISBN 0-333-22618-6 Pbk

Contents

Preface

This book provides a detailed statement of the policies, procedures and practices used in a wide variety of British manufacturing companies. It concentrates on describing what actually happens in the organisation — who determines the targets, who is responsible for delivery, how the shop floor works — in order to spell out the operational management tasks in detail. A range of manufacturing companies has been reported, covering most industries and contexts, and the managerial attitudes and requirements in these different situations have been distinguished. The book is intended as a practical and realistic casebook for students and teachers of management, and for managers interested in comparing company practice and performance. Its aim is to develop a greater understanding of the nature of the operations management function for the provision of customer service and proper resource utilisation; and in doing so to increase interest and confidence in the operational management skill in industry.

I am very grateful to the managers of the companies represented in these cases who have allowed me to study their manufacturing operations. I am particularly grateful to the staff in the companies, who have devoted a lot of their time to describing their procedures to me. It has often taken a long time to understand how things work in the companies, and I have persistently gone back to demand more of their patience in explaining the detailed points to me several times over. Some of the data and some details of the technology have had to be disguised for commercial security purposes, but the broad circumstances provide an accurate picture of the facts. Although the cases represent recent history some of the commentary is written in the present tense, reflecting the currency of the issues at the time they were investigated.

If Professor Bert Wood of Western Ontario had not originally pushed me into the study of production and operations management I would never have embarked on the task of creating a documented account of British manufacturing companies. Retrospectively I am grateful to him for forcing me in this direction and owe him an immeasurable debt of gratitude for his continuous encouragement as I struggled through the jungle of industrial practice. For the actual typing of the text and the creation and organisation of the illustrations (with the continuous revision to respond to student comments) I am permanently grateful to my sister and mother. In acknowledgement of their help I would like to dedicate the book to them.

T.A.J.N.

London Business School
February 1977

Questions on the Cases

Part A: Introduction to Manufacturing Operations

The introductory section contains two chapters. The first chapter states the objectives of the case studies and outlines their content and character. It establishes the priorities which have been used in creating the cases and suggests the particular emphasis which should be used for their analysis and discussion. It serves to clarify the expectations of both student, teacher and general reader.

The second chapter provides the first full case. It is a study of a small 12-employee plastics company which is well run by an energetic production manager. It is a useful introduction as it covers the whole field of operations management from company policy to daily work scheduling as displayed through the activities of a single manager and in a single month's records of the company. The main objective is to determine standards and targets and to ensure good performance for what is currently a very informal operation.

1 Objectives of the Case Studies

1. Purposes of the cases

The case studies in this book provide a detailed account of operational practices in a variety of British manufacturing companies. They are all based on an extensive period of study by the author of policies and practices in the companies concerned. The objective of writing the case studies has been to offer a basic source of information through which the student of management, the practising manager and the interested general reader can develop three skills:

the ability to understand how manufacturing companies work;
the ability to measure physical operating performance and recognise the interactions between those measures;
the ability to formulate a plan and identify responsibility and information needed to carry it out.

The cases focus exclusively on operating effectiveness. The major environmental factors such as the site, the management team, the product and process designs, the plant layout, the market and supply sources are all taken as a given context within which the operating position must be assessed. The frame of reference for success is the level of customer service being achieved in terms of delivery and product availability, the utilisation of physical resources and stock levels, and the motivation of the company supervision and employees.

The book aims to provide a useful and distinct contribution to education and training in this field. The subject of production and operations management is the least well documented of the major activities of a business and new educational materials are needed in this topic. The shortage of texts occurs perhaps because of the enormous coverage which the subject of production management can have. It can range across technology, production engineering, works management and production control. This set of cases concentrates on the task of organising production capacity to meet market plans. It deals with the administration of manufacturing capacity, not with the design or specification of the technology.

2. The case method in operations management education

The earlier books on production management tended to follow the approach of the industrial engineer and to develop precise quantitative skills for solving individual problems in quality, stocks, investment, scheduling and layout. More recent books on the subject have taken a management-oriented stance and treated the subject through case study discussions. This development seems appropriate. In the teaching of such a practical subject as the management of production operations it is difficult to see how the nature of the subject can be properly discussed without frequent reference to company situations. The reader can with advantage let his imagination work afresh on the pictures of individual practices and work gradually towards generalisations rather than learn direct theory in advance of applications. Besides, the operations management situations are not 'solvable'. One is always dealing with a changing situation and new difficulties will soon crop up. The operations manager has to learn to enjoy handling an on-going situation rather than hope for a once-and-for-all solution to his difficulties. Good production management is much more about being alert to the key questions rather than having ready answers.

Recently there has also been much emphasis on the 'systems' approach. In production terms the systems approach requires that all the factors − human, market, technical − should be considered collectively when dealing with a management problem. It takes a 'total' point of view and is a great improvement over the treatment of management issues in terms of isolated problems for solution by individual techniques. But there are new kinds of difficulties in teaching with the systems approach: in having to consider everything, the student may end up feeling decisive about nothing. This book aims to deal in two ways with this dilemma and with the general vagueness the student often encounters when tackling case studies. Firstly, the cases work through a structured sequence of issues right through the book and each case study uses a common frame of reference giving a structure to the subject matter. Illustration 1.1 at the end of the chapter shows this structure in diagrammatic form, identifying the thirteen issues with which the cases are concerned. The numbers correspond with the chapter numbers in Illustration 1.2. Secondly, although each case stands alone as a description of a complete system, each case focuses on a particular leading question relevant to the company's operating issues at that time. All the questions require the design of an appropriate operational procedure to achieve customer service and sales policy through a better organisation of capacity, stocks and schedules. Implicitly they are addressed to factors which affect the organisation as a whole and are less concerned with more isolated improvements in the production system in such fields as quality, maintenance and method study.

The studies are written as precise accounts of what actually happens in the companies concerned. Most of the original company names have been preserved. Aside from some minor alterations for purposes of commercial security, the data and presentation are genuine. The studies have not been 'doctored' for educational convenience around a specific difficulty. The student has to find the front on which to act. The text contains the complete picture and preserves the inconsistencies, the managerial doubts, and the muddled paperwork which is actually in use. The inclusion of much of the detail means that some of the cases are fairly long. Again this is realistic: it would be pointless to pretend that production systems are simple. It is against this background of messy and voluminous information that the practising manager has to act fairly quickly. The use of the cases therefore supports the practical fact that managers generally have to make decisions before they understand everything perfectly. The cases are not so much about what management could do, nor about what management ought to do, but about what operating management actually does.

3. The range of case studies and their construction

The set of studies has been chosen to provide a comprehensive coverage across different manufacturing situations. Illustration 1.2 at the end of this chapter shows the diversity of company contexts, products and technologies which have been included. It will be noted that the process and construction industries have not been expressly represented. The objective of the studies was to concentrate on systems dominated by labour-controlled processes and where management planning was engaged in an on-going situation rather than a series of one-off projects.

The studies have been arranged in a set sequence for educational purposes. After the introductory material in Part A, Part B examines how to set levels of customer service. The next part, C, deals with the dominant different internal process arrangements for manufacturing: the job shop, the product line, the assembly line, the product build situation. Part D examines the problems of coping with system variation in product, process and demand levels. Finally Part E deals with the major concepts about the whole operating system: its coordination, complexity, and the management driving force to keep it going.

Despite this variety, each case has been constructed in a similar way. Each study relates to a particular site, normally a profit centre, and to a relatively short period of time, normally within the annual accounting cycle. The operating context is described in terms of:

the company and its markets;
the products and their manufacturing requirements;
the processes, their layout and capacities;
the labour arrangements and supervision structure.

The central operating problems are then explained through a full description of the procedures and paperwork currently in use, together with an analysis of the responsibilities of the operating managers and the presentation of their opinions. The operating managers include sales administration, production control, purchasing, works management and foremen. These are the key people who run the companies; they are the people who place the daily orders both inside and outside the company and on whose planning and organisational skill the implementation of the companies' marketing plans ultimately depends.

An assessment of the successes and weaknesses of the operations management in the companies are communicated through the plentiful, though often disorganised, data on operating performance. Each study in effect puts the case for the particular system the managers of the companies are adopting and it describes an experiment in the management of operations for a particular context. The outcomes must be judged by the reader.

4. The place of technology and technique

The case material is suitable for students on courses for business diplomas, business degrees, engineering and economics degrees, Higher National Certificates and accounting qualifications. It is addressed to all teachers and students engaged in courses which relate to the practical issues arising in industry. It will prove helpful if students have an outline knowledge of statistics and accounting for the analysis of data in the cases, but no technical knowledge is assumed. In each case the products are described in terms of their design, their construction and quality requirements, and the processes are discussed in terms of their capacities, reliability and manning arrangements. An attempt is made to overcome the difficulty of visualising the situation through a careful but simple description of the technology.

It is important for students to realise that for operating decisions the necessary knowledge of the technology can be grasped without a very detailed technical background. For the non-technical student the subject of production and operations management often provides a point at which he can learn the context of a technology and develop an interest in the essentials of how it works. Indeed a major purpose of the book is to show that operating policies and practice are to some extent independent of particular technologies and the same operational issues can recur in very different industries. They depend on the sales policy chosen, the product complexity and the internal methods for allocating capacity and supplies rather than upon technology as such.

Just as the technology is only one factor in the situation, so the techniques of production management — on which there are plenty of texts — are simply aids to the decision maker. There is no 'solution' to an operating situation; there is only a capability to handle the current circumstances well. Successful decisions on the organisation of physical operations are fundamentally based on the use of imagination and common sense, the ability to think through all the details carefully and to sense what can and cannot be controlled. Success in the study of the cases is therefore achieved by observing the details carefully, and being able to choose an operational plan and policy for the company which can be translated into practice in a clear, logical and consistent way.

5. Teaching and learning approach

The most appropriate method for teaching or learning about the cases depends on the approach of the individual teacher and his students. The studies have been written so that they can be used in three ways: as orthodox case studies for student preparation and discussion; as an illustrative basis which the teacher may use as a lecturing vehicle; or simply as supportive background reading for the student. When used in the normal case study discussion approach, it has often been found effective to have two 'bites' at each case. In the first 'bite' the case is read in order to gain an understanding of the issues and to raise questions in class which can lead to a collective understanding of the company situation. It gives the teacher a chance to work through the material and to explain the illustrations. Indeed the plentiful illustrations are intended to provide a practical vehicle through which to teach the basics of production systems. In the following session, after further preparatory time, it is important for the student or reader to commit himself to a precise operational plan. Each case study has been given a specific question which is simple in content but comprehensive in its relevance to all the material in the study. It is important to use this opportunity of case discussion in the lecture theatre to ask students to give presentations in front of the class so that they gain practice in putting forward their thoughts persuasively to other people in a formal context. In the end, to be effective, they will have to be able to 'sell' their ideas.

The case studies have been analysed extensively by the author in the course of numerous class discussions. A full text has been prepared containing these observations, analyses of the questions, and proposals for operational improvement in the companies concerned. This is available through the publisher for teachers of management, managers in industry and individual readers who would like to make use of a tutorial guide. Some of the notes contain details of the subsequent actions actually carried out by the companies concerned. The book will have succeeded if it interprets to students and managers the successful practices adopted in the companies which have been studied, and if it helps them to become more sensitive, more persuasive and more immediately effective as production and operations managers.

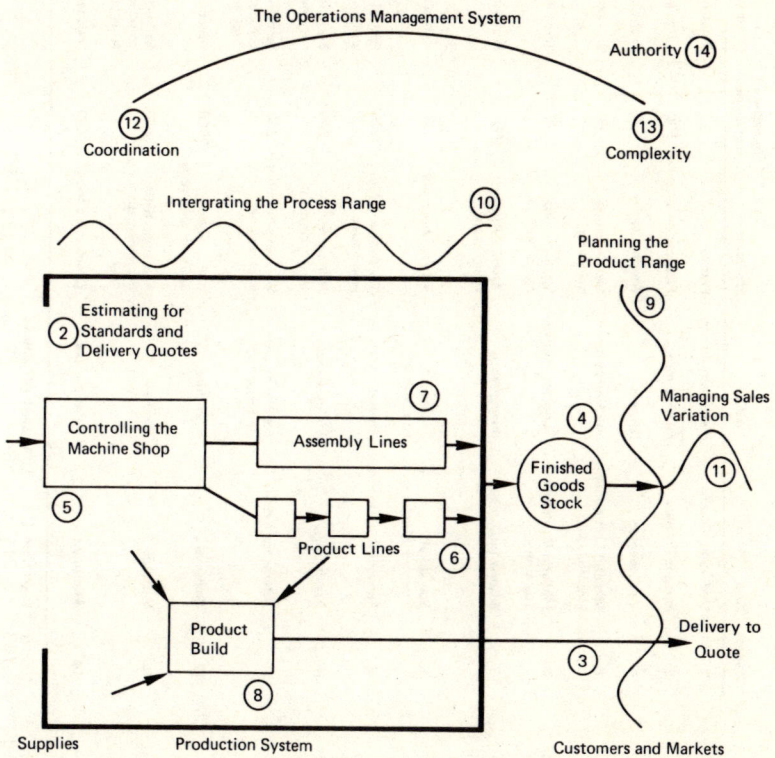

ILLUSTRATION 1.1   The sequence of operations management issues in the context of the production system

Chapter	Case	Product	Processes	Size (number of employees)	Context of company	Major issue
2	Medina Polymers	Plastic mouldings	Presses	12	Independent company	Standards
3	Parsons Peebles	Electric motors	Fabrication shops	600	Large group	Delivery date
4	Van Heugten	Carpets	Warehouse	30	Profit centre	Stock levels
5	Midland Components Machine shop	Machine parts	Metal-cutting machines	60	Service function	Work-in-progress Computer control
6	Midland Components Star-line	Tools for industry	Metal-cutting machines	20	Service function	Group working
7	Smiths Industries	Instruments	Assembly lines Hand tools	1600	Product centre	Assembly line and supplies organisation
8	Speedcraft Transport Ltd	Transport equipment	Fitting, assembly	150	Independent company	Contract management
9	Perivale Gütermann	Thread	Twisting machines warehouse	200	Part of international group	Product range
10	English Steel	Stainless plate	Rolling mill Heat treatment	600	Stage in steelmaking, nationalised sector	Process integration
11	Adams Ice Cream	Ice-cream and desserts	Blending, forming Packing lines	600	Semi-autonomous company within large group	Demand variation
12	Gommes	Furniture	Kilns, wood-working, assembly	2000	Independent company	Production co-ordination
13	Arnolds	Clothes	Knitting, dyeing machines, stitching lines	5000	Semi-autonomous company within large group	Complexity of planning
14	Micronair	Aviation sprays	Engineering shops	70	Independent company	Motivation and control

ILLUSTRATION 1.2   The range of issues

2 Developing Production Standards: Medina Polymers Plastic Mouldings

1. The Company

Medina Polymers Limited is a small company in the plastics and rubber moulding business located at Newport in the Isle of Wight. Under Dennis Welsh, the works manager, it has a total of 13 employees. The company was started by John Torrance in 1972 when he bought out Ray Mouldings (a London-based producer of plastic mouldings) for £20,000 with a year's work outstanding. John Torrance was already running a rubber moulding business at Shanklin on the Isle of Wight and he took a lease on a new factory of 3000 sq. feet on a new industrial estate at Newport. He brought the presses and tools from Ray Mouldings down to the Newport site so that he could manage both operations on the island. But running two separate sites was still a strain and in January 1974 he recruited Dennis Welsh by advertising in the local news-paper. Dennis Welsh was 31, had been trained as a toolmaker and later spent time in a large company doing industrial engineering, followed by a year in production management in a small company at Bembridge at the eastern end of the island.

In August 1974, John Torrance gave up the Shanklin site and relocated the rubber processing activities in Glasgow nearer to the customer base. He left Dennis Welsh in charge of the Newport operations, as Medina Polymers Ltd. Both companies traded under the parent company name of Thermosets Ltd. But by the spring of 1975 the Glasgow factory had not progressed well and the Newport site was the more effective operation. Dennis Welsh had even started to produce some rubber products as well as the plastic components which John Torrance had left behind.

When Dennis Welsh went into the Newport factory the situation was a mess. Labour turnover and absenteeism were high, customer orders (back-logged from Ray Mouldings) were not being met on time, and scrap rates were excessive. With Torrance trying to manage two separated operations and spending most of his time at Shanklin, there was no real authority at the Newport site.

Gradually Dennis started to improve the situation. One of his first jobs was to classify and examine all the outstanding moulding tools which belonged to the customers and identified the products. He created a file for the office recording all the tools and their physical locations by referencing a number denoting a painted square on the floor near the presses where they were to be kept when not in use. He sorted out the maintenance equipment, a lathe and a milling machine, and appointed a new maintenance engineer to look after the presses which had constantly been breaking down. He rearranged the location of raw material and the finishing operations and advertised for a girl to manage the complete finishing activities of collecting pressed products, inspecting, finishing and packing. The rearranged layout is shown in Illustration 2.1.

But his most important move was to develop a reliable labour force. For the press work he gradually reduced and replaced the operators until by the spring of 1975 only one of the oldest moulders, Fred Robinson, remained of the original team. 'I've chosen older men for the moulding work. They're more suited to the job; this kind of work is routine but requires care. The younger ones try to get the edge on you.' He increased the pay of the moulders from an average of £25 per week to £35 over the year of 1974, and worked on a basic flat rate not related to output. (The finishers' pay is about £14 less per week.) As he said, 'It's my job to make the men work, not the payment system.'

By the spring of 1975 the moulders' performance was good and there was no unexplained absenteeism or turnover. As Dennis explained: 'The men trust me and I trust them. I always work a bit harder than they do and I can attend to any of the technical difficulties. I often come in to finish off a job on Saturdays, and I turn on some of the presses on Sunday evenings to start them warming up. (Phasing your start-up cuts the electricity bill as it avoids a rush load on the Board.) I often come in and do a bit of moulding first thing on a weekday and then when they're all in I start organising and ringing round the customers. I like to be available for the customers to ring me at any time including lunchtime.' (Over the year 1974/75 Dennis had achieved a steady improvement in sales turnover, raising it from around £4000 per month in January 1974 to £6000 per month in January 1975.)

Dennis had got the work so organised that one man could handle two or

three presses, unlike many competitors in the field who work with one man
to every press. 'I want the men to produce to peak outputs all the time
without the 33 per cent allowances you get in the large company. I know the
maximum possible outputs by looking at the cure times and cycle times on
the work and generally I get the best results possible. In return the men
want me to secure the workload and help them with personal requirements.
For instance one man borrowed the company van for a removal, another had
paid time off for a funeral, and I lent my car to one of the moulders to get a
quick trip to the dentist. I always tell them about the situation, and get them
to realise that by producing good products at a good rate we'll get our
customers' respect and obtain further orders.'

2. The Manufacturing Operations

The first step in the plastic moulding operation is to create a 'tool' or mould
appropriate for the customer's product. The new customer will usually
supply a drawing of the plastic component to be moulded. Medina Polymers
will then determine how to make the tool for the pressing of the component.
The tool is essentially a pair of steel plates, the lower plate having a number
of recesses in it in the shape of the design of the component and the upper
plate having a set of matching projections. (A special difficulty in tool design
is the provision of bars for the ejection of the part without damage after
moulding.) Depending on the size of the component, tools can be made with
a number of cavities or impressions so that a set of products is produced in a
single pressing operation. The choice of the right number of impressions is
sometimes difficult. The more impressions, the lower the running cost on the
presses as output is faster, but the capital cost of tool manufacture is
correspondingly higher. Medina Polymers will quote the cost of tool
manufacture to the customer company. If the customer accepts the quote
the tool is manufactured — generally subcontracted to a local toolmaker.
When complete it is checked out with some samples and the customer retains
the ownership of the tool although it is held by Medina at Newport. The total
invoiced value of such work undertaken in March 1975 was £924.

Once the tool is approved, the customer will normally place a series of
orders for delivery. Illustration 2.2 gives the outstanding orders at the
beginning of April 1975 for the current list of active customers together with
their credit position. Often the order is expressed as a gross volume with a
known call-off rate per month although the orders will be subject to alteration
and cancellation more than three months ahead. The activities undertaken in
March are shown in Illustration 2.3, giving the total sales due together with

the initial stock plus production achieved and the despatches made by the end of March. All this data is drawn from the files of invoices, despatch notes, current orders and the completed production records which give the cumulative production and rejects on each order.

Illustration 2.4 gives the technical details for producing the products. Each product has a negotiated price, an estimated material cost and an appropriate choice of presses, 50, 100 or 150-ton indicated in Illustration 2.4 by the codes 1, 2 and 3 respectively. A product has a given minimum cure time in the press and a corresponding cycle time between successive pressing operations (assuming one man per press). The finishing rates are also given. All this timing data is based on estimates from Dennis Welsh.

The overall production sequence runs through material supplies, pressing, finishing and despatch. The required volume of plastic powder (black phenolic and various shades of urea) are purchased from Fergusons in London once a month and brought to Newport in Medina's own van. A quantity of rubber sheet is also bought from Hatchams for the rubber products. The cost of the plastic is £7 per 25 kilo bag (40 bags per ton) and supplies are generally plentiful, although the situation was critical in the autumn of 1974 when supplies ran down to three weeks. The appropriate material is distributed to the presses in cardboard trays by the maintenance engineer. Some customers also require small inserts such as brass terminals to be fitted to the moulding and these are usually supplied free by the customer for his orders.

The moulders work from 9.00 until 5.30 with half an hour for lunch. In March 1975 a four-day week was being worked except for a few key products. Normally one moulder will work two or three presses simultaneously and keep to those presses. Some products will be run continuously on a press month after month, but others will have a changeover several times a month. (A changeover will take up half a day.) The allocation of moulders and products to presses for March is given in Illustration 2.5. The products are indicated in brackets by the reference code given in Illustration 2.3. (This data has been assembled from the collection of production daily records completed by Jill Waterhouse during March.)

The opportunity to man several presses is provided by the automatic cure time in the press cycle. When the press is in the closed position and the cure is taking place the operator can set up, load and unload other presses provided the cure times are balanced across the set of presses which he works. Medina Polymers have also bought five radio heating devices which can speed up the curing process. The curing time can be cut by a factor of 3 if the pre-heating is done, but it makes the moulder less efficient as he has to load and unload the pre-heater. The curing temperature varies between 270°C to 410°C for the plastic products, and is around 300°C for rubber products. The sequence of activities is shown in the following list:

(1) Raise press
(2) Remove products and place in bin
(3) Clean cavities with air hose
(4) Place inserts in press
(5) Load pellets/powder with measured scoops
(6) Lower press
(7) Open for 'breathing' and immediately close
(8) Fill up measured scoops
(9) Go to next press and repeat steps, returning to step (1) on this press
    after the cure time is complete.

The completed work is collected by Jill Waterhouse who is in charge of the finishing section. The finishing section work from 7.45 till 4.15. She takes the bins to her inspection table, records the completed work, and notes the number of rejects, together with any machine breakdown times on the pink daily production records for each press. The rejects increase as the tool begins to wear and in due course Medina's maintenance engineer will refurbish the tools. Faults also occur in handling and due to undercuring in the presses. Jill Waterhouse goes round the presses at 9.30, 11.30, 2.00 and 4.30 to collect the finished products.

After recording the work Jill distributes the products to her finishing team of three assistants. The trimming and finishing operations include linishing, polishing, drilling, tapping, filing, rumbling and painting. The requirements vary for the individual products as shown in Illustration 2.4. (The times in Illustration 2.4 refer to one person doing the work.) Jill herself does a lot of work, working at a very fast rate. She has increased output and reduced the staff by a factor of two on finishing over her six months at Medina. She also eliminated the pile of work in progress between presses and finishing so that the finishing of all products is now done directly the pressing is complete. 'High productivity comes', she expained, 'from using both hands and eyes in a fast systematic way to suit the individual. People should determine their own methods and pace. Few people want to slack if you set a good example yourself.' Not all the finishing work is done internally. Some of it is done as 'outwork' although this is usually finishing done at home by the Medina finishing employees at an agreed price.

Finished products are despatched by post or by a fortnightly distribution round using Medina Polymers' own van. Occasionally a customer will make some returns but this is a rare occurrence. In the trade there is a general acceptance of ±10 per cent on volume on any order with an appropriate adjustment of invoices. The actual packing is organised and often done by

Margaret James who works in the office. She prepares the despatch notes and invoices and is responsible for maintaining the customer orders file, and general customer liaison on the telephone. She also prepares the wages statement and keeps track of the accounts due and payable. Although Margaret James prepares the cost statement, John Torrance still manages the bank account from Glasgow and signs the cheques. The bills from March included £1600 for wages, £1,259 for materials, £1,367 for rent, maintenance, electricity etc. and £310 for manager salary.

3. The Problems Ahead

Although Medina Polymers was running well as a production unit in the spring of 1975 the prospects ahead were not so favourable. Dennis Welsh considered that the order book was down to six to eight weeks outstanding work and new orders were not coming in. The situation was the same for many small companies supplying larger companies where forecasts of sales had turned down. 'I've explained the position to my employees', Dennis Welsh explained, 'and I'll do my best for them. It would be a crying shame if we cannot pull through now that everything's working well here. I've got to resolve both the immediate problems and the longer-term ones.

'My job now, at the beginning of April, is to prepare the schedule for this month. We have a number of alternatives: we could go flat out to complete all the work; we could reduce the multi-press manning level; we could go down to a three-and-a-half day week; we could lay off one or two employees. Whatever we decide on as our capacity, we then have to choose the right orders to work on. This is a tricky exercise. I have to balance the loads on the press groups, across all the presses and across the men. I also have to be sure that the finishing balance is right and that materials are available. Often we've had jobs coming off the presses with no finishing for days.

'A particularly immediate problem we've got is cash solvency. Fergusons say they won't supply more materials till we've paid the January account. Torrance says he won't pay Fergusons until we have more cash in the bank. So I'm chasing our larger customers to pay their debts. But the true cash position is obscure as I'm sure Medina Polymers more than pays its way within the overall company, Thermosets Ltd.

'In the longer term — say in three months' time — we'll have to be looking at one of several options:

(1) Increase the order book.
      We have got orders from several of our old customers recently, and I have

several quotations to do now for tools for new customers. We could divert effort into finding new customers, but getting out on the road selling is not very effective. I call in at ten places over the Industrial Estates and maybe get one half-hearted prospect promising to make a further enquiry. We cannot afford a full-time representative and I have to look after the works myself. It is better to pursue our existing customers. We've offered them good service recently giving good delivery and quality. Also our prices have been too low, which suited the customers. Most prices were inherited from Ray Mouldings. I put up some prices by 300 per cent and the customer still knew he was on to a good thing. But on the new quotes we'll again have to keep prices to a minimum to get the orders.

(2) Borrow cash for a limited period.

We could try to keep above water on our existing level of operations by borrowing cash for a limited period until the up-turn comes. But the bank limits us to £3000 overdraft despite our effectiveness. We might have to find other benefactors.

(3) Combine with Glasgow operations.

Another possibility is that John Torrance will transfer the rubber operations back to us here at Newport simply by transferring the tools and orders. He could lock up the presses and close down activity at the Glasgow site. It is a rough operation at Glasgow with vandalism, dissension and lack of co-operation from the workpeople, in stark contrast to us here at Newport. Perhaps if he combines with the Newport site he will make me a full partner in the business. He has also been mentioning the possibility of buying up some more small companies and setting up the whole operation at Glasgow where the development grants from the Government are so favourable.

(4) Sell out the business.

Finally I suppose we might have to sell out the business as a going concern. perhaps to one of our major customers and become a controlled supplier. We might get only £10,000 for it. The depreciation on the presses must be nil by now.

'Whatever happens we're going to have to prove we're a good going concern operating effectively. What I need is a clear statement of our current performance, and together with it an on-going simple information system so that I can see what the position is at a glance. And we'll have to do this without a lot of extra paperwork. At the moment with this size of operation I can keep all the customer requests, the production information and the plans in my head and leave the figures to Margaret and Jill. I simply aim at £6000 sales per month by generating £3 per hour per press. I also use this figure for estimating

prices allowing a penny a lift on the presses for materials and a penny for
trimming. In production terms this means I aim for 15 lifts per hour on the
presses. But all these rules need to be checked against our objectives and the
possibilities open to us. What I need is a simple formula to decide next month's
plan which I can use to tell me if any job is running at a profit on the day it
runs.'

Question for discussion

Assess the estimates used for production management at Medina Polymers.

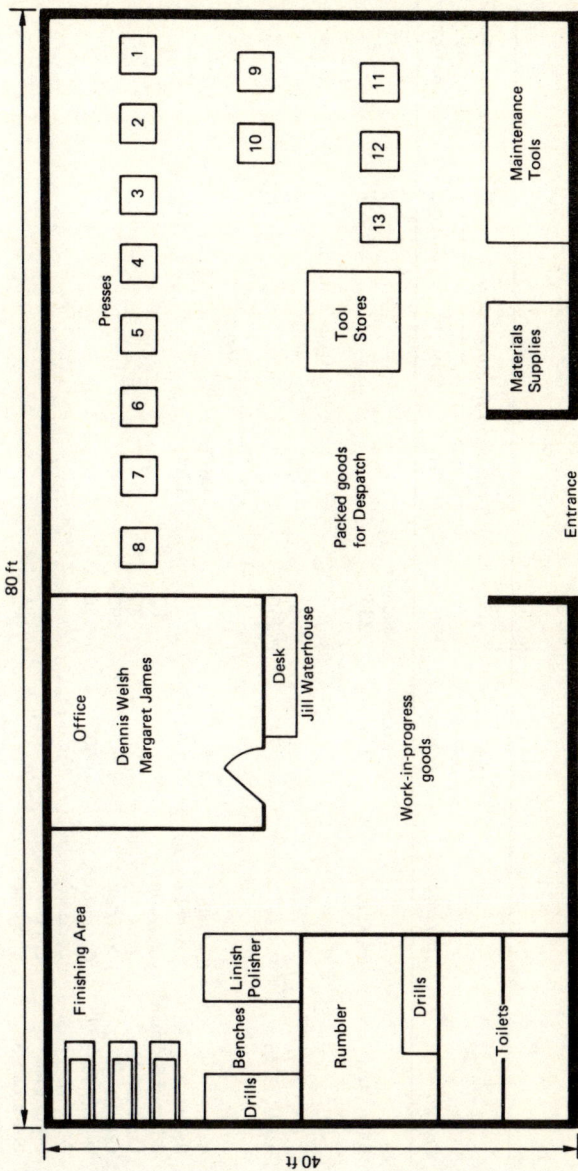

ILLUSTRATION 2.1   Rearranged factory layout

17

	Customer	Location	Accounts due (£)		Production Requirements			Vol. outstanding after June rec'd but not confirmed (000)
			Pre-Jan _Invoices_	Feb _Invoices_	Apr qty	May qty	Jun qty	
1	Allen West	St Albans	1276	236			1500	1.5
2								3.0
3								1.0
4					750	1000		
5	Assoc. Auto	Purley, Surrey	24	255		450		1.5
6					1750	2400		
7								
8	Belling	Enfield			1400			2.0
9	Brush	Loughborough	170		1300		500	1.5
10	Clifford & Small	Croydon		63				
11	Copperad	Milton Keynes		139				
12	Croydon Eng.	Croydon		153				
13	Cybernaut	Canterbury	600	975				
14	Duplex	London						
15	Edlin Elec.	London	65					
16	Edwards Vac.	Shoreham		186				
17	E.M.D.	Ealing	152					
18	E.M.I.	Hayes	200		90			
19	Groves & Gut	Isle of Wight			28			
20	Gulton	Brighton			500	500	500	3.5

21	Hanovia	Slough	55					
22	Hardinge	Exeter	583	36				
23	Interpet	Dorking	779	583				
24	J.M. Manuf.	Hitchin	952	339	120			80.0
25	Kenwood	Havant			20,000	20,000	20,000	30.0
26					6000	6000	6000	400.0
27	Lincass	Littlehampton	3066		6000	6000	6000	
28	L.P.A.	London	2519	1135	200	700	200	0.2
29					2000	200		
30					2000			
31					700			
32					5000			5.0
33	McMurdo	Portsmouth	150					
34	Pye Unicorn	Cambridge	68	122				
35	Secomak	London	203		5000		1000	0.05
36	Smiths	Witney						
37	Standard	Camberley	102	57				
38	Stanley-Bridges	Sheffield	254					
39	Sterdy	Cambridge	491					
40	Strainstall	Isle of Wight	152	576				
41	Tann	London	306					
42	Tech. Metals	Littlehampton			6000	6000	6000	100.0
43					6000	6000	6000	100.0
44	Ultra	Acton	565		100			

ILLUSTRATION 2.2   Outstanding commitments

Customer	Component	Sales due in March or before	Initial stock + Mar. Prod'n qty.	Rejects	Mar. qty.	Despatches: value inc. VAT	Date order placed
1 Allen West	Rim	1500	1374	50	1260	296	14. 3.75
2	Case						14. 3.75
3	Cover		105	39			4. 3.75
4	Small rim						29.10.74
5 Assoc. Auto	Denom block	5000	1918	3	1100⎫	178	14. 2.75
6	Denom block	2850	1464	2	1100⎭		28. 2.75
7	'A' Button						23.12.73
8 Belling	Fuse Holder					270	26. 3.75
9 Brush	Bobbin		2120	0	2111	228	31. 1.75
10 Clifford & Small							4.12.74
11 Copperad							
12 Croyden Eng.							
13 Cybernaut	Keynector block	2000	1807	26	1600	881	
14 Duplex	Bush cap						
15 Edlin Elec.							
16 Edwards Vac.	Ballast		843	25	754	112	
17 E.M.D.	Set of blocks	4200	4586	0	3530	248	
18 E.M.I.	Bobbin						16. 1.75
19 Groves & Gut	Rubber wheel						6. 3.75
20 Gulton	Gasket						3. 3.75
21 Hanovia	Cap						10. 3.75
22 Hardinge							
23 Interpet	Thermostat	20,000	21,000	0	20,000	583	11.11.74
24 J. M. Manuf.							
25 Kenwood	Camspeed	8000					21. 1.75
26	Uppers and lowers	10,000	4476	45	4296	137	12. 1.74
27 Lincass							
28 L.P.A.	Cable flats		829	162	584	380	1. 2.75
29	DMC plug		256	36			29.11.74
30	M.3 sleeve	60	107	0	78	524	1. 4.75
31	28V sleeve	240	207	0	205		3. 1.75
32	Neck insert	450	613	56	557		28. 3.75
33 McMurdo	Rubber boot		350	54	300	42	12. 3.74
34 Pye Unicorn							
35 Secomak	Terminal block						20. 3.75
36 Smiths	Bush	6250	1094	0	1025	56	4. 2.75
37 Standard	Ash bowl	1000	1089	0	1087	211	
38 Stanley-Bridges							
39 Sterdy	Telephone	1500	214	21	203	88	
40 Strainstall							
41 Tann	Bobbin	2000	2030	0	2030	133	
42 Tech. Metals	Iron handle	300 per day	4975	164	4800	1296	22. 1.74
43	Control knob	300 per day	8998	172			22. 1.74
44 Ultra	Term block						5. 3.75

ILLUSTRATION 2.3   March production data

Component	Price £/100	Material cost £/100	Cure Time (mins)	Cycle Time (mins)	Impressions	Press Choice	Finishing Rate (no. per hour)
1 Rim	17	2	1.5	2.5	1	2	400
2 Case	15	1	1.0	1.5	1	3	120
3 Cover	10	1	1.5	2.5	2	2	60
4 Small rim	25	2	1.5	2.5	1	1,2	60
5 Denom block 1	15	1	2.0	3.0	1	1	150
6 Denom block 2	15	1	2.0	3.0	1	1	150
7 'A' button	6	0.5	1.25	2.0	2	1	150
8 Fuse holder	15	1	2.0	4.0	2	1	30
9 Bobbin	9	0.5	1.5	2.5	2	1	30
10							
11							
12							
13 Keynector block	50	6	3.0	4.0	1	2,3	120
14 Bush cap	15	1	4.0	4.5	2	1	60
15							
16 Ballast	14	2	2.0	3.0	2	1,2	300
17 Set of blocks	8	4	1.5	2.0	1	1,2	12
18 Bobbin	55	4	1.5	3.0	2	1	30
19 Rubber wheel	2000	40	20.0	40.0	1	2,3	12
20 Gasket	12	3	8.0	10.0	4	2	20
21 Cap	30	3	1.5	2.0	1	1	100
22							
23 Thermostat	3	0.5	1.0	1.5	6	2,3	150
24							
25 Camspeed	3	1	1.0	1.5	4	1	1500
26 Uppers and lowers	3	1	2.0	3.0	6	2	2500
27							
28 Cable flats	60	2	10.0	12.0	2	2	40
29 DMC plug	8	0.5	3.0	3.5	2	1	50
30 M3 sleeve	86	36	10.0	12.0	1	2,3	40
31 28V sleeve	77	32	10.0	12.0	1	2,3	40
32 Neck insert	66	12	10.0	12.0	1	1	40
33 Rubber boot	13	11	2.0	3.0	1	1,2	60
34							
35 Terminal block	12	1.5	2.0	2.5	2	1	100
36 Bush	5	0.5	1.0	1.5	4	1	300
37 Ash bowl	18	3	3.0	3.5	1	1,2	360
38							
39 Telephone	40	2	2.0	3.0	1	1,2	13
40							
41 Bobbin	7	0.5	1.5	2.5	2	1	80
42 Iron Handle	20	7	1.0	2.0	1	2	400
43 Control Knob	25	1	1.0	2.0	4	1	200
44 Term block	130	4	2.0	2.5	1	1	40

ILLUSTRATION 2.4   Production specification data

Press no.	1	2	3	4	6	7	8	9	10	11	12	13
Tonnage	50	50	150	50	50	100	100	100	50	50	100	100
Regular moulder	Fred	Fred	Tony	Tony	Tommy	Tommy	Tommy	Colin	Colin	Jim	Jim	Jim
Other moulders: Dates				Colin 24	Stephen 3, 10	Tommy	Tommy	Jim 7 10, 13, 21	Jim 9 10, 14, 21	Tommy 13		
Day												
3	(17) 236	(1) 118	(39) 66	(36) 684	(32) 35		(28) 56	(42) 229	(43) 478		(13) 86	(26) 1226
4	251	123	163	410	36	0	70	273	572	0	96	240
5	246	123	(37) 42	(13) 112	35	0	64	262	516	(16) 155	97	0
6	255	110	98	111	37	0	27	245	588	263	82	0
7	(5) 143				39	0		123	408	159		
10					7			283	544			
11	190	(6) 58	29	0	52	0	57	269	572	88	106	370
12	168	166	216	129	42	0	64	297	546	(1) 108	128	100
13	182	183	156	138	8	0	22	257	514	91	65	0
14			211	134	30	0	52	426	306	0	0	0

Date												
17								141				
18	189	190	31	15	(33) 114	0 (28) 58	34	284	508	101	82	0
19	190	182	107	96	53	62	0	200	572	134	101	0
20	194	189	0 (3) 20	141	0	60	0	293	612	83	93	0
21	183	176		30	0		0	175	560	0	0	0
24				114				202				
25	181	178	8	0	30	63	0	360	610	79	108	374
26	184	180	113	90	76	50		166	488	88	85	532
Total down time (hrs).		1			21	21	19	14				
Rejects	3	2	60	6	37	36	62	154	152	75	20	45

Notes 1   Allocation of products is indicated by a number immediately above the date on which the mould started on the press. This number corresponds to the product list in Illustration 2.4. The product continues manufacture until a later entry occurs.

2   Press 5 has been converted by Dennis Welsh into a crude rubber extrusion process to prepare a cylinder of rubber for the rubber products produced on presses 6, 7 and 8. Usually the press is operated by Stephen or other moulders if their press breaks down. Twenty hours a week is sufficient.

ILLUSTRATION 2.5   Allocation of products and moulders to presses and daily output records, 3 – 26 March 1975

23

Part B: Setting Standards of Customer Service

The starting point for the analysis of a company situation is the sales policy in providing customer service. Customers choose to buy products from particular companies for a variety of reasons, amongst the most important being:

the product range on offer
the design flexibility
the price
delivery (or availability)
support services
convenience of location.

In examining any case studies a first vital step is to establish exactly which of these factors predominate in the sales policy of a company. Perhaps the most important operational variable in a company's short-term policy is the delivery or availability of its products. This in turn is expressed in terms of a number of sub-factors:

the length of the lead times offered after orders are placed
the accuracy of the deliveries achieved
the stability of the lead times over time
the flexibility offered to the customer to make changes.

Broadly, the products on offer fall into two groups: those that are made after the order is placed and those that have an intended availability from finished stock. In the former 'make to order' situation a company manufactures the product after the order is placed, whereas, in the latter situation of a 'make to forecast' company, the customer orders are made after production has taken place. The first will involve difficulties of quality and the controlling of lead times on individual orders, whereas the second type will face the risk of stockouts and surpluses.

This part contains two case studies to illustrate these two different contexts. The first case, Parsons Peebles, describes a manufacturer of heavy

electrical equipment facing delivery control problems with a large
manufacturing facility. The second case, Van Heugten, describes a carpet-tile
distributor's problem of reducing stock levels while at the same time aiming
to maintain high standards of service (availability) of the products. The two
cases respectively require schemes for quoting deliveries and for determining
the right level of finished goods stock to hold.

3 Quoting Delivery Dates: Parsons Peebles Electric Motors

1. The Company

Parsons Peebles Motors and Generators Ltd is a large manufacturer of heavy electrical engineering equipment with factories in Edinburgh and Birmingham. The Edinburgh factory shares some common facilities with the Power Transformer Company which operates on the same site. The manufacture of transformers has many of the characteristics of flow line production, and, although dealing with very large items, control problems in the transformer company are relatively straightforward in principle. The two companies are managed quite separately.

The rotating machinery factory in Edinburgh manufactures in relatively small batches, producing electric motors to individual customer requirements, and has more complex control problems. It has an annual turnover of three million pounds and an establishment of about 600 employees.

Most orders come from past customers, although the customers are not usually ordering duplicate products. Customers include end users and their consultants, mechanical equipment manufacturers, and plant contractors. There are about 250 customers at any time of which 30 represent key accounts. The electric machines produced are diverse in application and may, for example, be destined for a pump with flame-proof certification for the oil industry, for industrial ventilation equipment, for installation in a steel rolling mill, or for stand-by power supplies.

The major U.K. competitors of the company are G.E.C., Hawker-Siddeley and Brush, who also manufacture rotating machinery in smaller sizes more on a production line, standard product basis. Siemens and AEG (Germany) and A.S.E.A. (Sweden) are typical of continental competition. Parsons Peebles focus on custom tailoring of features within the framework of standardised optional features and can thus operate on a make-to-order basis without sacrifice of methods and benefits of batch production. Only one customer, the National Coal Board, places contracts on an annual basis for a fixed series of orders. The company consider that they often lead the field in price setting and that other competitors have usually followed the pattern Parsons Peebles set. Prices are based on costs rather than on beliefs about market levels of price. The total demand pattern tends to follow the business cycle although the Edinburgh order book does not seem to have fallen off too badly in recent recessions, no doubt partly due to increasing operation in a world-wide market. Traditionally, as an order book builds up, long delivery times are quoted, and extra overtime is introduced and more explicit recognition of extended financing of work in progress is made, raising prices only later on in the boom. But the sales manager considered that the alternative policy of raising prices to manage demand levels can offer a better alternative to keep delivery and capacity under control in the future, although it was more difficult to operate.

The motor and generator products are divided into three classes dependent on their kilowatt rating and speed and hence physical size. The standards for delivery together with the price range and the maximum and minimum monthly sales values vary for the different classes.

Class	Size (horsepower)	Delivery time (Weeks)	Price range (£)	Monthly sales value 1970 (£)	
				min	max
1	Small <100	16–20	1000–6000	15,000	100,000
2	Medium	26–35	3000–10,000	65,000	240,000
3	Large >1000	25–45	10,000 and above	–	–

[Class 3 motors were transferred to Birmingham towards the end of 1969 and there was a reciprocal transfer of certain smaller standard motors to Edinburgh.]

The delivery time is a critical factor in the motor market. Orders increased significantly in April 1970 when there was no backlog, and virtually all deliveries were being met on time. Sales staff also judged that prices could be increased if the delivery time could be reduced. Frequently a penalty of ½ per cent per week of contract price is imposed for late deliveries and less frequently a bonus can be obtained for early delivery. This can make a significant difference to the targeted net profit on individual orders.

2. Organisation and Facilities

The organisational structure is flat: all the major functional managers report to the Divisional General Manager of the Motor and Generator company. These include Sales, Contracts, Works Superintendent, Planning Engineer, Stores

Manager, Accounts, Computer, and Design. Of the total of 600 staff employed in the division about 450 are direct production staff reporting through foremen to the Works Superintendent. The Electrical Trades Union and Amalgamated Engineering Union are represented in the works. Labour relations have generally been good. Within the last year there have been two one-day stoppages in connection with national strikes on Government industrial relations policy. A strike of one day also occurred as a protest against an earlier bonus system. The absence of serious labour relations problems may be partly attributable to the lack of alternative employment in the Edinburgh area for the same types of skills as are needed in Parsons Peebles.

The Edinburgh Division is split up into nine major sections, each of which contains its own producing and testing facilities. The sections correspond to the various stages involved in the manufacture of motors and generators.

For costing purposes the sections are divided into 11 cost centres broadly corresponding to the major processing stages. These are listed in Illustration 3.1 together with the labour hours worked per week. Parsons Peebles reckon to achieve about a 75 per cent actual utilisation of all labour on directly productive work. All sections work a 40-hour basic week, together with, in alternate weeks, two three-hour evenings and eight hours on Sundays, giving 46/48-hour alternating regular weeks as a standard pattern in 1970. Operators are paid hourly on a weekly basis, earnings varying from £20 to £30 dependent on skill. Direct overheads are allocated to the cost centres at 40 per cent to 70 per cent of labour costs.

The departmental capacity figures may be altered from time to time by moving selected operators from one department to a neighbouring department within their skill limitations. Supervisors and foremen plan these manipulations as appropriate if the workload threatens to become out of balance in the different sections.

3. Orders Planning System

The average number of orders received each week varies from 15 to 20 although this figure had fallen to 13 by the end of 1970. When an incoming order has been negotiated between the commercial staff and the customer, and a contractual situation exists, the design and planning engineers prepare documentation for manufacture.

This is the first of the three stages in the production of a motor:

(1) Preparation of drawings and specifications

(2) Procurement of outside parts and materials
(3) Manufacture and tests and despatch

The first stage takes from one week to twelve weeks depending on the degree of novelty in the design, and is a full time task for 40 design and D.O. office staff. For each order a 'Shop Specification' is prepared which shows all the parts required to be purchased on the job, provisioned from stocks, or to be manufactured. There are approximately 300 different components in the manufacture of a single motor. The first sheet of a typical specification is shown in Illustration 3.2. Up to about 90 per cent of these parts can be standard design items, with the other 10 per cent requiring original detail design office work. Besides giving the description of all the items required for the manufacture of the product, the Shop Specification annotation shown in the last two columns indicates the assembly structure coding in brackets. The planning engineer enters the date of requirement of materials on to requisitions for outside purchased material, and these are obtained within four to six weeks. Many of the smaller and more popular items are bought by stores in bulk, and issued on to orders as required, but these seldom exceed 5 per cent of the sales value of the order. A few of these components also require additional processing at Parsons Peebles and these will be processed as a batch and go into stores for subsequent allocation to jobs.

The overall picture of the main manufacturing stages and the structure code identity is indicated in Illustration 3.3. It shows a stator, rotor and bedplate being made in parallel before final erection and test. This type of chart is used to progress the work through the separate stages. Broadly speaking, the total work content given in the fabrication department cost centres 503, 504, 508 and 202 is split 1:2 between the frame assembly and the combined stator and rotor units. The stator and rotor units require an approximately equal quantity of labour overall, but provide only a small workload on the pre-erection department, compared with final erection of complete machines. On average nine-tenths of the fitting shop effort is deployed at the final erection stage prior to test.

When the Shop Specification has been completed the production Planning clerks enter the number of operations for the manufactured items, referring to the drawing number, and prepare works tickets for the order. These tickets specify the material and the sequence of operations on the machines within each cost centre. They indicate the work times and set-up times for the operations. The operation tickets are used to describe and authorise the labour and therefore the costs on the total order. Each ticket also shows a 'month ending date' to indicate when the operation must be completed to meet the order due date. All this detailed preparation of manufacturing instructions may take up to four weeks for an order. The prepared tickets are then passed to stores.

Thereafter stores manage and coordinate the manufacture of the order. Some of the materials are stocked, such as electrical core steel and mild steel plate for fabricating the frames and bedplates, but some special parts such as castings, forged shafts and copper are bought-in specifically for the order. Stores initiate the purchase of the required materials, kit-up the parts for an order, and issue the work to the foremen in the manufacturing departments with the appropriate set of operation tickets when materials become available. Sometimes the purchasing of copper or steel or insulation is seriously affected by suppliers' labour disputes or import difficulties.

As the operations are completed on an item, the time spent in manufacturing at each cost centre is entered on the job ticket. The data on those job tickets which have been returned to stores is collected up at the end of each week, and transferred to the accounts section. Operators also have to notify their foremen of any lost time due to breakages, or time spent waiting for work, and the foreman keeps a weekly tally of this information. All this data is punched up and used on the 'Orders Cost Recording' weekly computer run, which is also linked to the computer payroll calculations.

After completing a stage of work on an item, it is moved on to its next stage in manufacture by bogey, crane or fork-lift truck. The lying time between successive operations typically varies between hours and one week. An order occasionally has to be passed back to earlier stages because of faulty work revealed by inspection. When an order has completed all its required manufacturing processes in a department, it is either returned physically to stores, or, when too large, stores are notified. As further materials become available it can re-enter production in the appropriate department for further manufacturing and assembly work. If all is going smoothly, the work on parts of a motor can progress on a parallel working basis in a department, e.g. if 100 total hours of work are involved in a particular department, the work may be completed in about a 40-hour time span. The total work content of an order varies between a few hundred and more than 1500 hours. The proportion of work in each department also varies between orders, irrespective of the size of the order, owing to individual design characteristics. Two orders with the same total work content may vary by as much as a factor of 3 in their demands on an individual department. Recent records of four orders are given in Illustration 3.4 showing the labour content in hours at various cost centres.

4. The Delivery Problem in 1970

Towards the end of 1970 Parsons Peebles were facing a serious production control problem in their Rotating Machinery Division in Edinburgh. The order book for electric motors had fallen by 20 per cent over the last six months despite a continued growth in the manufacturing industry generally. Criticism was coming from customers about late deliveries of their orders which were running on average four weeks late with some deliveries up to eight weeks late. Yet the more that was done about it the less effective were the results. The Managing Director, the Divisional General Manager, sales and contract staff had all been attempting to help constructively with the task of meeting deliveries. Whenever contacted about an order, they would tend to personally check with the works superintendent, progress chaser, foreman, and even operators to see how the work was getting along and even attempt to persuade the operator to switch priorities.

By September 1970 the Divisional General Manager recognised that this sort of approach was not really achieving any long-term results — if only because the selective pushing of one order probably only meant the post-ponement of another The records were showing that despite all the concern and activity, work-in-progress had been steadily building up, output was not, and the shop supervision and operators were being completely confused about their objectives. At one time he found that 112 out of a total of 370 were being treated as 'crisis' orders. He decided, therefore, that to bring order into the chaos he would appoint a production controller, a new position in the organisation with clearly defined responsibilities. He also considered that some form of computer-assisted scheme of handling of job work content data could prove helpful. As a first step in the analysis of the problem he checked on the distribution of lateness of actual orders despatched and also checked on the hours worked. These figures are shown in Illustrations 3.5 and 3.6.

Question for discussion

How should delivery dates be quoted at Parsons Peebles?

Cost centre number	Processing functions	Hours per week
202	Machining frames	3650
203	Stamping	966
204	Core building	1150
206	Coil preparation	3000
269	Light winding	1200
209	Heavy winding	2100
211	Erection	1650
213	Brass (light machinery)	900
503	Fabrication, tank making	500
504	,, , prep.	450
508	,, , general	1800

ILLUSTRATION 3.1   Capacity of sections

R. SHOP SPECIFICATION

PARSONS PEEBLES LTD.,

K

| ORDINARY MATERIAL TO BE ORDERED BY | 400 | MAIN & SPECIAL MATERIAL REQUIRED BY | 460 | SPECIAL MATERIAL TO BE ORDERED BY | 370 | WRITTEN BY | |

DELIVERY DATE 26-1-71   DATE OF ISSUE 16-10-70   WINDING SHEET No.   CHECKED BY

DESCRIPTION T.E.F.C. FLP. Sq. C. IND. MOTOR   APPROVED BY

| ORDER TYPE | GoH | FOR COMPLETE ORDER MULTIPLY QUANTITIES BY :- | 1 | PERIOD :- | 500 |

| ORDER No. 252864 | ON COST | NUMBER OF MACHINES | 1 | FRAME SIZE VBS 9354 | 3. | SHEET No. |

SPEC ITEM No.	QUANTITY PER MACHINE	DESCRIPTION of MATL. COMPONENT or ASSEMBLY	DRG. PART No.	DRAWING No./REVISION	MATERIAL REFERENCE NUMBER / weight lbs	Stores Class	No. of ops
		PACKING COSTS		(01)			
				AA1			
		CARRIAGE CHARGES		(02)			
				AA2			
		JIGS & TOOLS		(03)			
				AA3			
		OUTSIDE ERECTION		(04)			
				AA4			
		FINAL ERECTION		(0)			
	1	MOTOR OUTLINE		RE 2249			5
		S.G.					2
		NAMEPLATES					
1	1	C. BRS NAMEPLATE S# 3674		95561	38811-1016	SF	
		FLP No 4642 GROUP II					
		HP 60 RPM 2975 VOLTS 420 AMPS 74.5					1
		PHASES 3 CYCLES 50 INSUL 'A' RATING CMR					
		TEMP. RISE 55°C STARTING TORQUE 75%					
		STARTING AMPS 223.5 SPEC 2613/1957					1
		TYPE VBS 9354 CONN-DELTA SERIES No 252864/1					

ILLUSTRATION 3.2   Product specification and parts list

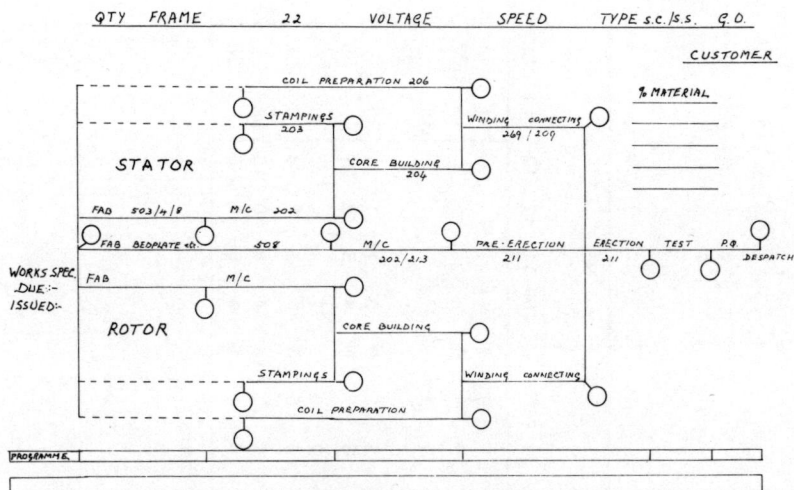

ILLUSTRATION 3.3   Structure for manufacturing a motor

KW/Speed	Stator/Rotor	departments										
		202	203	204	206	209	211	213	269	503	504	508
123/8	Wire/S.C.	169	51	58	–	2	30	32	130	12	20	69
276/4	DZA/S.C.	186	93	91	346	100	65	42	–	7	32	119
147/6	Wire/C.C.	133	6	18	–	5	29	20	116	4	14	25
201/4	VA/B	160	27	34	205	69	117	32	–	8	53	112

ILLUSTRATION 3.4   Work content by department for four orders

Date	Class of motor	Early	Weeks late														Cl.1	Cl.2	Total orders late
			0	1	2	3	4	5	6	7	8	9	10	11	12	>12			
Jan	I		2	0	2	2	0	0	5	1	9	7	4	1			31		53
	II				1	1	0	1	7	4	4	4						22	
Mar	I	3	35	9	9	7	5	13	1	1	1						46		67
	II	1	2	7	13	1												21	
May	I		1	0	2	4	5	6	3	3	1	0	0	1	1	6	32		68
	II						1	1	3	3	2	6	4	3	2	11		36	
July	I	22	2	1	1	13	4	3	4	2	0	0	2				30		64
	II	2	1	2	1	1	2	1	2	4	6	3	1	5	2	4		34	
Sep	I		1	0	0	2	1	4	5	2	12	13	4	8	0	10	58		86
	II							5	3	4	1	4	4	0	4	0		28	

ILLUSTRATION 3.5   Lateness despatches against due dates

	Department						
	202	203	204	206	209	211	213
Jan	3000	831	1135	3249	1980	1673	876
Mar	3267	1243	1146	3529	1985	2511	982
May	3700	1825	1090	4519	2419	1430	949
July	3996	1089	1439	4445	1934	1813	1017
Sep	3861	946	1321	4345	2103	1540	880

ILLUSTRATION 3.6   Capacity levels: times clocked for first week of month

4 Determining Stock Levels: Van Heugten Carpet Tiles

1. The Company

Van Heugten Brothers Ltd, Aylesbury, is a British company which sells and
distributes carpets mainly for use in offices, hotels and similar institution
buildings. All the carpets are obtained from the Dutch parent company which
manufactures the products and distributes worldwide. The British company
order their requirements from Holland, stock their products at a warehouse
at Ovington in Suffolk, and distribute through a single contracted transport
company, Lethems, at Halsted near Ovington.

The Aylesbury company started operations in September 1971, replacing
a previous agency in Essex which had failed to satisfy the Dutch Head Office.
The company's products consist of carpet 'tiles', each tile measuring approximately 20 inches square (or exactly 4 tiles per square metre). The scheme of
carpet tiles greatly facilitates the transporting and laying of carpets, besides
saving on waste incurred when cutting them and enabling worn or damaged
patches to be replaced.

Until the autumn of 1972 the company had been selling five main product
groups in carpet tiles, two of which are being phased out. Each product
group corresponds to a material type and has its own brand name. The price
of all products within the group is the same, and there is little difference
between group prices. The three product lines are further classified by colour
variants, creating a total range of 25 products, In October 1972 four new
product groups were going to be introduced into the market, again each
having their own colour variations so that the total number of lines would be
around 60 and it was anticipated that the present situation of run-down of
some groups and addition of new ones would continue into the future.

Although Heuga tiles were the first in this country and are widely regarded
as being of extremely high quality, competition is fierce and many similar

AUTHOR | REQUESTED BY P.7. | ORDER No. E

Nicholson, T.A.T.

TITLE & SERIES:

Manufacturing Operations (A Casebook)

ISBN | PUBLISHER Macmillan | INV. No. | PRICE £10.12

BOOKSELLER | DATE OF ORDER 22/7/82 | DATE REC'D £5.85

THE LIBRARY, REGIONAL TECHNICAL COLLEGE, LETTERKENNY,
CO. DONEGAL. Alex Armstrong

products are being introduced continually. A major competitive factor is the delivery performance to the customer of both quickness and reliability. The number of orders handled by the Aylesbury company has grown rapidly during 1972 and it has established a name for itself in meeting demand on time. Van Heugten aim to deliver to the customer within a week. They estimate that if the guaranteed delivery time were doubled to two weeks, many of the small customers on small orders would buy elsewhere. They have also had a number of enquiries about large orders where the customer has ordered elsewhere on discovering that insufficient tiles were available on the required date from Van Heugten. The continued success of the company therefore depends on the efficient management of its growing distribution system.

The company has a total of 48 personnel. Under the Managing Director, Mr Grant, there are three department managers for sales, marketing, and administration including distribution and accounting. The Sales Manager has a team of 16 sales representatives working for him. The Distribution Manager, Mr Flower, is responsible for stocks of goods, transport services and shipping to customers. He has a team of eight staff at the warehouse managing and loading the orders and two girls doing the data processing of the incoming orders at Aylesbury.

2. Customer Orders and Despatches

Van Heugten sells direct to 400 contractors and one wholesaler. The contractors are Heugten franchise customers and are approved purchasers of Heuga products. All customer orders come to the Aylesbury office. Each order specifies a customer name, a quantity required and a delivery location. The quantities required in an order may vary from a few (about 20) to 30,000 tiles.

Most orders are comparatively small and for one colour only, while a few orders are extremely large and many of these are for a number of colours. The distribution of order size for each colour within each product group is virtually the same, with some 'peaking' at multiples of five boxes. Illustration 4.1a shows the distribution for each product group: Felt, Flor, Lux, Lon and Laine. A special feature is a wholesaler who orders at least a hundred boxes in each order. The effect of this customer's ordering on stock level requirements is unclear, but the effect on the order size distribution of Felt and Lux products is shown in Illustration 4.1b, representing the distribution of all orders except those from this customer. Other product groups are unaffected.

Orders arrive randomly at the Aylesbury office, varying between 50 and

110 per day. The average number of orders per day for each product group is about 19 for Felt, Flor and Lux and 10 for Lon and Laine. The percentages of orders for each colour within each product group are given in Illustration 4.2.

One of the main concerns of a customer is to obtain a good match in the tiles. Inevitably there is some variation in the colour of different batches of a particular product produced by the Dutch company and it is important to try to send a customer his total order requirement out of a single batch of intake into stock. Most of the orders are for immediate delivery within the seven-day target set by the company although some orders are booked for forward delivery on a specified date in several weeks' time. These 'holding' orders are generally large because they are required for new buildings, and consequently the delivery date may be brought forward or put back at short notice by the customer, depending on completion of the building.

All distribution to customers is handled through Lethems' transport company. Lethems' vehicles go to all areas in the U.K. twice per week and guarantee capacity to cover their customers' requirements. The warehouse staff at Ovington prepare the customer loads at the warehouse and Lethems call to take the deliveries either direct to the customer or to any of 16 depots in the U.K. for a second stage. Lethems supply a base schedule of delivery runs, with a minimum service of twice a week, and daily for London and some other areas. Van Heugten are able to take advantage of this schedule by pushing orders through that can be loaded immediately: they also have the right to request additional lorries if their deliveries are too great for the capacity available. In general, lorries are loaded in the afternoon for a night run, and trailers are unloaded in the morning. One of Mr Flower's concerns is to ensure that the distribution service being provided by the depots is up to the standards required.

3. The Stock Replenishment Scheme

All products are ordered from Van Heugten, Holland, and shipped over to Britain in containers. The containers are docked at Felixstowe and transported to the warehouse at Ovington, Suffolk. The disadvantages of the geographical separation of the company management at Aylesbury from the warehouse at Ovington is considered to be more than matched by the transport savings achieved through having the stocks located near the port where incoming goods arrive. Each container holds 800 boxes and each box has 20 or 24 tiles depending on the product type.

Mr Flower makes an order each Wednesday to the Dutch company. The order is made in two stages. The preliminary order prediction is placed four weeks in advance of despatch from Holland. This order is then confirmed or adjusted two weeks later. Adjustments are limited to a 10 per cent increase on the prediction but may be reduced down to total cancellation. Each week, therefore, Mr Flower is making out a prediction order for four weeks ahead together with a confirmation or adjustments for the despatch two weeks ahead (on which a prediction was sent a fortnight previously). This is a recent revision negotiated with Holland on the previous rigid scheme requiring orders to be placed eight weeks in advance.

For making an order to Holland, Mr Flower examines the current stock level for each colour. He also has a table giving average weekly demand based on six months' previous data and records of previous predictions and outstanding confirmations (i.e. undelivered orders from Holland). He is therefore able to forecast the stock level for the week for which he is making a prediction or confirmation and decide whether this will be too low with too great a chance of stock-out to be acceptable. If he decides it is, a new order is made out, or an adjustment if he is at the confirmation point.

A minimum order of a thousand square metres is made for colours of Felt, Flor and Lux, the products for which larger orders occur. The minimum is set because of the colour-matching problem. In manufacturing tiles, Holland has a cycle of production runs for each colour using the necessary dyes. Because of the cycle, it cannot be guaranteed that the colour on one cycle will be identical with that on the next. Although the difference is slight, it is noticeable if two dye-batches are used in the same room. Holland store all tiles before distribution to customer countries, and it is possible to get as many as three different dye-batches in an order of a thousand metres. Smaller orders to Holland would increase the number of dye-batches held at any one time at Ovington, greatly increasing warehousing problems with no guarantee that a large customer order could be met. Also, of course, Holland prefers a few large orders for longer production runs, though there is no explicit cost penalty for small orders. Stocks at Ovington are kept in colour and dye-batch piles with efforts being made to finish one pile before going onto the next. The batch size for an order is therefore always greater than 1000 square metres for the three main lines and greater than 500 for the lesser lines, Lon and Laine. Beyond these levels, Mr Flower works up in units of 500 square metres until he considers the order size is large enough. After assembling his total load he adds an extra quantity to ensure multiples of complete container loads.

The time between the intended moment of despatch from the Dutch company until arrival of the goods in the Ovington warehouse varies from half a week to 1½ weeks due to delays in customs, timing of despatch, etc.

In addition, because of the production cycle in Holland (which is planned on the basis of the order predictions of the thirty or so countries which Holland supplies), some colours may be unavailable during the planned week. There is only a 19 per cent chance of a complete order being available. The distribution of delays for orders on any individual colour is shown in Illustration 4.3.

4. The Information System

The objective of Mr Flower's information system is to record the transactions accurately and transmit the incoming data on an order into a warehouse despatch note as rapidly as possible.

All orders are received at the Aylesbury office. The order is confirmed by sales, approved by accounts for creditworthiness and then expressed as a warehouse request and relayed to Ovington by telex line. The total time taken from order arrival to warehouse notification is about two hours and all incoming orders are cleared on the same day. Each order is taken in turn on a first-come-first-served basis. If a large order arrives which cannot be supplied from stock it must be delayed until adequate stock of the right style has arrived at Ovington. Orders are not split into part supplies and only sufficient stocks for some of the colours are available. For any of these requests which cannot be covered by existing stock a new order is made out to keep track of the backlog.

The recording of transactions is made on the daily despatch sheet (Illustration 4.4) and the stock sheet (Illustration 4.5) in tiles. Each of these forms is filled in daily by staff at Aylesbury to keep an exact picture of the current situation. The staff managing the data processing have to keep in mind the different units used for recording. Orders for stock replenishments from Holland are made in metres, the warehouse stock is measured in boxes and the customer orders are made out in numbers of tiles.

The 'holding orders' are treated in a special way. They are earmarked as being holding orders but are treated on paper as normal orders, and are 'despatched' with a consequent reduction in stock levels. In the warehouse, the equivalent physical stocks are tagged. In this way, there is no danger of despatching stock that may be required for a holding order. When an order is confirmed, the stock is 'unfrozen', returned on paper to the stock record, and then removed as a despatch, the physical stocks being despatched now as a normal order.

Whenever tiles are returned (the return rate is less than equivalent to an order a day) the stock sheet is adjusted accordingly in the same way as it is when stock is replenished from Holland. The completed transactions are analysed monthly by computer to provide total sales turnover by month and by style and to provide further information for accounting purposes.

5. The Request to Reduce Stocks

In October 1972 the warehouse at Ovington was nearly full, a situation that had arisen since shortly before the docks strike. Mr Flower was away on holiday at the time, and in his absence large quantities were ordered from Holland to ameliorate the expected effect of the strike. In the event, a too pessimistic view was taken, and stock levels were too high. Mr Flower succeeded in cutting these down to some extent and by the end of the year expected to have about five weeks' sales in stock. With the new products the capacity available for current products could be only seven weeks' sales, or perhaps even less. The capacity of the warehouse could be increased by inserting extra racking and in any case this could be needed for the new products.

The build-up of stocks during 1972 to seven weeks' supply had implied a considerable increase in working capital, and the Dutch Head Office had requested Van Heugten, Aylesbury, to reduce their stocks to a three-week supply level. However, Mr Flower attributed their success in meeting sales commitments and achieving sales growth largely to their promise of delivery within seven days and their ability to meet these deadlines. He believed that cutting stocks to a three-week supply would mean a lowering of their standards of service and a loss of sales. Very few customer requests had been missed in the first year of operation of the company.

Mr Grant decided to call in a consultant to work on the problem with Mr Flower and study the opportunities available for reducing the stocks to a three-week level and to assess the implications involved. With the growth occurring in the company he also believed that it was an appropriate time to set out a more formal procedure for the ordering system from Holland which one of Mr Flower's assistants could operate under his supervision.

Question for discussion

Determine the appropriate stocks levels for Van Heugten Carpet Tiles.

No. of Boxes	(a) Distribution of all incoming orders					(b) Distribution excluding wholesaler	
	Felt	Flor	Lux	Lon	Laine	Felt	Lux
1	23	22	30	55	60	27	34
2	11	15	12	6	5	16	17
3	7	11	9	6	16	11	12
4	5	9	6	6	6	8	9
5	7	7	8	3	2	8	9
6	3	5	3	4	0	4	4
7	2	4	1	3	1	3	1
8	2	2	2	2	2	4	2
9	1	2	1	1	1	1	1
10	11	3	13	4	1	3	4
11	1	2	0	1	0	2	0
12	1	2	2	1	0	1	2
13	0	1	0	1	0	1	0
14	0	2	0	0	0	1	0
15	4	1	3	0	1	1	1
16—20	10	3	6	2	1	2.5	2
21—25	3	2	1	1	0	2	0.5
26—30	3	1	1	1	0	1	0.5
31—40	1	2	1	0	0	1	0.3
41—50	2.5	1	0.5	0	2	1	0.2
50—100	2.5	3	0.5	1	0	1.5	0.5
Average no. of boxes	10.4	9.0	6.1	4.4	3.0	6.7	4.5

ILLUSTRATION 4.1   Percentage of orders demanded by order size

Product	Felt		Flor		Lux		Lon		Laine	
	Col	*%*	*Col*	*%*	*Col*	*%*	*Col*	*%*	*Col*	*%*
	101	16	302	11	703	14	501	15	402	6
	102	16	303	25	704	7	502	8	403	20
	103	8	304	8	705	18	504	13	404	6
	104	12	305	16	706	12	505	14	405	28
	105	26	306	10	707	9	506	4	406	25
	106	13	307	6	711	18	507	16	407	15
	107	9	308	7	712	7	508	7		
			310	5	713	10	512	10		
			311	12	714	5	514	5		
							516	8		

ILLUSTRATION 4.2   Percentage of orders for each colour of a product line

No delay	50%
1 week's delay	24%
2 week's delay	12%
3 week's delay	8%
4 week's delay	4%
5 week's delay	2%

ILLUSTRATION 4.3   Supplies delay

DAILY DESPATCHES
VAN HEUGTEN BROS. LTD.

C/FORWARD	HEUGAFELT							HEUGAFLOR					
INV. NO.	101	102	103	104	105	106	107	302	303	304	305	306	307
B/FORWARD	920	1000	260		2130		2275	240	1776		1392		
7524 ✓								240					
7630 ✓													
7632 ✓									24 ✓				
7642 ✓				80 ✓									
7628 ✓													
7638 ✓										480 ✓			
7653 ✓													
7395 ✓													
7652 ✓			60 ✓				20 ✓						
7648 ✓		40 ✓											
7663 ✓								72 ✓					
7647 ✓				40 ✓									
7639 ✓	40 ✓												

ILLUSTRATION 4.4   Daily despatch sheet

STOCK SHEET
VAN HEUGTEN BROS. LTD.

INV. NO.	101	102	103	104	105	106	107	302	303	304	305	306	307
BALANCE B/F Goods Received Note No.	12036	9118	34317	15396	59056	100	21997	34056	15019	22316	2619	15454	32622
Returned Goods Voucher No.													
TOTAL													
Less Daily Despatch Total	868	248	843	100	492	32	1076	24	688	72	524	840	48
BALANCE C/F	11168	8870	33474	15296	58564	68	20921	34032	14331	22244	2095	14614	32574

ILLUSTRATION 4.5   Daily stock sheet

Part C: Types of Manufacturing Organisation

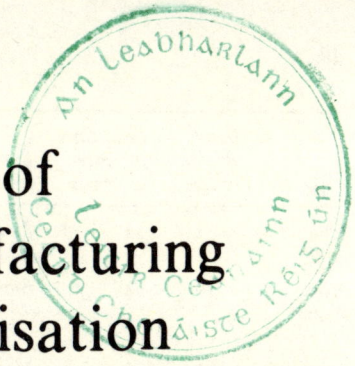

The managers of every company stress the uniqueness of their operating circumstances. They point to the special machines, labour skills and product designs which are theirs and theirs alone. And when it comes to the problems facing operating management they will generally claim exclusive rights to this complexity. However there are in fact important similarities between situations which enable useful groupings of situations to be reached for the purpose of studying operations management. The classification into different groups for operating purposes is not so much based on product or process, but by internal and external environment. In Part B we have distinguished two different sales operating policies for the external relationship with the market — make to order and make to forecast — and in this section different classes of internal manufacturing arrangement are considered.

For operations management we are not specially concerned with the technology as such but the way in which it is used for operating purposes. The operating conditions for manufacturing a range of products are largely determined by the frequency of manufacture, the average batch sizes used, the number of components in the product, and the lead times incurred between start and completion of a batch. In addition it is necessary to consider the significance of material supply problems for assembled products and the tolerances and loss rates being incurred for high-technology processing. These in turn lead on to certain kinds of skill requirements, material handling patterns, etc. The collection of these conditions for all the orders being manufactured in the plant determine the overall complexity of the operations management problems.

In this section we will distinguish four typical types of manufacture; their associated problems and characteristics are shown in the table.

Type	Batch size on orders	Lead time for batch in weeks	Supply problems	Materials handling	Labour skill	Design conditions
Product build	1	24	Significant	Bring to product	Very high	At time of manufacture
Process shop	10	12	Simple	Varied routing	Medium high	Immediately prior to manufacture
Product line	100	6	Moderate	Common sequence through processes	Semi-skill	Prior to sale
Assembly line	1000	3	Critical	Short line many bits	Semi-skill & low skill	Prior to setting up the facilities

We will study each of these types of manufacture, starting with component manufacture in a process shop and following this with a product line organisation, both cases coming from a traditional engineering works of a large manufacturing company. These will be followed by the assembly situations, taking firstly an intensive modern assembly line of an instrument producer for the motor car industry and then a slower moving product build company manufacturing hovercraft for world export.

Each of these situations has individual types of control problem which have to be dealt with by some special methods; the focus of operating difficulty in the four cases and the special treatments applied to them are:

Machine shop	progress control	computer-assisted schedules
Product line	capacity balance	group working
Assembly line	supplies and absenteeism	control of capacity and stocks
Product build	control of shortages and demand	material requirements planning.

Although many manufacturing companies have more than one of these types of facilities on their sites, generally speaking each 'shop' on the site will be found to approximate to one of these patterns.

5 Controlling the Jobbing Shop: Midland Components Machine Shop

1. The Machine Shop

The machine shop is the focal point of the activity of the Engineering Division of the Midland Components Manufacturing Company based in Manchester. The total facilities of the Engineering Division consist of the machine shop, a tool shop and a machine erection shop, with various storage points. The turn-over of these three shops in 1972 was respectively £1,150,000, £274,000 and £330,000. The machine shop provides the tool shop with pre-cut blanks for tool manufacture and the machine erection shop with machine parts; it also supplies the finished goods stores with machine parts for stock or spares for customers.

Traditionally the Engineering Division has simply acted as a service supplying tools, machine parts and new machines to Midland Components main factories at Stalybridge and Stockport where they mass produce metal fasteners (nuts, bolts, etc.). But in 1971 Dick Holmes was appointed Chief Executive of the Engineering Division with the brief to convert the Division into a more independent profit centre. Dick Holmes described his task as 'to break the gentle culture of a service function with its single capability of good engineering. We've got to sell our products now, not simply design them. We've got to concentrate more on delivery, prices and customer service than on productivity, costs and engineering skills.' Dick Holmes relied heavily on the management skills of Bill Harrison for achieving this conversion as he had three-quarters of the total employees under him and was accountable for three-fifths of the budget. Both men believed that the machine shop was an area ripe for improvement.

The machines in the machine shop are arranged in functional sections. The number of machines and the typical number of men in each section are given in Illustration 5.1. The machines are on average about 10 years old. About half the men in each section can operate any machine within the section and about 20 per cent of the men can be switched to two or three other departments if this is necessary. Others would need six weeks further technical training before they would be competent to operate the other machines.

The typical job on the machine shop is to process a small batch of metal parts or components through a series of cutting operations. The parts are transferred manually between operations in a standard metal tray; the operator takes the tray, sets up his machine, processes the batch and then the work is inspected.

The exact form of the final component is specified in a drawing which has all the details of tolerances determined by the design office. A drawing of a saw spindle part BT2 is shown in Illustration 5.2. Each component will have a specified sequence of operations for manufacturing the component determined by the production planning office. Each operation has a standard time per unit set for it together with an allowed set-up time for the batch which have been determined by the work study department. The routing and timing information is all set out on the job tickets which accompany the job as it progresses through the machine shop. In order to execute the operation the machinist will probably require special tools (jigs and fixtures). After the operation the work will be inspected by a separate inspector. Therefore the successful completion of an operation requires a range of seven types of resources:

> a supply of material
> an operator
> a specific type of machine
> a drawing of the component part
> tools to complete the cutting operation
> documentation on the operation
> an inspector to approve the finished job.

Between 30 and 150 orders (often called batches) are placed in the machine shop each week. About 60 per cent of these orders go into finished parts stores and are therefore stock replenishment orders rather than direct customer orders.

The overall management and workings of the machine shop are divided between the work-flow responsibilities of the production control and stock control functions on the one hand, and the line responsibilities of the superintendent and foremen on the other. The production control staff generate the paperwork and place the orders on the shop floor; the stock controller receives all orders for listed stocked items; the superintendent and foremen manage the labour and equipment on the shop floor. Excepting the stock controller, who is placed under finance and accounts, all functions report upwards through Bill Harrison, the works manager, who has a vast experience of the machine shop. He had started as an apprentice in the machine shop and has now spent 30 years in the Engineering Division and knew everything about it. As he remarked: 'I can still taste the cutting oil in the wind.' The comprehension of the machine shop depends on an understanding of the relationship between the control responsibilities and the line responsibilities and the detailed paperwork system.

2. The Production Control and Stock Control Functions

Tony Laker, the production controller, is responsible for placing orders and progressing the jobs through the machine shop. The production control offices are located on the second floor of the office block some 50 yards from the machine shop. Tony Laker has a staff of about 16 working with him, distributed between the offices, the machine shop and the tool room with a total budget of £35,000 of which one-sixth is attributable to tool shop progressing staff separate from the machine shop.

The main function of the production control group is to get the orders through the machine shop in a reasonable time. Traditionally the cycle time for work in the machine shop has been 14 to 16 weeks and the customers have come to believe that this is the norm. As Tony Laker remarked: 'Three to four months seems about right; six months is too long and nine months is much too long. We can't rush things too much as we have to keep some work in hand to keep the foreman loaded with about half a week's work on the section for distribution to his operators.'

The total load on the machine shop tends to vary with a four-year trade cycle and the load in the first half of the year is about 25 per cent higher than the second half. This is mainly a result of the owners of Midland Components machines preparing their maintenance schedules in January. 'We really do know quite a lot about what our customers are asking for and we can also tell when they're simply re-stocking with parts', remarked Tony Laker. 'Perhaps we ought to be able to manage the demand, but it's not easy to tell your customer when they should be making their orders. It also gets unstable: tell the customer factories that they can't have their work on time and they simply order more and then you can deliver even less on time.

'Besides I don't have too much control over delivery quotations. Someone up there in the sales department is concocting delivery promises and then I have to try to meet them. Later on when we haven't met the delivery, sales send me the list of overdues and we set some revised promises on delivery by giving a best estimate and hope the customer will be satisfied.'

In order to improve the forward planning system and therefore delivery service Midland Components' central computer staff had adapted the I.B.M. CLASS computer package for machine shop loading. The program claimed to be able to maximise the use of resources, smooth workload on work centres, and reduce manufacturing cycle times and work-in-progress. It also claimed to be easy to install and to simplify administration of production scheduling. Prior to his appointment as production controller in 1973, Tony Laker had been part of the central computer team working on the adaptation of CLASS to Engineering Division's needs. At the end of 1972 the basic files had been set up and the system started to operate live under Tony Laker. 'We are hoping the CLASS system will be able to sort out our problems', said Bill Harrison. 'It should build up a picture of the forward loads and then juggle the jobs into some sort of optimum fit on the machine shop. At least that's what the intention is.'

Both Bill Harrison and Tony Laker agreed that one of the continuing issues in 1973 was excessive work-in-progress. Tony Laker explained: 'There are about 3000 jobs on the shop floor. If I had known the orders were going to rise so much in 1973 I would not have accepted so much work. We now subcontract some of the work to other machine shops in the district. Generally I try to choose the incoming jobs which are making heavy demands on the sections already overloaded. I work on a primary load – what is on the section now – and a secondary load – the total load due for the section. These figures come from the CLASS output. I also try to subcontract the simpler jobs – those not requiring jigs and fixtures. Going outside is more expensive but we're limited by the number of men we have here. Subcontracting is estimated at 30 per cent to 50 per cent up on our costs; the outside man has to make his profits, he works on overtime (hence his good deliveries of four to six weeks), he has to add transport costs, and he pays his labour more as he provides no security. But despite the load here management will not take on people because of the difficulty of getting rid of them. The policy seems to be that you don't increase the labour force unless you can be really sure of retaining that level of production. That's one of the effects of a union in a large company.' [Redundancy agreements usually entitle a man to one week's wages for every year of service with the company.]

'Once an order is in the machine shop the only control left to me is the priorities which I can allocate through the CLASS system to the orders each week. These affect the output which guides the progressman about what he advises the foreman to do next. But there are other channels for influencing priorities – all the informal ones like the superintendent, the works manager,

even the customer visiting the site. Also the primary loads can get so large
that the priorities don't have much effect. Sometimes there are 50 jobs
waiting at a section. That suits the foreman because he has a wide choice of
work to dish out. It also suits the machinists because they'll keep on choosing
the jobs with the good piece rates for their bonuses.'

Both Tony Laker and Bill Harrison think that Jeff Yarrow in finished
parts store could do more to help with the load on the machine shop. Of the
50,000 machine part numbers for which drawings exist, the 5000 most popular are held by Jeff Yarrow for direct delivery to customer from stock. For
these parts the customers have come to expect a four-week delivery. Jeff
Yarrow also holds 2000 finished tools and the blanks made in the machine
shop which go on to the tool shop.

While Jeff Yarrow justifiably complains about poor delivery from Tony
Laker, Bill Harrison considers that Jeff Yarrow ought to be able to offer
longer runs on the shop and cut down the number of orders on hand. Bill
Harrison had recently uncovered a report from the British Productivity
Council giving a formula for economic batch sizes which he thought might
prove the point. It stated that:

$$\text{Batch size} = \sqrt{(2 \times \text{annual demand} \times \text{cost of a set-up}/ \text{cost of stockholding})}$$

To test this out he found out from accounts that it cost £2 per order for
planning and preparation in production control; that Jeff Yarrow's store,
150 ft. x 15 ft., with its precisely labelled racks, was valued at £0.40/sq. ft. p.a.,
and that Jeff Yarrow's paperwork system and the physical goods store was
run by four staff with a wage bill just less than £8000 per annum. 'Certainly
Jeff Yarrow has an immaculate stock control system', commented Bill
Harrison, 'all the i's are dotted and the t's crossed but we're not sure if we've
got the objectives right. Really Jeff's got a double ticket in the finished parts
store: he's got to provide good delivery from stock but he should also smooth
the load on the machine shop.'

3. The Paperwork System and the Physical Flows for an order

Getting to grips with the production and stock control functions means
getting to grips with the paperwork system which states the plans and records
the actions. This is mainly done through a system of job-tickets. The scheme
of job-tickets is similar from one machine shop to the next with a few special
features in the format to suit the particular situation.

Customer orders are received by sales and typed on to a five-part document set. At the same time a punched paper tape is produced which will establish the order on the computerised orders file. (This orders file was in use before the CLASS system was adopted.) If the customer order is for a non-stocked item it is passed direct to production control to raise the shop floor documentation. If the customer order is for a stocked item, the order first goes to Jeff Yarrow and he enters it on to the customer order record card related to the particular item and it may be delivered direct. If, however, this additional quantity to the total forward requirements lowers the stock balance (which Jeff Yarrow works out) below the re-order level (R.O.L.) for the part, a new order is placed on production for a batch of size equal to the re-order quantity (R.O.Q.). The R.O.L. and R.O.Q. are indicated in the Quarterly Forecasts of Usage cards held by Jeff Yarrow although the information on it is supplied by sales as the R.O.L. and R.O.Q. are determined in the quarterly sales analysis computer run. The order on production (called a Stock Replenishment Order) is recorded on the Stock Order Record Card for the part and is passed to sales for typing and entering on to the computer. A copy of the typed order after checking by the stock controller is then passed to production control. The Order Record Card, Quarterly Forecasts and Customer Order Card for the part shown in Illustration 5.2, BT2 9–20 is shown in Illustration 5.3.

For each production order production control staff retrieve the master document describing the process of manufacture. If no process master exists for the part the sequences of operations are determined by the planning department and the times are determined by work study. Also for each order a header master is produced giving the order number, batch number, batch quantity, due date, etc. From the process and header masters the following documents are produced, using line selector Banda machines in the offices adjacent to the production controller's offices.

(1)	Batch History Card	holds all the details of the order manufacture
(2)	Material Requisition (white)	identifies and authorises the basic material to be used in the manufacturing operation.
(3)	Identity Tally (blue)	kept by shop control to record where order is.
(4)	Operation Cards (yellow)	one for each operation used to specify the operation to the operator, record his time and results of inspection.
(5)	Delivery Card (brown)	sent to sales or stock control on completion of the order.

A batch history card for part BT2 9—20 is shown in Illustration 5.4. It shows the customer order heading, all the processing details as well as the results of the operation. It therefore gives both quality, quantity and timing information. The original date for launching the batch on to the shop is stamped on the left-hand side of the card.

Before the above documents are passed to shop control the raw material records are checked in raw material stores (under the purchasing function) to ensure material is available. If material is not available the job is held in the office until material arrives. Parts that are often manufactured will have their drawing kept in the drawing stores on the shop floor. Otherwise a copy of the master drawing must be obtained from the drawing office and issued. The shop floor is also forewarned if special tools or fixtures are required. All this preliminary preparation will take two weeks from the time the order reaches the production control office.

Central shop control (on the shop floor) receive the job documentation from production control. Later they also get a CONFOR card from the computer centre, which is a punched card specially for the CLASS system. This punched card is produced through the computer system when it receives details of the order at order entry stage from sales. It has a special order number on it (uniquely relating to the actual order number) and it is used by one of the clerks in shop control for keying-in job progress information to the computer system. Shop control keep the tally card and the punched card and pass all the remaining documentation to the progressman for the appropriate machining section of the first operation. (The two progressmen each cover half the sections in the machine shop.) The progressman passes the material requisition (and the other cards) to the material stores to sanction the release of raw material, and places the first operation card in his 'next operation' tray.

The material will be cut by material stores and taken by the stores labourer in a standard metal tray and placed (with all the cards, excluding the first one, in a plastic envelope) in a special rack at the appropriate machining centre. Meanwhile the progressman will examine his priority listings produced by CLASS showing the priorities of the various jobs and decide which of the 'next operation' cards to put in the appropriate trays. Once the next operation card has been placed in the tray of parts on the section it is available for work and the foreman will decide amongst such available jobs which job to allocate to each man when the operator is available to do more work. To undertake the work the operator will collect any tools necessary from tool stores together with the drawing.

On completion of the work on the batch the operator will enter the time taken on the job on the operation card, and with the approval of the foreman

the job will be parked in the finished jobs rack. The section labourer will take
the work to one of three inspection points in the shop and leave the work on
the inspector's table. The inspection policy is to examine all items in batches
up to five items in total. For batches in excess of five, a sample of five items
is taken and if any one is faulty the whole batch is examined; otherwise the
whole batch is passed. When the inspector has approved the work (re-work
may have to be done first and some items scrapped), the inspector will sign
the number complete on the batch card and the operation card and place the
job in his rack. The progressman's labourer will then take the job to the
section for the next operation and will remove the completed operation
ticket of the previous operation and also the next operation ticket which will
then go into the appropriate progressman's 'next operation' tray.

The completed operation card is handed to the clerk in central shop
control. The appropriate punched CONFOR card for the job is retrieved and
fed into a terminal, and additional data and the operation number and quantity completed are keyed in. The terminal produces a paper tape at the
central computer for updating the CLASS system. The central shop control
clerk also enters the details of the completed operation on the tally card as a
manual check. The operation card is then sent to wages for operator bonus
assessment and later to accounting for work-in-progress records. All the cards
are accumulated by accounts for the month and about six weeks later they
produce the department expenditure analysis. An example analysis is shown
in Illustration 5.5 for June 1973. Besides recording the spectrum of direct
costs incurred it also includes the indirect labour, most of which is attributable to materials handling activities.

When all the operations have been completed central shop control sends
the batch card, identity tally and delivery card back to production control.
For a customer order, sales department, on receipt of the batch card, produce
a multi-part delivery note against which the order is despatched. For a stock
replenishment order the delivery card is passed to parts stock control who
update the record, receive the goods from their labourer, check it, and
return the delivery note to sales. In either case, sales then delete the order
from the computerised orders file.

4. The Use of the CLASS Planning System

At the end of each week the CLASS computer program is run on the
company's computer. It prepares a statement of a plan for resource usage in
the immediate future. The computer program uses the data on new orders
fed in by sales in the course of the previous week, together with the paper

tape describing all the completed operations in that week. The computer refers to two permanent files of information:

a process routing file listing all the machine parts and giving for each of them the machine group sequence for each operation with a set-up time and processing time per operation.

a machine group file giving the details of capacities on the machine groups and a pre- and post-transfer time for movement of work between groups.

The computer creates an updated list of the current status of all orders, attaches the resource demands to the new orders and then prepares the resource plan by proceeding through the following steps:

Step 1. Firstly by working back from the due date the computer calculates the latest finish times for each operation on each job (as for critical path calculations), and secondly by working forward from the earliest start time (usually now) it computes the earliest start time of each operation. This provides a measure of 'slack' in the operation scheduling. Either of these calculations can be used to create a plan of operations on each order (see Illustration 5.6).

Step 2. The computer then calculates the implied loadings on the machine groups scheduling all the operations at their latest start dates and the results are printed out — called the loading to Infinite Capacity (see Illustration 5.7).

Step 3. Finally the computer calculates a schedule of the operations taking account of the capacity limits indicated in the machine groups file. This is the most complex part of the calculation. Orders are selected in priority order and their operations are loaded at their latest start times provided enough capacity is available. The priority for an order is defined by the nearness to the order due date of its first outstanding operation unless an external priority has been designated which over-rides the calculated priority. If insufficient capacity is available the order is moved to a time when each operation can be fitted in in a continuous segment of the required resource under the capacity limitation. After this stage any operations which can be moved forward in time are brought forward to fill up the available capacity. If an order is delayed beyond its due date the computer will reduce the transfer times between machines to a limit specified by the user in an attempt to meet the due dates. The results of these calculations give a loading of operations in priority order on the machine groups for use by the progressmen, (see Illustration 5.8).

All these calculations take about one hour of C.P.U. time on the I.B.M. 360/65 and produce a volume of folded printout approximately five inches thick each week.

On the whole Tony Laker considered that the CLASS outputs provided useful information. Midland Components had experienced no special labour relations problems in getting CLASS going whereas this had been a common difficulty on other applications he had heard of. On the other hand work-in-progress was still very high and orders were still coming out late and he was not sure how CLASS would solve this. As he remarked, 'CLASS can be very helpful if all the other factors are working out all right. It's primarily an advisory agent — it can never be gospel truth. It will take some time for us to get it meshed in with our overall loads so that its true potential can be realised. The only real problem I am having is explaining the errors which crop up from time to time in any new data processing system. Getting the disciplined data input and complete respect for the output from all parties will take some time to achieve. Also only 60 per cent of the actual output is on the CLASS system at present so that it is still far from complete. One of my objectives is to keep a record of the volume of output and the delivery performance so that I can keep an eye on what is happening to the workload as CLASS develops.' Illustration 5.9 gives a picture of the output and the lateness of batches completed each week which Tony Laker recorded over the latter part of 1973 and early part of 1974.

5. On the Shop Floor

Jeff Adams is the machine shop superintendent but he is also superintendent of the machine erection shop. Both the machine shop and the erection shop are independent cost centres and Jeff Adams has to answer for variances which show up on the departmental expenditure analysis. The budgeted figures on Illustration 5.7 are prepared at the beginning of the financial year by computing the total labour required for the expected work load in the machine shop. The overhead charges for the division are based on the proportion of labour assigned to the machine shop.

A significant proportion of the jobs in the machine shop are for parts for erection shop machines. Jeff Adams is not happy with the arrangement of responsibilities, as it gives him a divided loyalty, tending to make him give preference to jobs on parts needed urgently for work in the erection shop. 'The machine parts are worth a fiver whereas a tool blank is only worth 50p. And my machines which the parts go into are worth £5000. Still we've got to push all the jobs through the machine shop — it all depends heavily on the foremen and they do a good job.'

Under Jeff Adams the machine shop has three foremen — John Dougal, Henry Franks and Jim Cross. All the men in the shop are skilled, setting up their own machines, with a tight loyalty to their union, the A.U.E.W., and a clear interest in preserving their skill. The machine shop works a 40-hour week and in the late spring of 1973 was doing 10 hours overtime by putting in an extra half-hour at the start and end of the day on weekdays and working from 7 till 12 on Saturdays. Overtime levels can be altered by management with a few weeks' notice, but not normally by more than 50 per cent in six weeks. All men are paid a basic rate of £32 a week and typically earn £10 or more extra on overtime and bonus payments. On overtime the operators are paid at time and a half. The bonus depends on performance. Each job has a standard time (double the actual time — i.e. a 200 per cent efficiency rating) and the total work done by the operator is cumulated for the week and he is paid a bonus of 12p per point for any work above a 175 per cent rating. After a level of 250 per cent performance the bonus rate drops off to 8p per point. When the operators have to wait for work or work on jobs which have no allowed times they may be put on waiting time and their bonus is guaranteed for these periods at the average of the past few weeks.

The foremen were unanimous in their views about what the production control system should do. They like to have more than two weeks' work on the section although they will tolerate less on early operations such as turning. 'If you don't keep the section loaded you'll never get the output.' The foremen can move their own men around in the section to a limited extent. 'But if the work-load drops down to a week, they'll start being particular and finding reasons for delays.'

'The paperwork is more nuisance than it's worth', Jim Cross said. 'The progressman should be actually out on the shop floor, not over at the end in shop control. He could actually see what is happening then to ensure that the work is moving to the sections where the work-load is running down. There may be 2000 hours of work for a section somewhere on the floor but only 60 hours available to work on. It takes the progress people two hours to tell you where a job is when it is already in here, and two or three weeks to get it down here in the first place. Sometimes they think the sections are overloaded and the job is contracted out before we have a chance to get it. The foreman is much more help to production control than production control to the foreman.'

'But our worst bugbear is the time standards', said John Dougal. 'Eight out of ten times that I take a job to an operator he questions the time rating. Most of the time values are based on time studies of 10 to 12 years ago. In those days you forced a man to accept it. But now that management have let the ratings slip by 12½ per cent to build in a wage rise the timings are around

200 to 215 rather than 175 to 200 per cent of actual. I spend half my day going up to the work study department. I give the man the job to be going on with and I then go off with the operation card. Work study look over the synthetic timings and usually find something they've overlooked. They set the new rating and alter the card. It's all a waste of time because it's not altered on the master copy, and the whole business is repeated with the same job next time.

'The main objective is to keep the men happy — it's the only way. We don't get much trouble here — very little sickness or absenteeism and very little turnover, perhaps 5 per cent of each in a year. The men are loyal to us. Sometimes we get a bit niggled to find the shop stewards of the union and the convenor have arranged a meeting with Dick Holmes, the chief executive, without letting us know. But the shop stewards are good for the men. They get the best part of the bargain. On all the other problems we can usually settle it amongst ourselves.'

Question for discussion

What should the work-in-progress level be in Midland Components machine shop?

	Machine Type	Average replacement cost of the machine (£000)	Number of Machines	Typical number of men	Foremen
1.	Capstan lathes	8	12	10	John Dougal
2.	Ordinary lathes	5	13	10	
3.	Milling machines	6	8	5	Henry Franks
4.	Grinders	7	12	9	
5.	Gear cutting	15	3	2	
6.	Boring	20	4	3	
7.	Drilling	3	6	4	Jim Cross
8.	Shaping	2	6	4	
9.	Slotting	4	2	1	
10.	Planing	25	3	2	
11.	Marking out	—	2	2	

ILLUSTRATION 5.1   Machine shop section details

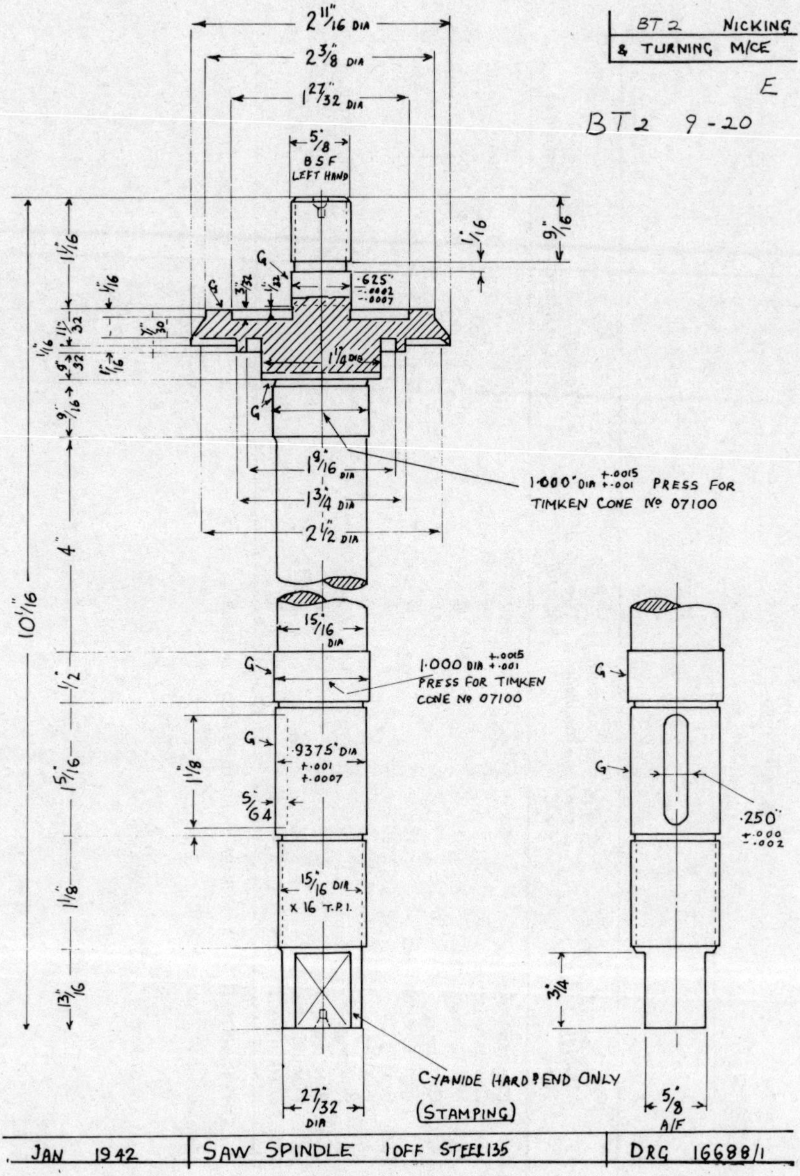

ILLUSTRATION 5.2   Drawing of a part

62

5/02/02

STOCK ORDER RECORD CARD

Part or T/S No: BT2 9-20 — Drawing No. 16688/1 — Description: saw spindle

Quantity	Week Issued	Week Required	Customer	Order Number	Batch Number
48	10	-6-1972	FPS	23704	7
48	16	28-1972	"	25804	9
48	26	52-1972	"	26552-74	-74
48	2	28-1973	"	31997-17	-17
48	7	33-1973	"	34100-22	-22
48	12	38-1973	6	32997-17	-17

CUSTOMER ORDER RECORD CARD

Part or T.S. Number: BT2 9-20

Customer	Order Number	Qty.	Week Req'd	Total Req'd	Total after Del's
115M	29312	6	6/73	6	3
Glasgow	30961	6	14/73	6	
Glasgow	31747	24	16/73	24	
Ereting Str	3013	20	18/73	20	
Ereting Str	3014	20	24/73	20	

QUARTERLY FORECASTS OF USAGE

Part or T/S No: BT2 9-20 — Drawing No. — Description

	YEAR	1972				1973			
	QUARTER	1	2	3	4	1	2	3	4
	ACTUAL DEMAND	86	98	85	6	67	-	-	22
	6 QUARTER MOVING AVG	50	63	67	63	64	57	43	30
	FORECAST	168	200	252	268	252	256	228	172
	COST RATIO								
	R.O.L.	112	132	168	178	168	170	152	114
	R.O.Q.	84	100	126	134	126	128	114	86

ILLUSTRATION 5.3   Stock controller's records

Order No.	Item No	Sched. Week	Finish Quantity	In Compl	Batch Qty	Comp Week	Qty Unit	Dept	N/L Code	Job No
25804	2	34			48	28	01	M	2102	

CUSTOMER'S ORDER No F.P.S.   PRODUCT TYPE/GROUP 399

D./S. No.   30 MAR 73

Description of Part: Saw Spindle   Drawing No. BT2 9-20

Description of Part: Saw Spindle.   Part No. Check BT2/9   20D

Div. Note No. 32478

Material and Identity: 0553   EN 39B. 2.3/4" Dia x 10.3/16". Drg. No. 16688/1

Date 20-3-73

ROUTE													
Machine	2 L4	4 CF	6 LS	8 K1	10 HW	12	14 GR1	16	18	20			
Machine	22 Cen	24 Cen	26 Cen	28 K	30 N	32 H.T	34 GR	36	38	40			

No.	Description of Operation	Section	Machine Group	Jig, Tool or Gauges Number	Set-up Time	Allwd. Time per Piece	P.W.	Date	Passed	Scrap	Viewed by
21	2 Face to Length & Centre	Cen	L4	11	30.	24.00		1/6/72	42		
22	Turn Dia's.	Cen	CF	33	240.	39.00		23/6/72	41		E
23	Face, Screw & U/c.	Cen	LS	26	60.	04.25		19/6/72	34		RQT
24	Keyseat	K	K1	8	60	7.50		25/7/72	34		K.C.
25	10 Mill Flats	M	HH1	7	60.	6.75		14/8/72	34		GT
26	12 Cyanide Harden End (EN 39B)			1							
27	14 Grind Dia's & Face	GR	GR1	12	60.	20.00		17/3/73	34		ZZ

ILLUSTRATION 5.4   Batch history card (completed)

DEPARTMENTAL EXPENDITURE ANALYSIS

for the 5 weeks ended 3rd JULY 1973

HP 1401   Stock

Total Employees	Actual	Budget	Department	Code	Month	Year
Direct	47	55	M/C SHOP	13	JUNE	1970
Indirect	12	13				

No. of Wkg. Days 123	No. of Wkg. Days 127	No. of Weeks 26			No. of Wkg. Days 25	No. of Weeks 5
No. of Weeks 20			Applied %			
			Non-applied %			

LAST YEAR Actual	THIS YEAR TO DATE Actual	Budget	% Act.	Hours Worked:	THIS MONTH Actual	Budget	% Act.
Hours	Hours	Hours			Hours	Hours	
52097	47713	58691	81	Jobs Completed & W.I.P.	9669	11553	83
1732	1145	1594	72	Own Work	200	314	64
53829	48858	60285	81	Total Machine/Man Hours	9869	11867	83
12414	9157	15336	60	Indirect Labour	1556	3019	52
66243	58015	75621	77	TOTAL Hours Worked	11425	14886	77

LAST YEAR Actual £	THIS YEAR TO DATE Actual £	Budget £	% Actual	A/c No.	EXPENSE CLASSIFICATION	THIS MONTH Actual £	Budget £	% Actual
6275	14464	6905	210	01-12	MATERIALS £	7100	1399	507
28281	30333	29827	102	18	DIRECT LABOUR £	7227	6044	120
					VARIABLE EXPENSES:			
954	1189	1003	119	22	Marking Out	304	203	150
2762	3231	2304	140	23	General Indirect	628	467	134
				24	Training			
				26	Inspection			
		241		27	Tool Service & Storekeeping		49	
				28/29	Stores			
3840	4662	4126	113	30	Supervision	831	836	99
1741	1167	1677	70	31	Own Work	235	340	69
157	282			32	Lost Time	57		
1333	1248	1288	97	34	O.T. Premium	290	261	111
246	225	234	96	35	P.U.G.	48	47	103
11033	12004	10873	110		Sub-Total	2393	2203	109
5167	5687	5304	107	36/37	Holiday Wages & Insurance	1212	1075	113
1728	1948	1894	103	38/52/3	Gas, Water & Electricity	338	384	88
892	734	675	109	50	Consumable Stores	125	137	91
967	336	1309	26	51	Machine Parts	16	265	6
6008	6711	4735	153	71/72	Production Tools	1114	518	215
				73	Tool Room Work		442	
705	740	760	97	74	Jigs & Fixtures	62	154	40
6670					HYDROPTIC M/C OVERHAUL			
1267	1970	1209	163	54	Plant Repairs & Maintenance	391	245	160
1826	1150	1803	64	55/60	Service Depts.	247	365	68
2	9			61	MISC SUPPLIES			
4580	5424	4778	114	63	Tool & Gauge Inspection	1139	968	112
				64	Pattern Shop			
583	985	799	123	66	Defective Work	201	162	124
112	88	208	42	67	Own Work Materials	28	42	67
41540	37786	34347	110		TOTAL VARIABLE EXPENSES £	7266	6960	104
69821	68119	64174	105		TOTAL CONVERSION COST	14493	13004	111
76096	82583	71079	114		TOTAL VARIABLE COST £	21593	14403	150
					Less Transfers			

s./d.	s./d.	s./d.		PRODUCTION HOUR RATES:	s./d.	s./d.	
10-11	12-9	12-6	10?	Direct Labour	14-11	12-6	119
15-11	15-10	14-5	110	Variable Expenses	15-0	14-5	104
26-10	28-7	26-11	106	CONVERSION COST RATE	29-11	26-11	111

ILLUSTRATION 5.5   Monthly cost statement for the machine shop

E.D. CLASS ORDER

Order	Item	Part no.	Quantity	Planned time	Time completed	External priority	Internal priority	Operation no.	Machine group	Earliest start date (Backward Schedule)	Latest start date (Backward Schedule)
30275	002	NSOL38-100	10	65.9	0.0		4				
30275	002							00	MTLS	3045	3045
								02	A220	3055	3055
								04	A450	3064	3064
								06	A928	3076	3076
								08	9000	3089	3089
								10	A928	3098	3098
								12	9000	3111	3111
								14	9000	3126	3126
								16	A500	3135	3135
								18	A500	3142	3142
30276	003	Adjusting screw									
30276	003	C11A15-64	68	26.3	8.7						
								08	A102	3045	3071
								10	B000	3053	3079
								12	A150	3059	3086

Note Dates are expressed as year (first digit), day (next three digits).

ILLUSTRATION 5.6   Order plan from CLASS system

E.D. CLASS Load graph   Small milling   A300   No. MCS   1   Act cap   8,0   Inf cap scheduling   Page

Wk no From To	Available capacity hrs	Load based on ESD hrs	Load based on LSD hrs	(graph 0–40–80)	hrs	(graph 0–40–80)	Unavoidable overload to meet LSD hrs
9 3045–3049	40.0	579.1	462.7	************+************* —	0.0	********************	422.7
10 3050–3054	40.0	205.6	162.0	***********+*********** —	0.0	******************	122.7
11 3055–3059	40.0	310.8	176.7	***********+*********** —	0.0	*******************	136.7
12 3060–3064	40.0	348.0	135.7	**********+*********	0.0	****************	95.7
13 3065–3069	40.0	117.6	54.9	***********+****	0.0	****	14.9
14 3070–3074	40.0	120.2	152.8	**********+********* —	0.0	*****************	112.8
15 3075–3079	40.0	49.1	80.6	**********+***** —	0.0	********	40.6
16 3080–3084	40.0	27.9	53.6	***********+****	0.0	***	13.6
17 3085–3089	40.0	20.7	61.7	***********+******	0.0	*****	21.7
18 3090–3094	40.0	29.1	85.2	**********+******** —	0.0	************	45.2
19 3095–3099	40.0	7.3	86.3	**********+********** —	0.0	************	46.3
20 3100–3104	40.0	21.9	42.0	**********+*	0.0	*	2.0
21 3105–3109	40.0	2.8	66.5	**********+*******	0.0	*******	26.5
22 3110–3114	40.0	0.0	44.7	**********+*	0.0	*	4.7
23 3115–3119	40.0	0.0	55.2	**********+*****	0.0	****	15.2
24 3120–3124	40.0	0.0	34.0	*********|	0.0		0.0
Totals	640.0	1840.1	1754.6		0.0		1120.6

Notes: ESD = Earliest Start Date; LSD = Latest Start Date

ILLUSTRATION 5.7   Loading on a machine group on basis of latest start dates

Loading sequence Order/Item		Part no	Op no	Qty	Total time	Time comp	Stt date	Fin date
X20069	001	C12A7-176	02	6	3.99	0.00	3045	3045
Y14467	002	GSDL3174	04	1	0.00	0.00	3045	3045
X20252	001	NSD18-13	10	4	6.43	0.00	3045	3046
X20417A	001	N1-6-8	04	1	0.88	0.00	3046	3046
X20794	001	NSDL22-18	06	1	0.95	0.00	3046	3046
Y11798A	006	C11A17-579	10	19	3.66	0.00	3046	3047
Y12819	021	NSDL312-1	06	5	11.41	0.00	3047	3048
Y21745	202	EM9000-766	04	2	2.40	0.00	3048	3048
28831	004	C11A24-14	06	264	73.10	0.00	3048	3057

ILLUSTRATION 5.8   Priority list for a machine group

Week	Batches	Hours	Av. batch	% on time	% < 10 wks late	Median Lead	Mean (Max Lead)	Std. Devn.	84% Lead
12	46	595	13	15%	72%	21	24.7(45)	9.9	34.6
33	85	1993	23	21%	55%	23	28.0(82)	10.7	38.7
34	44	473	11	27%	55%	24	26.6(43)	10.2	36.8
35	43	1202	28	14%	58%	25	29.2	10.2	39.4
36	37	554	15	24%	49%	26	29.0(35)	14.1	43.1
37	39	1845	47	36%	67%	24	26.2	13.4	39.6
38	61	828	14	39%	69%	25	23.2	12.5	35.7
39	70	1178	17	40%	69%	23	23.6(68)	13.6	37.2
40	30	465	16	23%	40%	29	30.6(28)	15.4	46.0
41	121	2229	18	11%	55%	28	27.6(119)	12.6	40.2
42	54	756	14	2%	41%	31	31.6(53)	12.9	44.5
43	92	1985	22	14%	63%	29	28.0	11.4	39.4
44	73	1064	15	10%	66%	27	28.1	13.3	41.4
45	67	991	15	22%	58%	27	26.1(66)	13.1	39.2
46	97	1882	19	18%	52%	27	28.8	13.4	42.2
47	118	2313	20	17%	52%	30	30.1	13.8	43.9
48	101	2511	25	18%	55%	30	31.1	15.9	47.0
49	113	4335	38	12%	11%	35	34.3	13.8	48.1
50	88	1797	20	10%	57%	28	31.7	15.0	46.7
.	.	.	.	.	.	.	.	.	.
.	.	.	.	.	.	.	.	.	.
1	37	1374	37	8%	30%	39	36.8	14.9	51.7
2	37	1379	37	22%	32%	31	33.6	15.0	48.6
3	74	2156	29	20%	34%	41	35.1	16.3	51.4
4	101	2268	22	22%	43%	33	34.3	17.5	51.8
5	70	2498	36	21%	43%	36	35.6	17.3	52.9
6	76	2242	30	26%	42%	36	34.9	15.8	50.7
7	104	2710	29	42%	47%	27	30.5	17.2	47.7

Notes:

Hours = total hours work + set-up time on the batches

Av. batch = Average batch size

Lead = Time between date of issue to shop floor and date of completion in weeks.

ILLUSTRATION 5.9 Output analysis — machine parts. Completed in wks 32 – 50/73 and wks 1 – 7/74

6 Group Working on a Product Line: Midland Components Star-line

1. The Establishment of the Star-line

Midland Components Engineering Division at Manchester supplies tools, machine parts and a machine repair service to a variety of companies in the fastener business including Midland Components' own factories at Stalybridge and Stockport. The customer factories require a steady supply of 'consumable' tools such as dies and punches for the manufacturing of nuts, bolts, clips, etc. The tool shop of Engineering Division, with a turnover of £1.2 million, is the major production centre for these tools. The number of tools produced each year include 115,000 rolling and heading dies, 52,000 punches, 400,000 saws and 9000 cutters. The manufacture of the tool requires a blank (often a bar or strip of metal) to be processed on a series of machine tools, lathes, presses, grinders, etc. The blank itself is manufactured from bought-in stock in the Engineering Division's own machine shop adjacent to the tool shop.

Up till 1968 the tool shop had been arranged on a functional layout by skill types. Each group of machines — milling, grinding, turning — occupied a bay in the shop with a foreman and a group of operators running the bay. Work on jobs would progress from bay to bay and generally there would be a pile of work-in-progress within each bay. But in the early 1960s a new concept called 'Group Technology' (coming originally from productivity studies in Russia) was being proposed for engineering manufacture which completely contrasted with the existing system architecture. The basic idea of Group Technology is to select families of similar components and to produce them on a flow-line production basis on an appropriately chosen set of machines which are collectively located together in a geographically small area. The aim is that the collection of a small team of operators with a small group of facilities manufacturing a family of products from start to finish will simplify control, reduce work-in-progress, cut set-up times and enrich the jobs of the operators by enabling them to make and see the whole product.

Midlands Components investigated Group Technology in 1965 by commissioning two members of staff of Engineering Services Group to study the relevance of Group Technology to their tool shop. They classified the tools by their shapes and processing specifications, examined the demand patterns and created two resource groups or 'cells', each of about 20 men with appropriate machinery. One group was to manufacture hexagonal 'star' forging dies and the other group was to manufacture a set of tools jointly constituting 70 per cent of the tools production. It was estimated that stocks could be cut by a third (the present stocks value of Star dies was about £40,000) and that delivery cycles of 16 weeks could be halved.

As it turned out the manufacture of some of the products planned for the second cell were transferred to another factory partly owned by Midland Components and it was never established at the Manchester site. However three cells were set up in 1968, one for the Star dies and two others for standard cutting tools and saw blades. The Star-line for the hexagonal forging die was located in the machine shop next to the tool room and undoubtedly this was the most successful cell in the works.

Bill Harrison, the works manager, considered that the adoption of the cell system was a radical transformation. 'Here we have several hundred machine tools in the works in a tool shop and a machine shop all operating to a centrally based production control system, to standard accounting schemes, and with a standard of 16 weeks' delivery. And then we pull out a dozen men and a dozen machines, put them all physically together and tell them to operate as a little plant within a plant doing their own progressing, inspection and management. It's a great idea.' Dick Holmes, the new chief executive of the Engineering Division, who was appointed in 1972 'to convert the Division into a profit centre', also regarded the Group Technology 'cell system' as a promising new method which should be extended further in his works if at all possible.

2. The Manufacture of Star dies

The Star die is a small steel tool about 4 cm long, used for forming nuts to a special patented shape. It is a product for which the works can forecast a reliable and continuing demand from major customers manufacturing fasteners.

There are 180 different Star dies classified into four series (noted as 1, 2,

3, 4) which produce 16 nut sizes in a range of 66 depths. The cost of a blank on entry to the Star-line is 30p. of which 20p is bar for the blank. The price of the finished Star die varies from £2 for types 1 and 2, to £2.50 for types 3 and 4.

Star die production starts with bar stock and ends in finished goods stores. Bar stock is made into blanks and held in blanks stores. There are 20 types of blank, the nut size and depth determining the type of blank needed. The blanks are then manufactured into Star dies, visiting the central heat treatment facility before going into finished goods stores.

The die is itself made by other tools in the pressing stage. The starting tool is a 'master die' which is machined from bar stock by precision tool makers. This master produces 50 formed intermediate masters. These are ground in the tool room into master tools for use on the Star-line each of which produce 400 Star dies. Each Star die will produce about 18,000 nuts. As in any machining operation the tools wear out gradually over their lifetime. One in 50 dies is inspected (and subsequently scrapped) to check whether the master tool is going out of tolerance.

3. The Operation of the Star-line

The cell system for the Star-line was set up during 1968 and it became a cost centre in its own right. The foreman appointed to manage the Star-line and the other two cells was Ken Wightman. Shortly after its establishment, Ken Wightman went on a N.E.B.S.S. course at the local technical college, and as a part of his course he prepared a report on the Star-line. His report portrays the nature of the Star-line and its benefits. Extracts from the report are given in Illustration 6.1 and 6.2. Illustration 6.1 gives the detailed process sequence for the manufacture of the Star dies. Illustration 6.2 reports the remarkable improvements which the cell system has achieved compared with the previous practice when the Star dies were just part of the products going through the tool room.

At the beginning of 1973 the Star-line was continuing to operate very smoothly. Ken Wightman was still in charge and he managed the two other cells as well. When asked how he coped with the extra load he simply stated that the Star-line 'ran itself'. The only major change to the equipment which had been on the line in 1967 was the addition of a further press for the type 1 and 2 dies. This press produces dies three times faster than the original press (which was retained for types 3 and 4). The extra press was an expensive addition to the line, costing around £10,000, whereas the other machines are valued at between £1000 and £3000. The line was working on a one

8-hour shift per day basis except for the presses, which were operated on two shifts per day.

There were now only 15 men on the Star-line of whom a third could operate any machine and very few could only operate one machine. The 15 included three inspectors and a labourer. This was a considerable reduction from the 21 men who had originally been assigned to the Star-line but they had only been on the line for 80 per cent of their time in the first instance, being used part-time on other work.

The men seemed to work well as a team and enjoyed the chance to inspect their own work: 'You can see how the work's going along', 'You see what you've made', were two of the comments from operators. Nevertheless some operators wanted to keep their individuality: one preferred to stick to the press operations and another was concerned about 'lead-swingers' if a group bonus system was introduced and team work applied to the limit. The men are paid on a piece-rate bonus system, using a standard rating of 200 (i.e. the actual times are half the allowed times), they get a fixed weekly wage for performance at 175 of standard and a bonus of 15p per point for faster work up to 230 ratings. Thereafter the bonus falls to 8p per point.

Despite the integrated character of the Star-line, the work flow to it was still part of the overall production control system. All customer orders for Star dies (about 15 to 20 per week) each having a batch size and delivery date pass through the sales department and from there to Jeff Yarrow, the stock controller. The order requirements are then entered on the stock record as a demand for stock. If it is a stock item Jeff Yarrow supplies from stock and checks to see if this order reduces the stock level below his re-order point and if it does he issues a new order through production control on the Star-line with a selected batch size. For non-stocked items he always issues an order. For types 3 and 4 the batch size rarely exceeds 100 whereas for types 1 and 2 the batch size is usually around 200 to 225. As Jeff Yarrow pointed out, 'I would like to order batches of 3000 on the most popular items to minimise the number of batches but that would tie the line down for a whole week and you've got to keep the flow of types moving.'

Most types of Star dies are held in stock so that orders for the Star-line are nearly all stock replenishment orders from Jeff Yarrow. The order passes to production control who generate the appropriate cards to authorise the work, taking about a week to do this. A bunch of five types of cards is produced (material cards, despatch slips, etc.) with a further card for each operation, giving all the production details. But Ken Wightman does not put these cards out with the work on the machine; he only uses the operation cards for the works operator payment system.

Jeff Yarrow summarises the more urgent order requirements for Ken

Wightman each week in two ways. Every fortnight he summarises the requirements in a stock requirements table. This list typically includes about a quarter of the total number of batches in progress. Then in the intervening weeks he gives a list of specific customer orders which are coming due. This list will have between 20 and 40 entries on it. This information enables Ken to judge his priorities for loading. 'I've got an easy relation with Ken', Jeff Yarrow remarked, 'because he knows where his work is and he can do something about it when an urgent job needs to be done. It's quite different in the machine shop.'

Jeff Yarrow keeps an accurate record of production levels, stocks, orders and sales summarising the statistics for all product groups on a weekly basis. Illustration 6.3 gives a graphical display of the weekly records of these quantities between September 1972 and March 1973 on the Star-line, smoothed into a four week moving average.

4. The Foreman's Job

Trying to find faults with the Star-line cell system in conversation with Ken Wightman is like trying to find a needle in a haystack. Not that he pushes the line as the best in the works — he simply wants to make it work well. He has a long experience in the company and has a straightforward, disarming manner. He would inspire immediate trust in anyone around him. When asked a question he will reflect for a moment or two and then give a short, precise, quiet answer which always settles the matter. These were his answers to some key questions:

'How do you keep the line loaded smoothly?'
Ken: 'It isn't very difficult: we always keep a little bit of work in hand and I start the jobs when they're needed.'
'Doesn't the line get out of balance? Don't you get bottlenecks?'
Ken: 'Sometimes work piles up a little bit at one of the machines but the operators help one another out. The press operators will usually stick to press operations but the rest of the men switch between machines and they get bottlenecks shifted themselves. They can see what's going on, they know the requirements and they make their own movements.'
'Doesn't this switching affect the quality of the product?'
Ken: 'No. They are all on the same skill rating. Inspection's carried on the same way. They do a lot of inspection themselves.'
'Surely their pay is affected by switching jobs when they are on a piece rate system?'

Ken: 'It doesn't really make much difference to their weekly pay. They all have their own personal targets. A '250' man will be on about 250 whichever machine he is on. Everyone has a little bit in hand. They end up with about 10 to 15 per cent more than the other operators in the tool room, so pay is not a problem.'

'How long does it take to get a job through once it's started?'

Ken: 'For a typical batch it'll take about a week on the line here but it can take two weeks in all. Heat treatment takes a while. It should take two days but often it can take up to four days. The actual operation only takes three or four hours. You see, heat treatment has to be shared by all the products in the works.'

'But you allow four weeks from Jeff Yarrow's issue of the order to completion. What happens to the other two weeks?

Ken: 'I hold about two week's worth of work in my card rack ready for starting on pressing. I've got to hold some work in hand to keep the line busy. If I get too many types 1 and 2 dies or too many types 3 and 4 at one time, one of the presses will be out of action or I might get too much or too little turning work. Jeff gives me his customer priority list and I try to push these priority orders through in front from the work I've got in hand. I can get the real priority orders through in three to five days if I push them.

'What about costing?'

Ken: 'That doesn't really affect me. It should though. I should really produce at the most economical cost. I have often asked what the real costs are. They give me the monthly expenditure analysis about three months after it's happened but I can never really understand it. That's the trouble with accountants. They parcel everything up their own way, wrap it up in brown paper and all you can see is the sealing wax. [The standard monthly departmental expenditure analysis for a month is given in Illustration 6.4.]

'You say the output is very steady but surely it must alter in response to changing market needs?'

Ken: 'Yes, we can increase the output with overtime or extra men. But we've got to keep the changes smooth. Given sufficient warning I can get it increased or I'll tell Mr Harrison what extras I need to increase output.'

All the evidence suggested that Ken Wightman was right about the flexibility he had on the line. At the beginning of 1972 total stocks of Star dies amounted to about 20 weeks' worth of sales and Jeff Yarrow, under pressure from higher management, was obliged to bring down the stock levels. Despite an order rate of about 2800 in the middle of 1972 the output target was set at

2500 to pull the stocks down. There was no overtime on the Star-line.
However by September 1972 marketing pressures mounted and some arrears
appeared on Jeff Yarrow's regular weekly production statistics (see Illustration
6.3.) At the beginning of November 1972 the output target was raised to
3000 dies per week and then again to 3250 and this target was achieved four
weeks later. However the inflow of orders continued and on 18 December an
output of 3500 dies was set. Ken Wightman made some specific written
requests at this stage, under this new pressure, for further resources but
once again this target was reached and recorded in the minutes of the regular
fortnightly production meetings chaired by Bill Harrison. However it was
noticed that the scrap rate was beginning to build up gradually to near the
budgeted 2 per cent limit with the steady increase in volume.

Generally Bill Harrison, the Works Manager, had been most impressed
with the performance of the Star-line. 'We add value at around £6000 per man
on average on the shop floor and the Star-line must show up well by comparison. The cell system really represents autonomous areas of management. The
difficulty is knowing how far to extend the ideas. Not everyone wants to join
the cellular style of production. Some of the other foremen wouldn't touch
Ken Wightman's job; they'd get bored stiff — the same for the operators. We
still have some open questions to resolve. Is the Star-line just a nice little cell
all on its own which we should leave alone, or should we have lots of cells all
over the factory? What are the conditions for setting up these cells? Perhaps
the Star-line doesn't really exploit the concepts of group technology at all or
perhaps it's the best cell that's ever existed. Perhaps there are some simple
ways to improve it. We don't know the answer to these questions and we've
got to sort them out before we can really decide whether to push the cell
system further into the tool room and the machine shop.'

5. Postscript to the hey-day

In the early summer of 1973 the Star-line was operating at its best. The output
had gone up to around 3750 dies per week. The operators were earning a lot
of overtime. Demand continued to increase until by August the required
output was nearing 4250 per week. But then things started to go wrong. Bill
Harrison traced the trouble to two sources.

'Firstly', he said, 'we've gone on to measured day work throughout the
factory so that pay is related to overall output now rather than the old piece
rates. This has had the effect of reducing the differential advantage the Star-
line men had over the rest in terms of pay. They were on especially high
ratings. Even taking 230 as the average efficiency rating for the jobs and adding

£4 on to their new basic rate meant that their pay packets had dropped. We pulled them back a bit with remedial payments extending over two to five years, but they say they want an incentive as the job is dull. Some of them threatened to leave; I doubt if they could find an equivalent job for the same money anywhere else.

'But the main cause of the trouble was the proposal for new machines. We just couldn't get the required output from the line as it stood and we had to put in a capital request for some new machines to add to the line. This is when the going got sticky.

'Because of the pressure on demand we had to rush through the proposal and perhaps we did not convert the men enough. But we were in a hurry for the output. First I proposed to add another press and a grinder with a couple of extra men simply to expand the capacity of the line. Ken Wightman and the Star-line men would have accepted that. But the company financial committee turned it down. Despite a promised 47 per cent return on capital, Head Office said they always worked to the rule that when you brought extra machines in you had to replace men – roughly: "get rid of a man for every £4000 invested." The board want us to push for extra-high technology on the Star-line, automatic feeding of blanks from magazines, transfer tables, automatic inspection, and perhaps some means of combining the processes. I've looked up some of the possible equipment. In the end we might go for some completely automatic machinery for all except the pressing stages for producing our Star dies, at the press of a few buttons. One possible machine we may get costs £22,000 and would save seven men on all operations other than the press. But I now have to make out another proposal to cut out some of the labour. And it will take another three months to get the decision.

'The proposals for capital equipment are put in under a fancy discounted cash flow procedure which I don't really believe in. It's too complex. It may be all right in theory for comparing completely different projects, but we're not in that situation. In most of the capital proposals we're putting in for essential replacement machinery which we cannot do without. D.F.C. is too complex for that. We should have a simple pay-back period scheme to act as a target on the investment in use. We would feel that better on the shop floor.

'I was surprised by the financial group's reaction to my first proposal. Perhaps it's because our chief executive of this works has just been made chairman of the financial Committee of the Midland Components Group and he has to appear to show a tough traditional line. It's amazing what they do spend money on. Midland Components have just set up a new works fifteen miles away in a copper plating operation. Everything's brand new and fully automated there. Yet we struggle to get a few replacement machines here. May be it's a tax dodge. In another of our works in Stockport we have really old machinery where the screech of the old screw-cutting machines and the banging of the presses goes on all day. I've watched one of the press operators jump every time his press thumps down. I've seen a similar near-silent operation in Germany. The men on these machines in Stockport are nearly all deaf by the time they are forty. Of course the company supplies ear-covers but they won't wear them — they think it's too soft. 'Dad didn't wear them so I won't,' they say. Another show of the conservatism on the shop floor.

'But back on the Star-line we're in difficulties. I've got to get new machines. The major trouble is that the foreman of the Star-line, Ken Wightman, has turned sour. Straight after the change in payment system he disappeared off to manage his other cell in the tool room. He wouldn't discipline the men. He's not so good as we thought he was. The cell system may be only appropriate for stable situations. What suits one man at one time doesn't suit him at another. That seems to be the way Ken is. Even the peak output of 3750 has turned down without any change in facilities. Now we're sometimes below 3000 on our weekly records. That's no good.'

Question for discussion

Evaluate the group working system of the Star-line.

SEQUENCE OF OPERATIONS ON THE G.T. PRODUCTION STAR-LINE

Also showing reviewed piece-work values. Obelisks denote operators who have been trained to perform more than one operation when the need arises. Asterisks indicate which operators do other work as well as Star Dies. Types 3 and 4 dies take 50% longer to machine than the smaller varieties 1 and 2.

Op.	Type of machines	No. of operators	Description of operation	Time values per operation	Inspection
1	2 Presses	8†	Press form	4.5 mins 3 & 4 per die 3.0 mins 1 & 2	1st. off 1 in 20 and final 100% visual check
2	5 Lathes	5†	Turn to remove excess metal face ends, and chamfer	From 4.25 mins to 10 mins/die 60/90 mins set-up according to size and style	1st off and final 100% check
3	Centreless grinder	1†*	Centreless grind O/D. (2 passes in soft state)	From 4.5 mins to 14 mins per dozen	No inspection
4	Broaching m/c.	1†	Cut locking grove	From 4 mins to 18 mins per dozen according to size	No inspection
5	Marking m/c.	1	Mark symbol No's	Day-work (1hr. per batch of 100)	1st. off Check
6	Heat treat	2*	Harden, temper and vapour blast	Process operation	100% check
7	Centre grinder	1†*	Centreless grind O/D final pass	From 2.5 mins to 7.5 mins per dozen	1st. off and final random check
8	Face grinder	1†	Grind front face	5.75 mins. per dozen 60 mins set-up per batch	1st. off and final 100% check
9	Heat treat	1*	Tufftride	Process operation	100% visual only

Note: These are 'standard times' which are approximately twice the actual times.

ILLUSTRATION 6.1   The Star-line process sequence
Extract from N.E.B.S.S. course: Report by Ken Wightman (1969)

SUMMARY OF IMPROVEMENTS THROUGH THE CELL SYSTEM

Using the G.T. Production Line method has reduced the distances travelled by,
OPERATORS — from 1,088 yards to 236 yards — saving 852 yards per batch.
Material   — from 1,669 yards to 269 yards — saving 1,400 yards per batch.

   Two operations in the original method, (Grind Back Face, and Grind Locking Flat)
have now been eliminated.

   In the event of any threatening 'bottlenecks', 12 of the 21 operators have sufficient
experience to be able to undertake 2 or more different operations. The operators are all
on the same piece-work rates, consequently payment problems do not arise.

   Fastener factories at Stalybridge and Stockport previously kept 10 weeks supply of
dies in stock and 10 weeks supply on order. Now the Engineering Division holds 8 weeks
stock, with a further 4 weeks supply being made on the production line. This enables
the Finished Tool Stores to meet all orders from stock, and for the Planning Department
to issue further orders to the Division for more realistic cycle times.

   These factors, together with information received from the Work Study Department,
confirm an overall 25% reduction in piecework times, reduced Work-in-Progress by 72.8%,
from 27,500 Dies to an average of 7,500 Dies, and cycle times by 62.5%, from 16 weeks
delivery from issue to completion to 6 weeks maximum.

   Production has increased 50%, — from 1200 dies to 1800 dies per week.

ILLUSTRATION 6.2   Results from adopting the Star-line
Extract from N.E.B.S.S. course: Report by Ken Wightman (1969)

Totals across all products

Stocks = I
Production = P
Sales = S
Orders = O
Arrears = A

I

O
S
P
A

18
17
16
15 000
14
13
12
11
10 000
9
8
7
6
5000
4
3
2
1

38 39 40 41 42 43 44 45 46 47 48 49 50 51 52 1 2 3 4 5 6 7 8

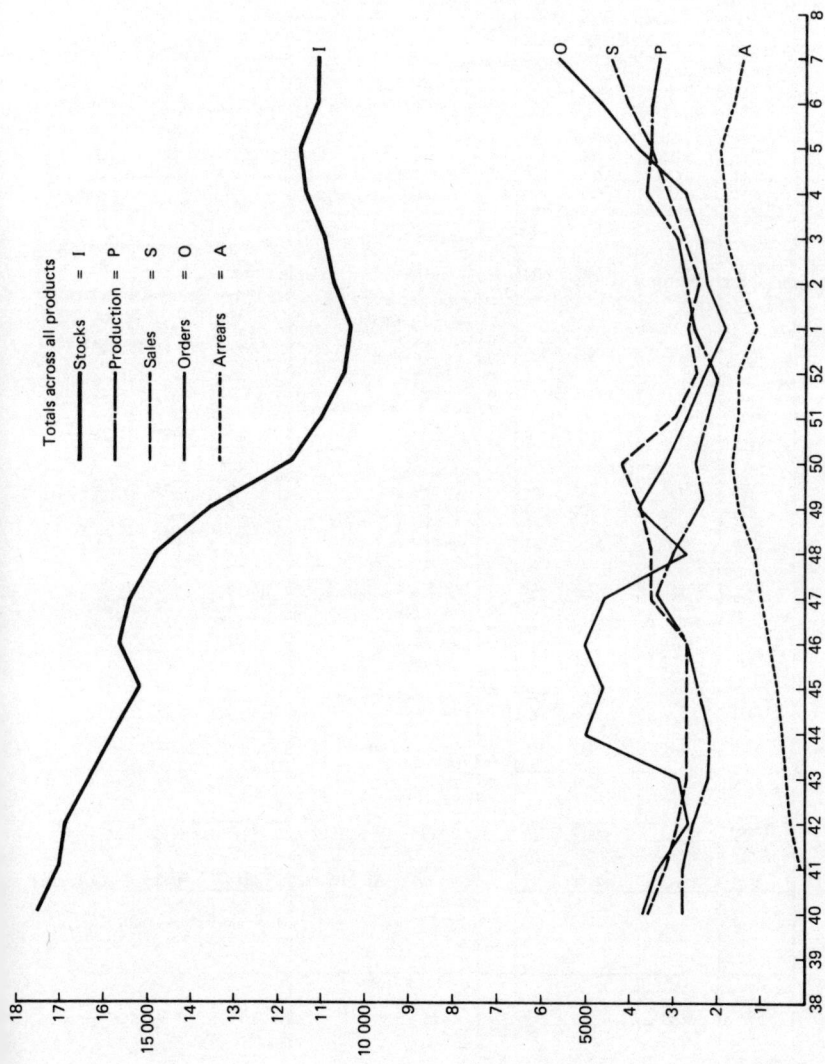

ILLUSTRATION 6.3 Weekly statistics of Star die production,
week 28, 1972 to week 8, 1973

81

Total Employees		Actual	Budget	Department	Code	Month		Year 1972
	Direct	10	12	Star Line	11	December		
	Indirect	7	1					
No. of Wkg. Days 242	No. of Wkg. Days 242	No. of Weeks 52		Applied %		No. of Wkg. Days 23	No. of Weeks 5	
No. of Weeks 52				Non-applied %				

LAST YEAR	THIS YEAR TO DATE					THIS MONTH		
Actual Hours	Actual Hours	Budget Hours	% Act.	Hours Worked:		Actual Hours	Budget Hours	% Act.
23381	20880	21614	97	Jobs Completed & W.I.P.		2124	2055	103
				Own Work				–
23381	20880	21614	97	Total Machine/Man Hours		2124	2055	103
2,150	3030	1896	160	Indirect Labour		197	180	109
25531	23910	23510	102	TOTAL Hours Worked		2321	2235	104

LAST YEAR	THIS YEAR TO DATE			A/c. No.	EXPENSE CLASSIFICATION	THIS MONTH		
Actual £	Actual £	Budget £	% Actual			Actual £	Budget £	% Actual
				01-12	MATERIALS £			
21296	21906	27286	80	18	DIRECT LABOUR £	2351	2776	85
					VARIABLE EXPENSES:			
				22	Marking Out			
1001	1234	894	138	23	General Indirect	132	91	145
				24	Training			
				26	Inspection			
				27	Tool Service & Storekeeping			
				28/29	Stores			
1619	1296	1445	90	30	Supervision	113	147	.77
				31	Own Work			
				32	Lost Time			
383	356	342	104	34	O.T. Premium	70	35	200
214	689	190	363	35	P.U.G.	7	19	37
3217	3575	2871	125		Sub-Total	322	292	110
3528	4201	315.	133	36/37	Holiday Wages & Insurance	551	321	172
				38/52/3	Gas, Water & Electricity			
344	684	307	223	50	Consumable Stores	59	31	190
96	159	86	185	51	Machine Parts	9	9	100
1359	581	1213	48	71/72	Production Tools	42	123	34
	2266			73	Tool Room Work	172		
120	148 (4)	107	138	74	Jigs & Fixtures		11	
37	254	33	770	54	Plant Repairs & Maintenance	94	3	
373	412	334	123	55/60	Service Depts.		34	
5424	6045	4844	125	63	Tool & Gauge Inspection	686	493	139
				64	Pattern Shop			
2589	2082	2311	90	66	Defective Work	399	235	170
				67	Own Work Materials			
17087	20411	15257	134		TOTAL VARIABLE EXPENSES £	2334	552	150
38383	42317	42543	99		TOTAL CONVERSION COST	4685	4328	108
38383	42317	42545	99		TOTAL VARIABLE COST £	4685	4328	108
					Less Transfers			

s./d.	s./d.	s./d.		PRODUCTION HOUR RATES:	s./d.	s./d.	
0.97	1.05	1.31	80	Direct Labour	1.11	1.31	85
0.73	0.98	0.73	134	Variable Expenses	1.10	0.73	150
1.64	2.03	2.04	99	CONVERSION COST RATE	2.21	2.04	108

ILLUSTRATION 6.4   Departmental expenditure analysis for the Star-line for the five weeks ended 31 December 1972

old machinery where the screech of the old screw-cutting machines and the banging of the presses goes on all day. I've watched one of the press operators jump every time his press thumps down. I've seen a similar near-silent operation in Germany. The men on these machines in Stockport are nearly all deaf by the time they are forty. Of course the company supplies ear-covers but they won't wear them — they think it's too soft. 'Dad didn't wear them so I won't,' they say. Another show of the conservatism on the shop floor.

'But back on the Star-line we're in difficulties. I've got to get new machines. The major trouble is that the foreman of the Star-line, Ken Wightman, has turned sour. Straight after the change in payment system he disappeared off to manage his other cell in the tool room. He wouldn't discipline the men. He's not so good as we thought he was. The cell system may be only appropriate for stable situations. What suits one man at one time doesn't suit him at another. That seems to be the way Ken is. Even the peak output of 3750 has turned down without any change in facilities. Now we're sometimes below 3000 on our weekly records. That's no good.'

Question for discussion

Evaluate the group working system of the Star-line.

£4 on to their new basic rate meant that their pay packets had dropped. We pulled them back a bit with remedial payments extending over two to five years, but they say they want an incentive as the job is dull. Some of them threatened to leave; I doubt if they could find an equivalent job for the same money anywhere else.

'But the main cause of the trouble was the proposal for new machines. We just couldn't get the required output from the line as it stood and we had to put in a capital request for some new machines to add to the line. This is when the going got sticky.

'Because of the pressure on demand we had to rush through the proposal and perhaps we did not convert the men enough. But we were in a hurry for the output. First I proposed to add another press and a grinder with a couple of extra men simply to expand the capacity of the line. Ken Wightman and the Star-line men would have accepted that. But the company financial committee turned it down. Despite a promised 47 per cent return on capital, Head Office said they always worked to the rule that when you brought extra machines in you had to replace men — roughly: "get rid of a man for every £4000 invested." The board want us to push for extra-high technology on the Star-line, automatic feeding of blanks from magazines, transfer tables, automatic inspection, and perhaps some means of combining the processes. I've looked up some of the possible equipment. In the end we might go for some completely automatic machinery for all except the pressing stages for producing our Star dies, at the press of a few buttons. One possible machine we may get costs £22,000 and would save seven men on all operations other than the press. But I now have to make out another proposal to cut out some of the labour. And it will take another three months to get the decision.

'The proposals for capital equipment are put in under a fancy discounted cash flow procedure which I don't really believe in. It's too complex. It may be all right in theory for comparing completely different projects, but we're not in that situation. In most of the capital proposals we're putting in for essential replacement machinery which we cannot do without. D.F.C. is too complex for that. We should have a simple pay-back period scheme to act as a target on the investment in use. We would feel that better on the shop floor.

'I was surprised by the financial group's reaction to my first proposal. Perhaps it's because our chief executive of this works has just been made chairman of the financial Committee of the Midland Components Group and he has to appear to show a tough traditional line. It's amazing what they do spend money on. Midland Components have just set up a new works fifteen miles away in a copper plating operation. Everything's brand new and fully automated there. Yet we struggle to get a few replacement machines here. May be it's a tax dodge. In another of our works in Stockport we have really

SEQUENCE OF OPERATIONS ON THE G.T. PRODUCTION STAR-LINE

Also showing reviewed piece-work values. Obelisks denote operators who have been trained to perform more than one operation when the need arises. Asterisks indicate which operators do other work as well as Star Dies. Types 3 and 4 dies take 50% longer to machine than the smaller varieties 1 and 2.

Op.	Type of machines	No. of operators	Description of operation	Time values per operation	Inspection
1	2 Presses	8†	Press form	4.5 mins 3 & 4 per die 3.0 mins 1 & 2	1st. off 1 in 20 and final 100% visual check
2	5 Lathes	5†	Turn to remove excess metal face ends, and chamfer	From 4.25 mins to 10 mins/die 60/90 mins set-up according to size and style	1st off and final 100% check
3	Centreless grinder	1†*	Centreless grind O/D. (2 passes in soft state)	From 4.5 mins to 14 mins per dozen	No inspection
4	Broaching m/c.	1†	Cut locking grove	From 4 mins to 18 mins per dozen according to size	No inspection
5	Marking m/c.	1	Mark symbol No's	Day-work (1hr. per batch of 100)	1st. off Check
6	Heat treat	2*	Harden, temper and vapour blast	Process operation	100% check
7	Centre grinder	1†*	Centreless grind O/D final pass	From 2.5 mins to 7.5 mins per dozen	1st. off and final random check
8	Face grinder	1†	Grind front face	5.75 mins. per dozen 60 mins set-up per batch	1st. off and final 100% check
9	Heat treat	1*	Tufftride	Process operation	100% visual only

Note: These are 'standard times' which are approximately twice the actual times.

ILLUSTRATION 6.1   The Star-line process sequence
Extract from N.E.B.S.S. course: Report by Ken Wightman (1969)

SUMMARY OF IMPROVEMENTS THROUGH THE CELL SYSTEM

Using the G.T. Production Line method has reduced the distances travelled by,
OPERATORS — from 1,088 yards to 236 yards — saving 852 yards per batch.
Material   — from 1,669 yards to 269 yards — saving 1,400 yards per batch.

Two operations in the original method, (Grind Back Face, and Grind Locking Flat)
have now been eliminated.

In the event of any threatening 'bottlenecks', 12 of the 21 operators have sufficient
experience to be able to undertake 2 or more different operations. The operators are all
on the same piece-work rates, consequently payment problems do not arise.

Fastener factories at Stalybridge and Stockport previously kept 10 weeks supply of
dies in stock and 10 weeks supply on order. Now the Engineering Division holds 8 weeks
stock, with a further 4 weeks supply being made on the production line. This enables
the Finished Tool Stores to meet all orders from stock, and for the Planning Department
to issue further orders to the Division for more realistic cycle times.

These factors, together with information received from the Work Study Department,
confirm an overall 25% reduction in piecework times, reduced Work-in-Progress by 72.8%,
from 27,500 Dies to an average of 7,500 Dies, and cycle times by 62.5%, from 16 weeks
delivery from issue to completion to 6 weeks maximum.

Production has increased 50%, — from 1200 dies to 1800 dies per week.

ILLUSTRATION 6.2   Results from adopting the Star-line
Extract from N.E.B.S.S. course: Report by Ken Wightman (1969)

7 Running Assembly Lines: Smiths Industries

1. The Company

Smiths Industries is a major manufacturer of instrumentation in the United Kingdom. Their instruments are closely related to transportation, going into motor vehicles, locomotives, aerospace and shipping. Although the company has created new divisions for diversification into clocks, watches and more recently into distribution in order to sell directly to the public, the main field for manufacture and marketing continues to be vehicle instrumentation.

The vehicle instrumentation division has factories at Cricklewood (London), South Wales and Watford. The Cricklewood site has a turnover of £12 million per annum and employs 800 direct and 800 indirect staff. The staff at Cricklewood provide an engineering, design and planning service for the other two sites.

The instruments produced at Cricklewood go mainly to the motor industry — to British Leyland and Ford. Smiths supply over 90 per cent of the British Leyland needs. This in turn constitutes approximately 60 per cent of the Smiths output; Ford take a further 20 per cent and the outstanding 20 per cent goes on specialist applications. Ford in fact buy through another company, Autolite, but Smiths supply the instruments to Autolite. Smiths also compete for business from Chrysler and Vauxhall. Their main competitors are Autolite and A.C. Delco in Great Britain, V.D.O. in Germany, Jaeger in France and Borletti in Italy.

The supplier—customer arrangements in the motor industry inevitably stay fairly stable as they form working relationships on the design phase of the products. British Leyland are charged for the tooling costs of setting up a line for a new set of instruments. Leyland will then continue to buy from Smiths provided they offer a reliable, high-quality product and respond successfully to changes in the demand pattern which the customer makes at short notice.

2. The Tachometer Shop

Instrument production is generally organised in assembly lines with machine shops and stores, and sub-assembly areas feeding the supplies into the final assembly location. Smith's factory at Cricklewood is the final assembly area for a wide variety of instruments and a typical instrument production area is the tachometer shop with a floor area of 8000 square feet and accommodating about 80 staff.

The tachometer shop assembles rev-counters of a variety of types for the main panel of instruments in motor-cars. Some of the rev-counters go direct to customers fitted into cases and are known as the 'case' type, some are produced to include in a customer's (Ford) instrument package and are termed 'non-case type'. A third group goes into a second stage of assembly within Cricklewood – the 'Panel' type – for a whole panel of instruments. The sales price for the various tachometers is around £12.00.

The tachometer shop is organised into five assembly lines together with a sub-assembly area. The lines are designated 551, 552, 553, 554, 555 and are known as 'Mini-tachometer final assembly'. Each of the assembly lines consists of a 'herring-bone' arrangement of work stations placed on either side of a moving conveyor. The conveyor length is approximately 40 feet with work stations located on either side at 5 ft. intervals down the line. The line is designed entirely by industrial engineering staff who prepare in advance for the variations in production by setting up arrangements for between 6 and 17 operators on the line, each arrangement specifying the parts needed and the fitting operations at each work station together with an expected output rate.

The function of each of these assembly lines is to fit together a collection of approximately 30 parts (many of which are sub-assemblies in their own right) into one final tachometer using hand tools supplied at the work station. All the parts are designated in assembly lists made out by the drawing office who in turn have received detailed instructions from design staff. There are many different variations of tachometer but the actual difference may be as small as the colour of paint on a particular part of the dial. Each variation is carefully documented by a specific code which is referred to as the assembly list number. Normally the first two numbers in the code refer to the sub-assembly level, the '41' codes being final sub-assembly items. The last two digits in the code refer to the issue number giving the latest versions of the product or component. Illustration 7.1 shows the list of parts for the final assembly of the Ford Capri tachometer RVC 6417/00F and the two lists for the movement assembly and the thick film assembly.

All of the parts for the assembly are obtained from stores. They are supplied to stores from three sources: Cricklewood production facilities, other

Smiths factories such as South Wales, or brought in from external sources. It is the job of production planning and control staff to ensure that all the 'set' parts particular to the product are available for the lines when required in the assembly programme, although many of the common items such as screws are 'bulk issue items' which the line chargehand will requisition from stores in lots covering two weeks' supply. Normally the customer forward schedule extends for six months ahead, the first three months being a firm programme and the next three months being tentative.

Each individual line is identified in the budgeting process and is given a planned output. The actual running of the line is accounted for by a detailed reporting system which records the achievement on the assembly lines. Many variations can occur due to absenteeism, shortages, customer schedule changes, etc. The total responsibility for the lines extends through a long chain of command from the production director to the chargehand on the line. The production controller, Neil Kenney, the manufacturing manager, and the industrial engineering manager report through Cricklewood works manager to the production director. The chargehands in the tachometer shop report through the shop senior foreman Ron Shail to the assistant assembly superintendent. He in turn reports through the assembly superintendent Bob Fairman to the manufacturing manager.

3. Designing the Assembly Line

When a new product range has been established and Smiths are entering the market in substantial volumes, the industrial engineering department is responsible for estimating the costs, establishing the tooling required and specifying the organisation of the line. The first task of assessing the cost of production in terms of labour, materials, etc., as well as estimating the total investment in setting up the line, is especially tricky as it must be done before any products have been produced or even before the product specification has been finalised. The estimating problem is tackled through the resident skill accumulated in the engineers at Smiths and also by the methods which they can use to break the estimate down into standard 'blocks' on which costs are more precisely known. Getting the estimate right is a critical step as the quoted prices and operating margin will be based upon them. The setting up of a tachometer line could cost as much as £50,000, three-quarters of which would go in capital costs of tooling, etc., and the rest in wages for a project engineer over twelve months, a production engineer, a tool designer and half a year's work from a work study expert.

The vast majority of the work of the industrial engineering team, however, consists of developments of existing lines for adaptations and refinements of existing products. Their job is to search constantly for ways of reducing costs through improved methods, improved tooling and generally through tidying up the processing arrangements. In Smiths Industries the industrial engineering department also carries the responsibility for collecting and publishing the statistics of physical performance on the line so that they are kept directly in touch with areas of concern.

Once the broad stages of the assembly have been determined, an industrial engineer will prepare details of the individual assembly operations. For the tachometer these involve a series of fitting, calibration and inspection operations as shown in Illustration 7.2. These details will be laid out on process sheets consisting of a set of papers describing the steps of each major stage. This proposed construction of the product is used for technical purposes of tool design, quality control and for initial discussion with supervision.

When details of the physical operations have been agreed between industrial engineering and supervision staff, the line is set up with the appropriate tooling and its initial operation is begun. Once the major 'bugs' have been sorted out, industrial engineering conduct a work study exercise on the individual operations to establish precise times, output levels, balances of work content along the line and the bonus ratings. For the work study task the whole assembly operation is broken down into elementary operations which can be timed. The tachometer assembly is analysed into about 40 such elementary operations (normally a number of elements on each of the operations shown in Illustration 7.2) and each element is timed by means of a stop-watch study. The time studies in standard minutes per hundred for attaching the thick film to the tape and mounting it on the bridge plate are shown in Illustration 7.3. It gives the standard time as 17.00 minutes per 100 for the first operation. The illustration shows the series of 14 detailed observations of the operation 'Pick up thick film', giving in successive columns the actual time in minutes, the rating for the operator doing the operation, and the allowed time in 'standard minutes' (which is approximately double the actual time).

The total set of standard times for all the operations is now used to allocate groups of work elements along a proposed line for a given number of operators. Various 'lines' are designed for different numbers of operators on the line. The arrangement for sixteen operators on the tachometer line is shown in Illustration 7.4. The intention is to try to arrange the groups so that each operator (or small group of operators) has the same total 'work content' by adding up all the standard times in the groups.

The line will then be 'balanced'. But the grouping pattern is restricted by the need to sequence the elements of the assembly in the correct technical order and to consider the tool availability at the various work stations.

Inevitably some imbalance on the line results. In Illustration 7.4 on the sixteen-operator system, the second last work station will be the bottleneck as there is a total of 1.354 standard minutes of work there, which is longer than the total at any other work station. All the other operators have a 'personal allowance' as indicated in the final column. On a line with six operators the bottleneck operation requires 3.735 standard minutes. These assembly line layouts provide the shop supervision with a detailed plan for organising the line with different combinations of operators present. It also gives an expected output rate and feed rate for operating the line at the base of the sheet. For example, on a six-operator line four instruments will be produced every 380 seconds with total standard minutes of 22.56, whereas a sixteen-operator line will produce four instruments every 145 seconds requiring a total of 22.07 standard minutes.

The design and amendments of these line layouts are the major responsibility of the industrial engineering department. The skill of the design requires a variety of factors to be taken into account. Firstly the instrument design must be so organised that the manufacturing operations can be properly managed by line supervision using low-skill operatives. Secondly, and partly because of the low skill, complex technical requirements have to be broken down into elementary 'foolproof' tasks. On the tachometer line, for example, the calibration of the instrument invokes some fine mechanical balancing principles to handle the variation in the distribution of mass in the assembled instrument. The industrial engineers have found that correct calibration can be achieved by using simple instruments to give a three-way classification of the tachometer which leads the operator to pick out a screw-on balancing weight of the appropriate kind selected by a corresponding three-way colour code.

Thirdly, the design must consider customer aspects even when they seem to incur unnecessary expense. Often the design engineers have to arrange the face of the instrument to suit the changing customer requirements of appearance although this may conflict with cost-reducing objectives. For example the bridge plate of the tachometer could be screwed on through the dial, thus saving one operation, but two screws would then show on the face of the dial which it is presumed would appear unattractive to the final customer. The industrial engineer thus forms a key interface between product, process and job design requirements; and he must minimise costs as a balance of these different interests.

4. Production Planning and Supplies

The planning process starts with the annual budget prepared for the period 1 August to 31 July of the following year over a 52-week period. The budget is prepared on the basis of the forecast of demand for products which, in the case of Smiths, depends on the predicted demands for the various car models. The Motor Industry prepare a detailed trend at the end of each year which Smiths find valuable in their own forecasts. From the forecasts the average monthly demands for individual lines are prepared, the required labour levels are estimated and the total budgeted costs are computed to provide a cost centre-based budget.

The budget is however only a guide to what actually happens. Sales department receive orders from customers for the products on an on-going basis for a monthly schedule of deliveries, but this will be firm for at most three months ahead. Ford place their demands for only two months ahead. The actual required time for the total cycle from ordering to despatch for tachometers is about 20 weeks so that the production controller has to rely on flexing the pipeline of supplies to the changing requirements. This is facilitated by the presence of many 'common parts' for the final instruments which can be switched to different end needs, and the fact that each assembly line can manufacture many of the products within a product group.

Incoming customer orders are received by sales liaison staff who are product- and customer-based and work in the production control offices. As customer orders are received they are entered up on the master ledgers for final products. Each ledger page holds 13 weeks of order intake data and corresponding records of despatches in each week. The demand for any particular week is amended as the customer changes his mind. For example in week 40 of 1975 the original requirement was for 1060. It then became 969 and finally was set at 1710 causing corresponding changes in the assessment of the current arrears position which changed from −276 to +474 on that product. In fact in week 40 a total of 2617 were despatched. In week 50 a total of 1376 were despatched whereas 281 were finally requested and the arrears stood at 814. The changes occur randomly and the actual demand over time varies substantially. In fact the demand was zero for tachometers of this type for the first 11 weeks of the next budgeting year.

The production control staff who manage the ledgers 'interpret' the demand picture into what they believe will be the final requirement, and manually create an 'input sheet' once a month for final products over the next six months. This is used to create a punched card representation of demand for the monthly computer run. The purpose of this computer run is to decide

output rates for final instruments
stock status and orders to be placed for final instruments
stock status and orders to be placed for bought out parts
stock status and orders to be placed for made in parts.

These calculations use a vital product structure file which is resident in the computer and specifies the relationships between products and components (many components are shared between the same end products) together with the lead times for ordering and the economic quantities to order on components for final product demands.

The monthly computer run prepares several key documents for planning and control purposes:

(1) Average monthly requirements for all 270 final instrument groups for six months ahead. This is discussed between production control and assembly departments to agree smoothed output targets. The target levels in the Autumn of 1975 for the mini-tachometer group was set at 7000 per week. These output targets form the basic output rates against which assembly supervision will be judged.

(2) A 'cover' sheet for final instruments giving total stock followed by gross requirements on the basis of orders on hand. This is given by week for the next four weeks and by month for the next five months. By subtracting current stock from the successive gross requirements the net requirements can be computed and this is used by production control to monitor incoming physical final stock into stores.

(3) A 'cover' sheet for bought-out parts which go into the final product. These are computed as monthly net requirements in the same way to meet final product demand. The requirements are timed to allow for the lead time of placing orders on suppliers and standard batch sizes are chosen.

(4) A 'cover' sheet for internally made parts calculated in the same way as for bought-out parts. The batch entries on this form show orders for which paperwork has been prepared, orders in progress and the quantity in stock which enables the netted-off requirements by period to be presented on the report.

(5) A complete 'centre' stock list giving the total stock picture for all 6000 items.

(6) A complete list of new manufacturing orders to go to the section for printing up the order documentation.

(7) A list of revisions to order documentation for those orders for which documentation has been prepared last month but which have not yet been released.

The total elapsed time between placement of manufacturing orders and the receipt of goods into stock is about 12 weeks, split down into:

1 week – list from computer to order documentation section;
4 weeks – preparation of documentation;
4 weeks – queueing before release of documentation;
1 to 4 weeks on shop floor running at two operations per week.

The long time an order spends in documentation queueing means that the revision list can be prepared each month to make further changes in plan.

The 'net' effect of these computations means that new orders are placed on suppliers in the form shown in Illustration 7.5, giving quantities and dates. Also orders are prepared for placing on manufacturing parts in the machine shops and for the final assembly lines. All completed work is returned to centre stock.

When the paperwork has been released and the products are produced, production control record the completion of the work on the batches by making manual entries on the cover sheets, and in due course they go into stock and are entered on the stock records in the computer. Theoretically the machined parts, the outside supplies and the assembly batches should enter central stock on the due dates stated on the job tickets. But owing to the long lead times and the disturbances which occur to the plan, production control staff need information on the progress of batches inside the monthly recalculation periods. In the machine shop progress is tracked by a computer-linked data collection system which requires a booking clerk to fill in details of a batch each time it passes from one work station to the next. This enables the computer system to print out a 'Daily Batch Status Report' which shows production control where the components are, grouped by product type. It also prints out a 'Daily Job List' by resource group which gives a list to the foremen and superintendents in location of the preferred sequence of jobs to work on in their particular location. Many jobs on this list are late or urgent and it is difficult to get the priorities implemented. The situation is better on the assembly lines where the progressman responsible for the area manually writes out a list of jobs which could be done (i.e. for which orders have been issued) with a preferred sequence for the week 'subject to change' (see Illustration 7.6 for the list for the tachometer shop for week 6 of 1974). Generally the 40 progressmen spend most of their time responding to pressures and trying to keep the system running smoothly.

Neil Kenney, the production controller, is clear about some ways in which the planning and control system might be improved. 'Firstly', he says, 'progress and customer liaison staff should be of a standard and status appropriate to those with such an overall responsibility. Secondly, means must be devised whereby machine shop supervision is more aware of customer's priorities. Their most relevant information, the daily job list, has fallen into disuse, leaving a very insensitive priority planning system.

'Thirdly, there must be some method for tightening up the paperwork discipline. The stock figures are not well maintained and figures printed out are not always right. Two men continually check stock quantities against stock computer records but they never have time to search out the cause of the errors they find. Often the forms are simply not filled in correctly. We have a purge on paperwork every so often but then people get lazy about it and the same mistakes occur.

'The computer system is necessary for the sheer slog of doing the parts explosion into net requirements and preparing the monthly reports. But we're not sure if the daily job list is workable. The computer can prepare reports quickly but it relies on a basically stable set of data and this does not hold true. We are at the whim of a very volatile motor-car industry and the production control system is at the centre of the market variation, the production system inertia and the supplies variability, and this really calls for a great deal of flexibility and accuracy. The responsibilities in the production control job certainly seem to stop nowhere.'

5. Running the Tachometer Line

The running of the assembly line itself appears to be a very smooth operation. Under the foreman of the tachometer shop, Ron Shail, each line has a charge-hand to ensure that materials are available, that quality is being maintained, and that labour performance is up to scratch. For any given team of girls the normal pattern is to set the pace of production with an efficient girl at the front of the line who will feed the conveyor with a tray of four tachometers (partly built) every time the light goes on at the head of the line. The frequency for the light depends on the number of girls present and is based on the pacing agreed with industrial engineering for the line layouts. There is usually one extra girl associated with each line to take over for breaks.

The principal task for line supervision is to ensure that planned output levels are met at the required quality levels. The main problem in achieving this is the random absenteeism (running at around 10 per cent) and the high turnover of labour per annum (currently at around 25 per cent). This means that the line has to be constantly re-balanced in terms of the set of employees who happen to be there on the day. It also creates continuous training problems. The operators are mainly female and are classified into three grades, A, B and C, and are paid 80.9p per hour for grade A with a 1p drop for grade B and 2p drop for grade C. In the tachometer shop three lines are run full-time and two others part-time. Bonus amounts to 12 per cent of take-home pay and a full-time operative will obtain about £36 a week.

The materials rarely constitute a problem to the continuity of the line. The 'set issue' items for particular product types are generally made available by production control and the common 'bulk issue' items which the foreman requisitions from stores depend on the foremen having a good relation with the stores position. As further cover Ron Shail usually holds a fortnight's worth of the bulk issue items and keeps a spare drawer of dials (set issue items) in case of difficulties. On the question of quality, if problems occur, Ron Shail will first assume that the equipment is at fault, next he assumes the materials, and only thirdly does he blame the operator. The main problem on quality is getting good results from the first and the last batch of the day's production.

The formal recording of the performance on the line is undertaken in two ways: direct reporting from the line and an overall retrospective assessment by industrial engineering. On the line itself the line chargehand keeps a daily record of attendance for each operative against their clock number giving all absences from the line. He also keeps a Line Booking Sheet (Illustration 7.7) of all events over a period of a week on the line. The line booking sheet records the particular line 'set-up' used during each day of the week caused by any change in circumstances on the line during the day. Any paid 'lost time' is recorded with a code of reasons. For example, in Illustration 7.7 giving the activity in week six on line 553 N72 means a stoppage caused by a product design problem; D12 means no operator available. Halfway through the week the assembly superintendent totals up the estimated deliveries to be made in the week for comparison with the agreed targets with stated reasons. The estimates are within 10 per cent of target in total volume but vary much more by line. The actual achievement on the line is then confirmed in a final weekly statement and entered manually by the assembly superintendent on the 'Anticipated Shippings' statement sent to the works manager. These results are very close to the estimates made mid-week.

Industrial engineering prepare detailed statements of efficiency on the line in terms of labour, lost hours, scrap rates and quality performance. Firstly an Excess Hours Analysis (Illustration 7.8) is prepared, to account for labour hours and the cause of the lost time. Lost time is called 'excess hours' and the total is accounted for against a coded excess group analysis. This is further traced to its source in terms of the control responsibilities shown in Illustration 7.8. The Excess Hours statement is prepared weekly through the shop booking clerk on the basis of the returns from the shop supervision. They also prepare a statement of the scrap incurred on the lines on a weekly basis, giving the implications in material and labour value. This may be about £100 on the tachometer lines.

Finally a quality statement is prepared in two ways: quality performance on the line and quality as detected at a subsequent audit. Each line normally has a quality viewing station providing 100 per cent testing of all finished products and this provides a quality record for the line. The quality results

on different tachometer lines vary between 7 per cent and 10 per cent. Also
a random audit of 10 per cent of finished products is carried out as an
independent quality check which is recorded separately. Faults detected at
audit are classified into three groups:

A — will cause a customer complaint
B — may cause a customer complaint
C — unlikely to cause a customer complaint.

If any 'A' faults occur in the audit a complete recheck is made of the
immediate batch. A and B class faults are usually both below 2 per cent.

Bob Fairman, the assembly superintendent, considered that the tachometer
shop had a particularly successful set of assembly lines. The lines were well
designed from many physical dimensions. A line containing 15 to 20 people
was about the correct size in his opinion: 'If they get too small there are
endless training problems and if they go too big the quality control can
become difficult.' Smiths have tried getting an operator to make the whole
instrument with various carrousel arrangements, but generally the volume of
production and the requirements of a conveyor for materials handling restrict
layout and work task arrangement.

In Bob Fairman's view the main factor in a successful line is getting the
right foreman with the appropriate social sense. 'The foreman has to be firm,
fair and friendly all at the same time: he is treading a tightrope. We've got the
right supervision in the tachometer shop and it works well. They only have
problems from 7.30 to 8.00 in the morning. They are fortunate in their
product and their location. The tachometer is a good instrument to make and
they have a clearly defined small shop. We're not so lucky in the other
assembly shop which spreads over a much larger area with no clear single line
of management command and large numbers of operations. Complexity and
confusion can break any foreman, however willing he is, and it immediately
creates a "them and us" situation. For success with people it must be clear
what their area is and who they're responsible to without any possible
interference.'

———————————————

Question for discussion

Evaluate the performance of Smiths' Tachometer shop.

⊟	FORD MOTOR CO. 72 CAPRI (4-cyl) 1972	compiled E.D.	Checked CA	Approved Smith	Sheet 1/1	Code RVC 6417/00F

Site MA1	Description FINAL ASSEMBLY

Panel mounted Impulse Tachometer contact breaker. Integrated circuit.
Thick film. 12-volt. 4-cylinder. Neg. earth. Floodlit illumination.
Black dial. White print. Rocket red pointer. Clockwise.
Frequency 173.61 Hz.

Parts List	No. OFF or Qty/1000	CODE (EXISTING)	CODE (NEW)	
Case assembly	1	31-713-139-00		(6)
Movement complete	1		41-16 0-849-15	(4)
Screw slotted ch. hd. M3 x 5 mm. long br. mf.	1 (5)	20-232-5096-01		(5)
Dial printed	1	31-648-702-00		
Pointer assembly	1	41-164-143-00		
Screw	2	31-337-551-01	31-871-185-15	
Label	1			
Label	1	31-871-186-03		
Label	1	31-871-528-00		

ILLUSTRATION 7.1   Parts list for a tachometer

ILLUSTRATION 7.2   Drawing of tachometer components

WORK STUDY SHEET	Study No:

Department ....552..................... Ref.No. RV1 108 A

Operation ..Affix T/film to Tape and Cut = 17.00 SMS/100...
    "   "   " Mounting Plate.= 27.00 SMS/100 Date ..12: 3: 73....

Machine .... Time Started ....

Observer .... Time Finished ....

Job Specification (Elements):- RV1 109B				P/u Mounting Plate		·13	120	260
				Locate over 2 pairs		·11	120	·220
						·11	·20	·220
	·06	120	·120	of AT 18059		·20	10	·230
I/u Thick film apply	·06	120	·120			·13	120	·230
	·06	120	·120					
to tape and cut off	·06	120	·120	P/u thick film Peel off		13	120	·260
	·07	120	·140			·14	120	·260
	·08	120	160	Backing and apply		14	120	·240
	·06	120	120			·12	·22	·240
	·07	120	140	to Mounting Plate 1 wrg		·12	120	·240
	07	120	140			14	120	·240
·149	·03	120	160			·13	120	·258
	·09	120	120			14	120	·240
·528 2½	·12	120	·180					·258
·165 + y²	·09	120	·140	·2435				
				·2495 2½				
issue 17·00 SMS	·07	120		·2695 8				3658
				issue 27·00 SMS/				
			2·086					

ILLUSTRATION 7.3 Work study records for fixing thick film to tape and mounting plate

ASSEMBLY LINE LAYOUT FOR   PER   HR.WEEK

DEPARTMENT 553
CODE   RVC   6417/00F

DESCRIPTION   Panel Hatch Tacho c.BC.   T/F   12V   6C42
         CAPRI

Spec. No.	Operation	S/MS Inst.	No. of Op'rs	S/MS Oper'r	P.A.
142	View Pointer and Broach	·261			
108 B	Assembly compensator plated with moulded base to movement	1·080	1	1·341	·013
109	Fix anchor plate tags and solder wires	·700			
108 B	Affix tape to thick film. Peel off backing paper and affix to bridge	·440	1	1·140	·214
112 B	View movement for damage. Assemble bridge.				
112 A	View pointer. assemble and zero.	·901	1	·901	·453
112 B	View dial for damage. Assemble to movement. check tightness. View pointer Assemble zero. Touch up as necessary.	·769 ·228 ·303	1	1·300	·054
109	View movement for damage. Solder 4 leads to T.F.	1·130	1	1·280	·074
117	Torque test pointer.	·150			
125A	Balance weight selection and assembly	1·284	1	1·284	·070
X3A	View line soldering.	·100	3	3·680	·127
111	Check movement for damage + cleanliness	3·680		1·227 1·226 1·226	·128 ·128
113	Check movement / calibrate	2·560	2	1·280 1·280	·074 ·074
110	Check base + movement. Screw tightness. Affix Fords Label.	1·257	1	1·257	·097
117	Invert pointer. Check freedom. Test, check Calibration.	1·354	1	1·354	*
110	Affix Smiths Label.	133			
116	Pack. Seal and Label.	1·030	1	1·163	·191
	Reject and Relief		2		
			16	17·260	1·697

	S.M. VALUE			PRODUCTION DATA	
B	LINE S.M.S. PER INSTRUMENT	17·260	A	NUMBER OF OPERATORS	16
C	REJECT & RELIEF OPERATOR/S	2·708			
D	PROCESS ALLOWANCE (D x 100)=% (B)	1·697		PRODUCTION Rating x A = Hours) H @33⅓%	
E	CHANGE TRAYS (·025 x 16 OPERS)	·400		RECOMMENDED FEED PER HOUR (97 x A) H.F)	A = 102 B = 104
F	CHANGE SETS (x OPERS)				
G	CONTINGENCY FOR			FEED FREQUENCY A = 142 4 INSTRUMENTS PER SECS. B = 149	
	TOTAL S/MS EACH	22·065			
	ISSUED S/MS EACH 100	2207		WORK STUDY ENGINEER .... DATE ... 18·2·74	

ILLUSTRATION 7.4   Specification of assembly line for 16 operators

SMITHS INDUSTRIES LIMITED

VEHICLE INSTRUMENTATION DIVISION

DELIVERY SCHEDULE

FOR SI PRODUCTION PERIODS 03 TO 08

1. This schedule is your authority to manufacture the FIRM Requirements shown below and, where essential, to order material for the Estimated and Tentative Forecasts.
2. Arrears listed are overdue and MUST be delivered within two weeks of the date of issue of this schedule as shown below. After this date they may be cancelled at our option without liability.
3. The SI Purchase Order Number and Material Code shown must appear on the outside of each package delivered to us.
4. This schedule supersedes all previous schedules FROM THE FACTORY LISTED UNDER DELIVER TO BELOW ONLY.

ORDER No. B32502	DATED		
	ADVICE NOTE No.	QTY. ACCEPTED	
LAST	63831	1890	
RECORDED	63882	25	
DELIVERIES	63883	685	

THORAN IND. LTD.
SHAFTESBURY ROAD
EDMONTON
LONDON   N18 1SS

SI PART No.	31-648-782-01		
DESCRIPTION	PRINTED DIAL		
SCHEDULE REFERENCE No. 03		DATE PRINTED 24/09/75	
SUPPLIER A/C No. 329282		RESP. CODE EA73	CLASS B

REQUIREMENTS

	F I R M				ESTIMATED		T E N T A T I V E		
	DELIVERY	WEEK COMMENCING			DELIVERY	WEEK	PERIOD	COMMENCING	
	29/09/75	06/10/75	13/10/75	20/10/75	27/10/75	24/11/75	22/12/75	19/01/76	16/02/76
ARREARS									
-214-	-0-	-0-	900	900	2400 1424	1400	1680	1600	1600
					6-29- 29				

INVOICE TO:
SMITHS INDUSTRIES LIMITED
VEHICLE INSTRUMENTATION DIVISION
CRICKLEWOOD WORKS, LONDON NW2 6NN

DELIVER TO:
SMITHS INDUSTRIES LIMITED
MAI FACTORY
CRICKLEWOOD, LONDON NW2

CONTACT AT SI:
TELEX: 922981
NAME: MR. G. BIGLAND
TEL: 01-452-3333 EXT: 2239

This schedule is subject to the terms and conditions shown on the reverse. See Purchase Order.

DELIVERIES

DATE	ADVICE/DEBIT NOTE No.	ORD REF	G.R.N. No.	QUANTITY DELIVERED	QUANTITY RETURNED	QUANTITY OUTSTANDING	ADVICE/DEBIT NOTE No	ORD REF	G.R.N. No.	QUANTITY DELIVERED	QUANTITY RETURNED	QUANTITY OUTSTANDING
29.9.75	64332		43751	1385								
15.10.75	64356		45075	600								
.. ..	64359		45086	1005								
	RVC 6614.00F											

ILLUSTRATION 7.5   Supplies order form

Mini Tacho Programme — Week 6 — Subject to Change

Final Code	Seq	Qty	Storages	Assy	Final Code	Seq	Qty	Storages	Assy	Final Code	Seq	Qty	Storages	Assy
RVC 6414-00^F	804	540 BAL		553	RVC 6414-00^F	805	1250 BAL		552	RVC 6414-00^F	807	1050 BAL		554
" " "	806	2000		"	IM 1810-01	"	500		"	" 2612-00^F	805	700		"
" 6613-00^F	"	400		"	RVC 6419-00^F	804	654 BAL		"	" 1410-00^AF	804	157 BAL		"
" 1002-00^F	"	150 50 BAL		"	" 6010-00^F	806	350		"	" " "	806	900		"
" 1003-00^F	804	152 BAL		"	IM 1809-00	"	200		"	" 2414-00^AF	"	500 + 85 BAL		"
" 6417-00^F	805	1,113 BAL		"	RVC 6417-00^F	"	596 BAL		"	IM 1807-01	804	1000 170 BAL		"
										RVC 2010-01	806	500		"
										" 2612-01^F	"	200		"
										" 1410-00^AF	807	1000		"
FVP 5104	803	12 BAL		558										
" "	806	100		"										

Week 6

ILLUSTRATION 7.6   Orders on the tachometer shop for week 6

CODE NO.	S.Min. Value	Seq.	Qty.	Day	Running Time On	Off	Operators Set Up	In Use	Excess Ops. Qty	Excess	Feed in Seconds Rec.	Act.	Paid Lost Time On	Off	Ops	Reasons	Unpaid Lost Time Mins.	Reasons
RVC 6414.00F	23.61	Excess N72 276	40 Rework 276	FRI.	7.30	12.45	13	13+1		N72	185	180	9.00	9.10	14	N72		
RVC 6414.00F	23.61	Excess 12 Rework 216	216	FRI	12.45	4.15	13	12+1		N72	165	180	3.00	3.10	13	N72		
RVC 6414.00F	23.61		16	MON	7.30	7.45	13	13+1		N72	-	-	4.05	4.15	13	D 40 CLEAN DOWN		
RVC 6444.00F	23.61		496	MON	7.45	4.15	13	12+1		N72	185	180	9.00	9.10	13	N72		
											180	160	10.30	10.45	13	D01 PAUSE HEAD		
											185	180	11.00	11.10	13	N72		
RVC 6414.00F	23.61	16	16	TUES	7.30	7.45	13	12			185	180	3.00	3.10	13	N72		
RVC 6414.00F	23.61	15-2	152	TUES	7.45	10.10	13	13					8.00	8.15	12	D01 LOCTITE MACHINE		
RVC 6010.00F	21.79	254	254	TUES	10.30	3.05	12	12+1		DM51	184	180	10.10	10.40	13	99999		
RVC 6413.00F	23.61	68	68	TUES	3.20	4.15	13	13			165	160	3.05	3.20	13	99999		
RVC 6413.00F	23.61	356	356	WED	7.30	12.45	13	13			185	180						
RVC 6413.00F	23.61	24	24	WED	12.45	1.05	13	12			185	180	1.05	1.15	12	99999		
RVC 6444.00F	23.61	216	216	WED	1.15	4.15	13	12			165	180	2.35	2.50	12	R06 CAL HEAD		
											180		3.00	3.10	12	D12		
RVC 6414.00F	23.61	16	16	THUR	7.30	7.45	13	11			186	180	3.00	3.10	11	D12		
RVC 6414.00F	23.61	548	548	THUR	7.45	4.15	13	12			185	180	9.00	9.10	12	D12		
													11.00	11.10	12	D12		
													3.00	3.10	12	D12		

ILLUSTRATION 7.7 Output records on line 553 for week 6

S 1 HOURLY PAYROLL — DIRECT LABOUR ANALYSIS

PAYROLL CODE 61   PROD.WK. 06   16/05/75   PAGE 47

COST CENTRE	SHIFT	CUMLTV STANDARD	WEEKLY % STANDARD	AVERAGE % EXCESS	STANDARD HOURS MEAS'D	UNMEAS'D	J.C's	TOTAL	EX/STD %	TOTAL EXCESS	NON PRODUCTIVE	TOTAL EARNED	ACTUAL HOURS	E/A %
552	1	0	0.0	0	0	0	0	0	0.0	0	0	0	29	0
553	1	878	20.6	.181	1068	0	19	1062	9.0	95	0	1157	513	226
534	1	1237	12.0	148	1214	0	0	1214	8.2	100	0	1314	636	206
557	1	585	12.5	73	604	32	0	636	10.8	69	0	705	340	207
558	1	408	14.5	66	445	77	27	549	16.5	90	30	669	465	144
TOTAL		3168	14.8	469	3510	109	41	3460	10.2	356	30	3845	1983	194

EXCESS GROUP ANALYSIS

COST CENTRE	SHIFT	0	1	2	3	4	5	6	7	8	9	OVERTIME
553	1	14	0	0	3	9	0	69	0	0		0
554	1	12	23	60	4	0	0	0	0	0		0
557	1	5	0	24	0	14	0	0	0	25		0
558	1	0	0	32	0	1	17	4	28	8		0
TOTAL		32	23	117	0	8	39	4	97	34		0

CONTROL RESPONSIBILITY OF EXCESSES

COST CENTRE	SHIFT	A	B	C	D	E	F	H	J	K	L	M	N	P	Q	R	S	T
553	1	0	0	0	13	0	0	0	0	5	0	69	0	0	0	0	0	0
554	1	0	0	0	34	0	0	13	0	12	41	0	0	0	0	0	0	0
557	1	0	0	16	25	0	0	0	0	2	24	0	0	28	0	0	0	0
558	1	0	0	0	26	8	0	4	0	24	0	0	0	0	0	0	0	0
TOTAL		0	0	90	34	0	0	17	0	19	89	97	0	28	0	0	0	0

Excess group
0 Waiting (Various)
1 Waiting Work
2 Rectification
3 Miscellaneous
4 Training
6 Temporary Allowance
7 Modification
8 Unmeasured
9 Changeover

Control Responsibility
D Assembly
E Process Study
F Tool Manufacture
H Production Control
K Electrical Dev
L Quality Control
M Training Dept.
N Application Eng

ILLUSTRATION 7.8   Labour time analysis in tachometer shop for week 6

8 Building Complex Products: Speedcraft Transport Ltd

1. Development of the Company

Speedcraft Transport is a small company of less than 150 personnel engaged in the manufacture and development of fast sea-based transport exploiting the hovercraft principle. The original idea of hovercraft — floating a vehicle on a cushion of air just above the land or water surface — was formulated by Christopher Cockerell in the early 1960s.

Usually the cushion of air is contained in an inflated skirt running right round the craft. However, one of Cockerell's assistants, Bill Wilkinson, developed the idea of a rigid skirt in which the sides of the boat could be made deeper to form rigid edges containing a cushion of air. This would offer increased control of the craft, cheaper construction, but limit it entirely to marine use.

Wilkinson with a number of colleagues formed a separate company, Speedcraft Ltd in 1967 to design and sell this craft. Their manufacturing was based on two sub-contract companies for the hull and the outfitting. But despite the zeal of the small group of designers the company was not a commercial success and went into liquidation. It was bought up in January 1969 by an American company, Specialist Transport Inc. and became Speedcraft Transport Ltd. Starting with some 20 people, the aim of the new company was to build up its own manufacturing facility and a suitable site was purchased at the waterfront at Portsmouth. Despite a continuously changing and nervous sales position, the company has matured to a strength of over 100 personnel in 1975, undertaking its own complete manufacturing and fitting operations with the exception of some specialist subcontract operations such as the machining of propeller shafts.

The managing director of the company is Ted Rowlants. He took over in 1974 from Al Larner, who came from the American company and remains as chairman. Rowlants is supported by a full management team covering material control, accounting, marketing, inspection, manufacturing, design and customer service. Ted Rowlants operates an 'open-door' policy for all staff. He meets all the management at a regular monthly managers' meeting in a nearby hotel, and sees the direct labour representatives monthly, always encouraging immediate communication of problems.

Under the guidance of David Hall, the manufacturing director, and Ian Tyler as works manager (later in charge of material control and reporting), the works have moved towards a more professional style in their manufacturing operations. They have built up a team of skilled labour grouped by trades — each trade reporting to a supervisor. The numbers in each skill are indicated in Illustration 8.1 which is the personnel report from the November management meeting. Labour is paid a flat rate without any significant bonus system — the pay rates competing favourably with the many other companies in the local boatbuilding activities. The company has no union on the site. Although some efforts have been made to organise a union it has not proved attractive enough to the employees.

Normally the target level of activity is to complete a craft every six or seven weeks, but it is very difficult to balance the production and sales rates. In 1974 the company were building craft for stock and ended up with a significant surplus which led on to redundancies. For 1975 they made craft only to order. The building of a Mk.2 boat consumes about twelve and a half thousand man hours and it sells for around £200,000, raising about £50,000 profit on the sale. Each sale is highly significant, being equal in value to the whole capital base of the company.

Much of the company's effort goes into development activities. The standard craft in 1975 is the SC Mk. 3, which is a 65-seat version of the original 50-seat Mk. 2 customised to some extent with fittings for each sale. A 'stretched' version of this craft is also being called the SC Mk. 4 which will accommodate 92 passengers. The first of these stretched craft was due for launch in April 1976. This was being financed from Speedcraft's own resources. Finally a 200-seat prototype is being built, called the SC Mk. 5, occupying a third of the total hangar space, due for launch in 1977. The finance for the design of this craft was being supplied on a contract from the National Research and Development Corporation. The N.R.D.C. will also cover half the costs of building the first craft. Some of this finance is repayable as a loan and the remainder will be repaid as royalties on the craft sold later. This new craft should be able to operate at one-third of the cost of the SC Mk. 3 — the stretched version should operate at half the cost — and the large craft will be able to operate in much rougher sea conditions.

Other research and design activities include fan and skirt developments for improved control, cavitation studies on the propeller and rudder, and investigations into glass reinforced plastics for hull construction. The works activities are closely linked to the design function and supervisors are encouraged to communicate any problems back to design staff. This strong development activity indicates the general optimism about the future of the company's new products. As David Hall, the manufacturing director, put it: 'We are confident of the future ahead provided our existing products can get us there; we have to survive on Mk. 3 to reach the commercial potential of Mk. 4.'

2. Selling the Product

The selling of the hovercraft is a very unpredictable business. Each sale has to go through many stages of approval before the final contract is signed and the craft is delivered. The sale can fail at any stage. Each sale is a new situation: no sales have been made to previous owners of this type of marine craft. There is therefore no known market. The hovercraft is not really in competition with any other equivalent product. The S.R.N.6 full-skirt hovercraft made by the British Hovercraft Corporation is mainly designed for military purposes and costs double the Speedcraft boat. The nearest rival is the hydrofoil boat which travels at the same speed and rides on a ski-foil in the water; these are made in Italy and now also in Russia.

The marketing staff of three key travelling salesmen and the Managing Director have to search out likely possible situations for a sale. Sites such as Rio, Hong Kong and Sydney are chosen where a lot of people move over water in concentrated numbers either for commuter or tourist purposes. The salesmen cover most areas of the world except North America, where a similar manufacturing operation of the parent company has been set up. Generally an approach is made to existing ferry operators using conventional craft and the challenge is to prove that the faster boat makes good economic sense. The success of the sale depends not only on convincing the ferry operator but also on convincing the relevant Government departments on safety and environmental factors, and establishing the appropriate insurance cover.

Ted Rowlants' aim at the end of 1975 was simply 'to sell as many craft as possible and preferably to sell in multiples as it saves so much of the agonising selling effort.' Every sale is only a prospect until the craft is actually despatched. The time taken to clinch a sale is between six months and a year and the sale can apparently progress rapidly or recede as the problems crop up. The status of the sales at the end of 1975 is portrayed in the marketing and the finance report of the November management meeting (see Illustration 8.2).

The actual sales achieved over the last few years are recorded in a wall chart in David Hall's office (see Illustration 8.4) which also records the production hours booked against craft. The random points of sale together with the varying levels of production activity indicate the difficulty of formulating a reliable sales and production plan. A plan was proposed for 1974 to build boats at the rate of one per month, but as the months went past they were only selling at half the rate, and in August the company had to go into reverse and cut the labour force by 20 per cent through declaring redundancies. (The reduction in monthly productive hours achieved is shown in Illustration 8.3.)

For 1975 the company did without any plan at all, but a new tentative sales plan was formulated for 1976. This proposed the start of a Mk. 3 craft every six weeks, each craft taking 18 weeks to complete. The plan would start at craft number 334, craft numbers 331, 332 and 333 still being in production. It also proposed the start of three new Mk. 4 craft besides the one already under construction. Each Mk. 4 requires 7 months construction time. On this plan, craft 331 and 332 are certain sales, 333 is 85 per cent secure but none of the other Mk. 3s is more than 50 per cent secure. The first of the stretched craft 435 is sold but the remainder have still to be found definite destinations. Fortunately craft are eventually sold, even if it means changing the fittings and the colours. One craft was sold three times and resprayed for each occasion as successive political or technical difficulties blocked the sale.

David Hall had been involved in a sale to Hong Kong where a craft was originally leased and incentives had been offered to the operator to buy the craft by the end of 1974 prior to the end of the lease. Getting the operator to buy meant changing the air conditioning equipment, searching for bank guarantees of signatures, getting Export Credits Guarantee Departments loan arrangements set up and closing the deal at 3.30 p.m. on 31 December. He considered that the only help you could give yourself in selling a craft was to identify the factors which a particular customer considered important in your commercial practice; these factors varied dramatically from one part of the world to another.

But the selling remains a chancy business. As he says: 'Sales and marketing can worry all day and night about their prospects and it may come to nothing: they get 100 per cent or zero results. The Hong Kong operator, for example, took four craft ultimately signed for in one afternoon, and that is half a year's production settled in a day. At least on the production side your efforts are likely to lead to 90 per cent of the results you want. The trouble in production is that you want to run at a steady pace and therefore you are either ahead of sales or behind them. Applying the brakes or the accelerator too quickly can lead to a lot of problems and the wrong final decision. Much of the difficulty arises because of the inertia characteristics of production capacity: you are asked to speed up the rate of working but it takes three months to do it and by the time you've got there sales may be asking you to cut back to the original levels of output.'

3. The Organisation of Manufacture

The organisation of manufacturing is divided into three steps:

The specification of how to manufacture the craft;
The authorisation of work;
The procedure for undertaking the actual physical tasks.

The manufacturing procedure for the SC Mk. 3 craft is defined in terms of eight 'stages', each stage having a set of jobs or activities (job card numbers) classified by the different trade groups. Each job has a list of appropriate drawing numbers to indicate to the workforce exactly what is required. Each job also has a parts list. All internally designed components are given part numbers and access numbers are also given to all other items. There are over 3500 different types of parts in a standard craft. There are about 150 'standard' jobs on a craft, constituting about 12,500 hours work. The 500 hours (approximately) of customisation on each craft is not specified in these standard jobs. The total build time for a craft will be approximately 18 weeks, the first six weeks being required for the moulding of the hull.

All work is authorised by means of Internal Works Orders (I.W.O.). These can vary from the I.W.O. for a complete new craft involving 16,000 hours to the replacement of a damaged engine involving 40 hours (see Illustration 8.4). Generally I.W.O.s are initiated by David Hall. The work content is estimated by Mr Sandys, the Production Engineer, and agreed by David Hall, involving Tony Whittle (the works superintendent) in the estimate where appropriate. The material costs are assessed by Ian Tyler (the material controller), the I.W.O. is then given a start date and a completion date by the initiator; it is costed by the accounts department and the overhead rates at 200 per cent are added on. It is then returned to the initiator for any reconsideration in the light of costs and finally authorised by Ted Rowlants.

When approval has been given, Mr Sandys makes out the standard job set from the printed set of 150 cards of standard tasks plus any extras not covered by the standards which are written out manually. All work done on that job is booked against that I.W.O. number. The only other form of work issue originates with Ian Tyler from Material Control when he issues 'Detail

Cards' which are orders for the manufacture of components which go into stock prior to assembly. These are all booked to a fixed I.W.O. number.

All the standard job cards and the 'detail jobs' go to Tony Whittle, who racks the incoming jobs by trade group. A copy of the parts list also goes to Ian Tyler's material control section to organise the appropriate materials. Whenever the supervisor for the trade requires work, the job cards are issued in plastic envelopes. The operator doing the job will draw on materials with the job ticket as authority using a requisition form for drawing from stores. The requisition form is returned to material control with the I.W.O. and job number on it. Inevitably shortages occur and a progress chaser keeps in close contact with the material control department to identify critical items which are needed urgently.

On completion of work on a job, the job card (and job if appropriate) is passed to the inspection department and either approved or, if necessary, reworked. Inspection department are responsible for defining the inspection and quality assurance procedures for the incoming goods, the in-house manufacture, and the incoming purchased items which all go into a 'quarantine' area until they comply with quality and paperwork standards. The November Management Report indicated that they had inspected 662 items from subcontractors of which 3 were found faulty, 403 fabricated items of which 7 were faulty, and had raised some 330 Stores Return Notes.

The Inspection team are backed up in the field by a customer service department which is responsible for providing replacement parts, covering claims on guaranteed items, and going into the field to help out and advise on the operation of the craft in use. This is a vital function as it is very much in Speedcraft's interest for these operating companies to succeed as they may then buy up further craft.

David Hall has also made provision on the standard job sheets for booking the actual hours expended against the estimates which he and Mr Sandys provide. This is to facilitate more accurate estimating for better cost prediction as well as to help set targets of achievement for shop floor personnel. David Hall wants to set targets which are fair but tough to meet. But he has no intention of tying the targets into a bonus-related work-timed system. They are estimates, not work standards. Not only does he consider it inappropriate to adopt a piece rate system when so much work is essentially concerned with development but he makes it a matter of principle. 'Once you start hitting a man in his pocket you can never win with the blokes on the shop floor. They'll beat you every time. In production management you've got to have an understanding of what happens on the shop floor and to know exactly what you're asking other people to do.'

4. The Organisation of Supplies

Ian Tyler was appointed to the position of materials controller and purchasing manager in the spring of 1975. He had previously been works manager, with Doug Fowler as his assistant, and had been subcontracts manager in the original Speedcraft company. He was asked to take over the materials control task to sort out some serious stock control problems. As works manager he had noticed various deficiencies in the stocks position. For example the store-keeper would be asked for parts which he said were not present, but later turned out to be simply not racked properly. The stock records clerk might report that the missing parts were on his books. As a further check one could contact the buyer to see whether he remembered purchasing the parts but he would simply pass the enquirer back to the stock records clerk.

Ian Tyler determined that the materials control job involved three conditions for success:

A clear single source of authority over buying, physical stock control and stock records;

The provision of an easily operated manual stock card system which would enable the stock controller to state with complete reliability and immediacy the precise stock position on any item;

A simple means for the manager to check that his stock control policies were being implemented.

In formulating a plan and a policy for stock control he considered that it was an advantage not to have had any previous experience in the subject. However this same innocence could raise doubts in the minds of the existing stock control staff about the new manager, and Ian Tyler spent much of the time in the first few months seeking advice, comment, and debate with the staff who had been in the job on how to formulate a new system.

The basic objective of the stock control system was to provide availability of parts for production. The engineering parts requirements for an order (I.W.O.) reach Ian Tyler's team prior to the job cards being issued to the works. Each I.W.O. refers to a particular craft, and, knowing the due date for the craft, they have to order parts depending on the stock situations and the lead times so that they are ready for production when needed.

After the discussions had taken place and an enthusiasm for a new system had developed, Ian Tyler took a number of decisions. First he decided that there was no alternative to getting rid of the existing storeman; this was an initial, necessary, but uncomfortable step. He classified and re-established a unique access number (or part number) on every item used on the craft (excluding basic fastenings — nuts and bolts), and claimed the sole right to allocate future part numbers.

He purchased a new set of Remington Rand Cardex filing cabinets with one card for each part. A 'strip' at the base of the card is used to indicate both the status and the policy on stock holding. Coloured plastic tags are placed on the left-hand side of this strip which show up on opening the drawer and a coloured plastic slide can be moved over the right-hand side of the strip to indicate the stock status: 'Max. Stock', 'Re-ordered', etc. All this information is revealed 'at sight' on opening the drawer and the following codes are in use:

Pink Tag   = A Class items (Class A = item value > £100
                                            Class B = item value > £5
                                            Class C = item value < £5)
Red Tag   = Item to be subcontracted
Black Tag   = Spares
Yellow Tag = Greater than four weeks' lead time on ordering the item.
                   (Some products such as engines can take up to six months to
                   obtain.)
Orange slide = Current part needed for SC Mk. 3 (2000 in total)
Green slide = The rest (1500 in total) e.g. Mk. 2 spares

By the autumn of 1975 Ian Tyler had got the system fully set up with a card filled in for every item and a bin location clearly identified. In order to guarantee the authenticity of the card records he designated one member of staff to 'cycle count' continuously (at about 20 items per day) and to check that the number of items on the cards were a correct representation of the number in the bins. Ian Tyler has designed a special form to record the cycle counting procedure. Each time an item is checked a green line is drawn across the stock record card. Whenever an error is found an amendment is made and an accounting variance is communicated to the accounts department for their stock account records. (This variance is turning out to be so low that it seems that the auditor will accept the statement from the records without requiring a separate physical check provided that the variance on the cycle count lies within a 3 per cent margin.)

The establishment of the system had made the stock position much clearer. In August 1975, when the system was started, the value of 'orange band' parts (current for SC, Mk. 3) amounted to £72,000 with £121,000 worth of other items, many of which would have to be sold off, and a total stock value of £216,752. Prior to the end of 1975 all stock had been valued at standard cost, but from 1976 onwards stock was to be valued at the latest invoice price plus 2 per cent per month for inflation. A stock check was carried out in December

which gave the following stock valuations in £ classified by category A, B, C
and by current Mk. 3 craft (orange band) or other (green band).

	A	B	C
Orange Band	62,293	94,178	15,283
Green Band	16,186	30,307	18,085

Ian Tyler also found that £38,788 worth of stock was attributable to 'detail
jobs', i.e. internally manufactured parts which could be significantly reduced,
he believed, as their production could be timed to fit in with their demand
pattern.

Essentially, as Ian Tyler pointed out, stock control is a trade-off between the
ceiling on money tied up on the one hand and the problem of shortages for the
production programme on the other. On the first issue the new system would
help especially with the classification system as Class A items represented
78 per cent by value of a craft and Class B items 20 per cent by value. But the
policy to meet the production programme was more difficult to determine.
'Suppliers don't always deliver on time and Ted Rowlants may bring a craft
forward by a month, which can mean several hundred telephone calls to
expedite orders. In these changing circumstances of supply and demand it's
very difficult to tell when you've got your stock policy right.'

5. The Reporting System

Besides his responsibilities in the material control function Ian Tyler is also
responsible for running the management reporting system on operational
achievement. Firstly he provides a weekly statement of how labour time was
used on the various internal works orders compared to budget, distinguishing
between 'basic time', 'overtime' and 'double time'. The raw data is provided
by the labour time sheet bookings. The total direct and indirect hours of
factory time is around 2250 per month. Special I.W.O. numbers are used for
booking labour waiting time and set-up time on tools, fixtures, etc. An
example of the weekly statement is shown in Illustration 8.5. Secondly this
factory hours account is supported by a staff hours account of a similar
nature showing how the time of the design staff is booked. Finally, Ian
Tyler prepares a monthly Financial Report showing the total value of
expenditure, hours and materials, booked against the various I.W.O.s (see
Illustration 8.6) and related to the total financial budget.

The other main source of recorded information on the production side is
the 'production progress report' prepared by David Hall for the monthly

management meeting. This records the state of progress on the various craft and the shortages which may be slowing up production (see Illustration 8.7).

'But', as Ian Tyler explained, 'it is one thing to be able to record where you have got to on a product, it is quite another to know that you are pointing in the right direction. With the uncertainty of the sales and the complexity of the product you really need a way of knowing that the policies and plans for production, purchasing and stockholding are all in balance, cost-minimised and flexible at the same time.'

Question for discussion

Assess the risk in Speedcraft's production plan.

STARTERS:	DEPARTMENT	NAME
Staff:	Marketing	V. Ogilvy
	R & D	S.G. Palmer
		J.M. Jones
	Sub-Contract	
	Design	1 Person
LEAVERS:	R & D	F. Hobson

LABOUR TURNOVER:	FACTORY	STAFF
Number of persons leaving over the last twelve months	37	41
Expressed as a percentage of number employed:	(51) 73%	(87) 47%

RATIO - FACTORY : STAFF

1974			1975		
June	1.38 : 1		Jan	0.87 : 1	
July	1.38 : 1		Feb	0.53 : 1	
Aug	1.06 : 1		Mar	0.58 : 1	
Sept	0.95 : 1		Apl	0.56 : 1	
Oct	0.94 : 1		May	0.57 : 1	
Nov	0.94 : 1		June	0.59 : 1	
Dec	0.86 : 1		July	0.59 : 1	
			Aug	0.59 : 1	
			Sept	0.61 : 1	
			Oct	0.58 : 1	
			Nov	0.59 : 1	

S/LEEJ
4.12.75

	At Comm. of Mth.	Starters	Leavers	At End of Mth.
FACTORY				
Woodworkers	19	2	-	21
Laminators	5	-	-	5
Detail Shop (Sheet Metal Workers)	3	-	-	3
Fitters	8	-	-	8
Electricians	5	-	-	5
Plumbers	2	-	-	2
Skirt Shop	2	-	-	2
Painters	1	-	-	1
Labours	4	-	-	4
	49	2	-	51
OVERHEADS				
Stores	3	-	-	3
Production	4	-	-	4
Production Engineering	2	-	-	2
Inspection	4	-	-	4
Customer Service	3	-	-	3
Field Service	4	-	-	4
Operations	5	-	-	5
Marketing	7	1	-	8
Buying & Material Control	8	-	-	8
Engineering	4	-	-	4
SC5	15	2	1	16
SC5 Contract Design	13	1	-	14
M.D.	2	-	-	2
Financial Accounting	7	-	-	7
Reception	1	-	-	1
Printing	1	-	-	1
Speedcraft Finance	1	-	-	1
	84	4	1	87
TOTAL	133	6	1	138

ILLUSTRATION 8.1   Personnel report for November 1975

The policy of concentrating effort into the six Category 1 negotiations has enabled the Department to identify its priorities, and it can be seen that both nature and priority have changed in the last four weeks.

Category 1

Philippines
Subsequent to approval being received from the Central Bank, several alternative finance options are being evaluated.

New Zealand
The hearing for Mr Pit's licence application is scheduled for December 9th, and in anticipation of his visit to the UK, an operational analysis has been prepared. A visit from the Deputy Director of Marine for the NZ Government proved very fruitful, as a great deal was learnt about the proposed operation, and Mr Gay.

France
STL has received a letter of intent from Havroute Cote d'Azur for the purchase of 2 craft. Langeard has presented one study to the French Banks, this is to be supported by the one prepared by HTL. David Nicholson will be visiting the Marine Marchand to progress the legal licensing aspects of the proposed operation.

Egypt
1) Tony Elwood will visit the Suez Canal Authority evaluation committee to encourage their deliberations. According to our agents they have said 'yes' to two Fire boats. A visit from the SCA proved most successful.
2) Quotations have been sent for two survey craft, and interest looks strong.

Nigeria
A 'glossy' brochure is being prepared

Japan
The sale of the first craft to HovPac is imminent, but it is understood that structural tests on the craft are still to be carried out (these are essential for Japanese Government approval)

Category 2

Slow progress with Seaspeed who need conviction that our craft can operate to a half-hour schedule.

Cairo City Transport are still potential customers for a fleet of modified SC2s — personnel changes rate a decision less immediate. The Egyptian Ministry of Tourism is another potential large scale purchaser. These are being given attention on CAB's impending visit.

Also being considered are sales in Teheran: Italy, where a joint study is still to be made: Thai Seaspeed, where we have asked for the balance of a deposit by 15th December: Fiji, where Edmond Lau had an enquiry for tourist craft: Turkey, where the new director of DB has been approached: and India.

Category 3

Potential sales to Israel are now considered to be fairly long term, this being ascertained by Graham Gilliat's visit. Enquiries have been received concerning the Balearics and Tristan da Cuna.

Following a visit from Royal Dutch Shell (whose enthusiasm for the SC2 was encouraging) STL have been invited to make a presentation in The Hague.

Publicity and PR
STL has had more good press, with even better to come. Several features on the company are being assembled, and the COI is considering recording SC5 progress on film. The Newsletter has been produced in an improved format and is being distributed.

December 1975

Activities planned for December include: CAB's visit to Egypt and Turkey, DWN to Paris, GAG to Teheran. We expect visits from: Ron Pit, Langeard and Pasco. The Department intends to prepare a study on the Calabar—Oran route, to revise HM2 specifications, to assemble a slide presentation and to update the Bermuda study.

Summary

Visits from: Suez Canal Authority (Egypt)   Visits to: Cottell (ARC Marine)
            Directorate of Marine (NZ)   Kamel Bros (London)
            Roy Bartlett (South Africa)   Egypt
            T. N. H. Wells (Carribbean)   Iran
            Press   Israel
            Students   France

A. ELWOOD
2.12.75

SPEEDCRAFT FINANCE REPORT

Management Report for November 1975

1.   *BR Seaspeed Limited*: 1 x SC (Mk III)

    Our offers are still under consideration.

2.   *Landoil, Philippines*: 2 x SC (Mk III)

    Negotiations continue and we anticipate finalising these shortly.

3.   *Havroute, Cote D'Azur S.A., France*: 2 x SC (Mk III)

    Contract of sale now looks more likely than a lease contract.

    This company is to be incorporated in early December and the contract may be financed from money to be made available by Midland Bank to a French Bank. This is dependent upon the French Bank's attitude to the viability of the proposed routes.

4.   *H.T.T.L., Bolivia*: 1 x SC (Mk III)

    Arrangements for altering the financing terms for this contract are being implemented following M.R.R.'s visit to La Paz.

5.   *Hong Kong and Yaumati Ferry Company Limited, Hong Kong*: Up to 4 x SC (Mk IV).

    Terms for straight purchase (as previous contract) have been quoted but subject to a bank guarantee because of a weakening of the company's Balance Sheet.

6.   *Waiheke Island/Auckland Service, New Zealand*: 2 x SC (Mk III)

    No progress with contract but more information on proposed operator found and financing methods suggested.

7.   Indication in principle and financing possibilities suggested for the following enquiries:-

    Singapore: Baltic Fleetmasters Limited: Interested in 2 x SC (Mk III)
    Canada: Union Steamship Limited: 1 SC (Mk III)

J. E. STONE
2 December 1975

ILLUSTRATION 8.2   Marketing and finance reports

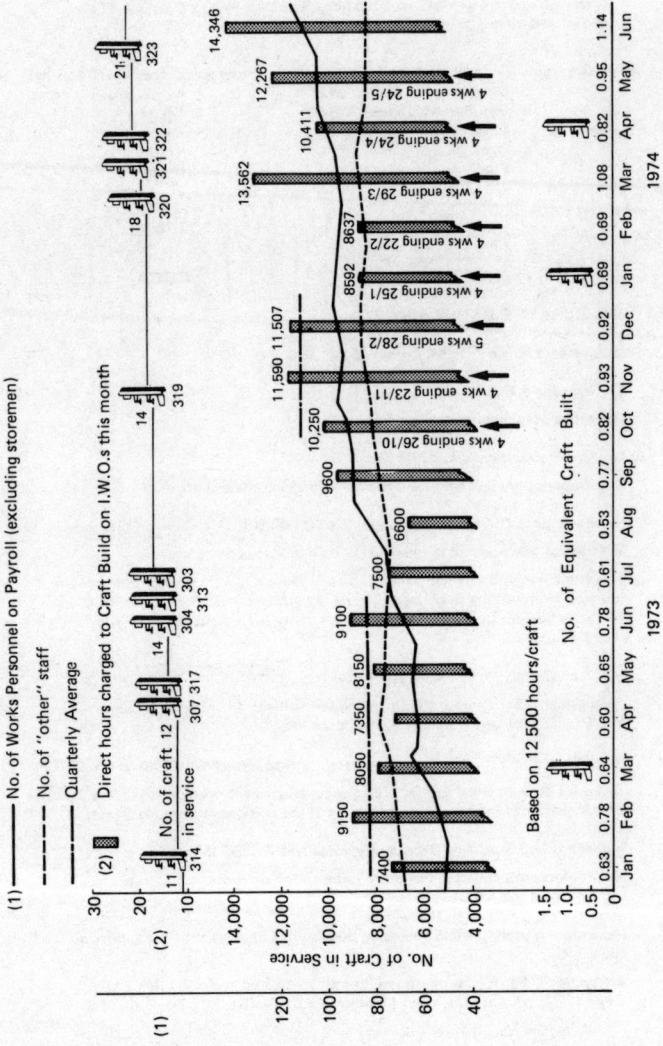

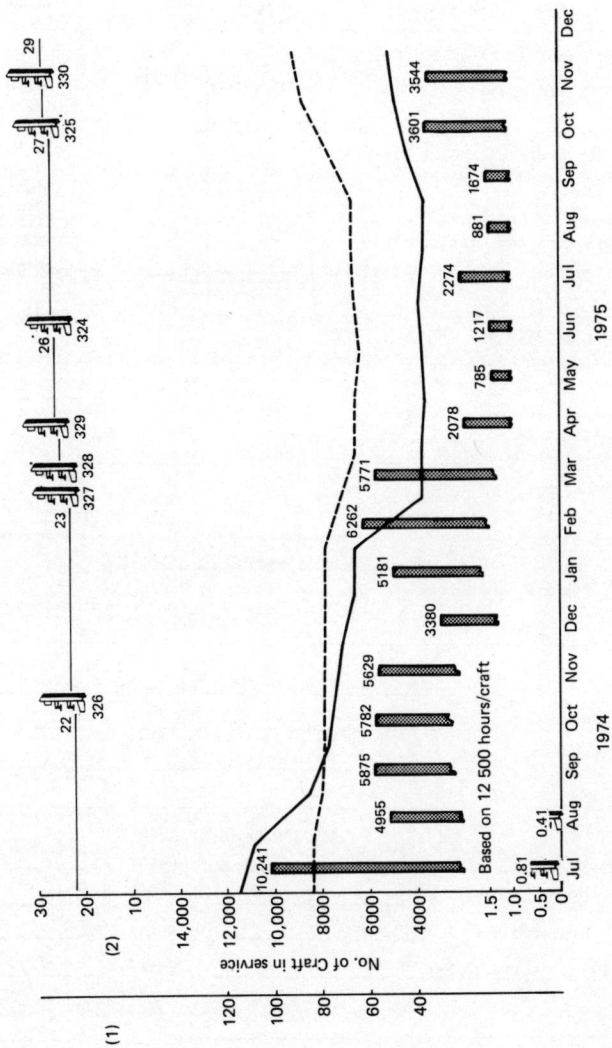

ILLUSTRATION 8.3   SC 2/3 Production and sales 1973 to 1975

115

SPEEDCRAFT TRANSPORT   INTERNAL WORKS ORDER NO. 4512

JOB DETAIL	Budget Staff hrs.	Budget Labour hrs.	Budget Mat: Cost
(1) Construction of first SC. Mk.IV Hull/Superstructure. G.R.P. assembly.		11,400	£ 4152 (Mk. 111 plus 20%)
(2) Fit out craft with G.M. Diesels Prop. Cummins Diesel Lift.		5,470	n/a (design unspeci- fied.)
(3) Manufacture new Lifting rig.			£900.00
(4) Manufacture 4 off. Craft stands.			£850.00
		16,870	

Reason for expenditure:

    Management decision to construct craft for launch. April 15th, 76.

                           Customer Order No: n/a

Proposed Restart Date   10 10.75   6194
Latest Completion Date   15 · 4 · 76   Charge to Account Code: 1931

    Initiated By: D. J. Hall

          Dept: Production   Date: 13.10.75

A.   ALL ABOVE TO BE COMPLETED BY INITIATOR

B.   ROUTE: 1 & 2   Accounts   4. Managing Director
              3   Initiating Dept.   5. Accounts for No. Allocation
                                        & Circulation

	Hours	Rate	£	o/h rates	£	Mat: £	TOTAL
1. Staff Personnel						94.000 1.752	
Works Personnel	2000	1·60	3200	20·00	2840		
	14270	1 80	25696	22·58	57947		
					61787	95.752	157,533

                       Additional Budget Costs   £

2. Cost Dept.   Costed By: C.S.R.   Date: 5 · 11 · 75

3.   Confirmed By: Dept. Head.   Date: 24 · 11 · 75

4.   Approved By: Date: 20/11 : 75

5. Cost Dept. Actioned By: Tyler   Date: 24/11/75

ILLUSTRATION 8.4   Form of the works order

MANAGEMENT REPORT WEEK ENDING: 28th November '75 FACTORY HOURS: DIRECT

I.W.O.	Initiator	Account Code		BASIC	OVERTIME		Total this week	Total Cum	Budget Total	COMMENTS
					1½	D/T				
			New Craft Build SC2.							
0471	DJH	6194	Trim 330	14	2	0	16	779	950	
311211	"	6194	Craft 331	370¾	39¾	0	410½	9711½	11545	
3114	"	"	Customer Extras	100½	8	0	108½	714¾	716	
321211	"	"	Craft 332	19½	0	0	19½	6369	11470	
4512	"	6194	Craft 435	249%	64¾	0	314¼	612¼	16870	
				754¼	114½	0	868¾			
			Stretched Craft							
6001	DJH	1113	Mould Extension	26	8	0	34	1243½	1500	
			SC5 Project							
5018	MERC	1152	SC5 Model GRP Hull	29	4	0	33	33	20	Over-spent
5050	DJH	1153	Manufacture of hull plug	422¾	54½	0	477¼	3981	13429	
				451¾	58½		510¼			
			Miscellaneous							
1000			Major Mlds	4	0	0	4	806	0	
0023	DJH	1040	Manufacture in-house details	165½	0	0	165½	7520¼	0	
0214	"	1120	Revision of Engine Shop	12½	0	0	12½	20½	45	
		A/c 3055	Egyptian Demo	8½	0	0	8½	8½		No IWO
				190½	0	0	190½			
			Engine Shop							
0225	DJH	1031		54	1	0	55	462¼	255	
8184	TW			0	3	0	3	75		
8193	"		Eng. 330 to Hydca.	0	2	0	2	122½		
			RP	1	0	0	1	80½		
				55	6	0	61			
			Total Direct Hours =	1477½	187	0	1664½			

MANAGEMENT REPORT WEEK ENDING: 28.11.75 FACTORY HOURS: INDIRECT

I.W.O.	Initiator	Account Code		BASIC	OVERTIME		Total this week	Total Cum	Budget Total	COMMENTS
					1½	D/T				
0478	TW	6197	Vesper Service	85	91	30½	206½	4681½		
0020	DJH	2033	Maintenance	18	12	15	45	1149¼		
0021	IT	2017	Stores Transport	40	9½	0	49½	1279¼		
0022	"	2202	Stores Personnel	96	10	4¼	110¼	6999¼		
0027	DJH	2005	Supervision	47½	4	4	55½	2223¾		
0028 }	"	2012	Factory Cleaning	65½	7¾	0	73¼ }	3084¾		
0031 }	"		Craft Movement	1	3½	2	6½ }			
0030			Tooling	3	0	0	3	970¾		
0042	"	2013	Waiting Time	5	0	0	5	299¼		
0064	"	2001	Time Keeping & Progress	40	8	0	48	2092¼		
0220	TW	2589	Assist. Training STL personnel	23	0	0	23	35½	50	
				424	145¾	55¾	625½			
			Total Hours Worked =	1901½	332¾	55¾	2290			
			Sickness:- 104 Late :- 5¼ Lost-time:- 6½ Leave:- 8					I. Tyler		

ILLUSTRATION 8.5 Weekly labour and job records

I.W.O. FINANCIAL REPORT   MONTH ENDING   November

I.W.O.	Intr.	DESCRIPTION	Hours	Hrs. Expen.	Purchase Expen.	Total cm. Expen.	Budget Total	Account Code
				£	£	£	£	
		NEW CRAFT BUILD SC LK 2						
3112/2	DJH	CRAFT BUILD 331		33,977	52,932	86,909		6194
3114	"	EXTRAS 331		3,431	800	4,231	5,835	6194
3212	"	CRAFT BUILD 332		19,200	19,041	38,241		6194
3312	"	" " 333		17,517	10,903	28,420		6194
3412	"	" " 334		11,441	2,523	13,964		6194
		Total		85,566	86,199	171,765		
		SC LK N STRETCHED						
4512	DJH	CRAFT BUILD 435		2,595	554	3,149	192,339	6194
6001	"	TOOLING		5,969	303	6,272	7,725	1113
6002	LERC.	TASK 1 POWER & PERFORMANCE		877	-	877	2,872	1154
6003	"	TASK 2 PROP. DESIGN		36	-	36	800	1154
6004	"	TASK 3 STRUCTURE		4,898	5	4,903	14,324	1154
6005	"	TASK 4 SEAT DESIGN		52	-	52	584	1154
6006	"	TASK 5 MECH. & ELECTRICAL SYSTEMS		7,664	-	7,664	18,142	1154
6007	"	TASK 7 MAINTENANCE MANUAL		-	-	-	11,120	1154
6008	"	TASK 8 LEGISLATIVE REQ.		-	-	-	3,500	1154
6009	"	TASK 9 DATA SERVICES		50	-	50	411	1154
6010	"	ENG. SUPPORT OTHER DEPTS.		-	-	-	8,753	1154
6011	DJH	PRODUCTION ENG.		347	-	347	14,325	1154
6012	JHC	SERVICING SCHEDULE		-	-	-	4,465	1154
6013	JOB	TRIALS		-	-	-	4,575	1154
		Totals		22,508	862	23,370	283,935	

ILLUSTRATION 8.6   Monthly financial statement

SC2. PRODUCTION BUILD STATUS.
Week ending: 12.12.75.

Craft No.	Start Hull Lay Up.	Actual Launch Date.	Delivery Date Required.	No. of Shortages.	No. Systems Not Yet Preselected.	Works Hrs. Charged Last Week.	Total Charged to Date.	Craft Compl. State. %	Craft Under Construction for Weeks.	COMMENTS.
330.	---	---	---	---	---	---	---	---	---	
331.	21.5.74.	--	3rd Venez. craft a.s.a.p.	7	nil.	445¾ / 143½ / 919.	10,512¾	85	81.	Launch due 5.1.76. Shipping due 15.1.76.
332.	13.6.74.	---	unknown.	488.	nil.	27¼	6505¾	57.	80.	Work held for parts.
333.	11.7.74.	---	"	unknown.	100%	5694.		48.	75.	no action.
334.	6.12.74.	---	"	"	100%	170¾	3340½	30.	53.	Clearing mould for 435 superstructur
435.	25.11.75.		"	"	unknown.	251¾	1206¼	5	3	'
336.										
437.										
338.										
439.										
340.										
441.										
342.										
443.									D.J. Hall. DJH/JDS. 18.12.75.	

ILLUSTRATION 8.7   SC2 Production Build Status. Week ending: 12.12.75.

Part D: Managing System Variability

In Part B the two types of sales policy were examined and in Part C the four main types of manufacturing organisation were studied. Both these parts were concerned with a better understanding of delivery and productivity. through analysis of individual orders and capacity centres. The next two sections are concerned with the integration of the total company operations in the face of variation and the demands of overall company policy.

The simplest type of manufacturing operation which can be envisaged for management purposes would be a simple process producing a single product for a single customer demanding a steady rate of production for the product. The plant could then be designed and operated at maximum efficiency with perfect delivery and predictable cash flows. However, those circumstances are unreal (and incidentally not very interesting to manage), and companies in fact operate with many products, many processes and with an uncertain sales picture. The consequence of these kinds of variation and variety is that not all products are equally important in their contributions, not all processes are used with equal productivity, and sales have to be forecast with some uncertainty. All three cases in this section concentrate on the cost and benefit of this variation, whether it is internally chosen by the company or externally imposed by the customers.

The first of the cases examines the problem of scheduling a product range in a thread manufacturing company. The operational task is to decide how to launch production orders in a product range on to the works to achieve an appropriate stock level for a given sales policy on thread availability subject to constraints on production capacity.

The second case examines how to control the flow of customer orders through a steel plate mill with many processes. The mill consists of a number of independent processes which will still have to be run like an integrated manufacturing facility to achieve high total productivity despite the need for delivery of small individual batches for customers.

The third case is concerned with sales variation in the classical seasonal activity of ice-cream manufacture. The challenge is to find a finished goods stock-holding policy which achieves an appropriate balance between sales and production needs in the light of the uncertainties in the sales and distribution system.

9 Producing a Product Range: Perivale Gütermann Threads

1. The Company

Perivale Gütermann Limited is the fourth largest manufacturer of sewing threads in the United Kingdom with a sales turnover of £3 million per annum, following English Sewing Cotton, J. & P. Coats Ltd, and Barbour Threads. English Sewing Cotton and J. & P. Coats together control 90 per cent of the thread market. The company is located in Perivale, Middlesex and manufactures a range of threads for industrial and domestic use. It has 300 staff of whom 130 are machine operators. The distribution operates through a warehouse at Perivale in the factory premises and through depots at Manchester, Leeds and Nottingham.

Perivale Gütermann consider themselves to be a specialist thread manufacturer concentrating on major outlets and particular types of thread. As the marketing director described it, they aim to provide advantages with their lines in terms of 'quality, delivery, article availability and flexibility to market trends and pressures'.

Apart from the silk threads, which constitute only 1 per cent of turnover, they manufacture four other types of thread: Tera and Skala from polyester continuous filament fibre, Mara from staple polyester fibre and Bulon made from nylon. Tera heavy counts are used in bookbinding and the carpet trade, fine counts in shirts etc. Mara industrial is used for clothes and retail Mara for domestic purposes. Bulon goes into the manufacture of swimwear, knitwear, corsetry, stretch tights and skirts.

As one of the smaller producers, Perivale Gütermann has broadened its market base so as to reduce fluctuations in earnings and sales. Accordingly in recent years the emphasis has been on overseas and retail home sales. The export area has progressed and the retail area has grown in volume by 100 per cent in 1971/72 and 50 per cent in 1972/73 though not so much in profit contribution. The only retail threads are Mara and silk. In 1973, although retail Mara accounted for some 15 per cent of total sales it only contributed 3 per cent of gross profits. In industrial Skala and industrial Mara on the other hand the percentage of gross profits (30 per cent and 20 per cent respectively) matched their percentages of sales turnover. An important issue for the company was therefore to organise their manufacture of retail Mara in the best possible way to achieve good profit margins on this new area of their activities.

2. The Retail Thread Product Range

The retail thread range consists of 370 Mara polyester threads covering a full colour range grouped into two classes: Class 1, labelled M303, has 250 colours and is used for seam sewing; Class 2, labelled M1003 and called Polytwist, with 120 colours, is a heavier, decorative thread for button holes.

The range of colours has been fairly stable over the years 1971—5. The number of shades is not so high as the range produced by some of the other manufacturers on the retail side. The competitors generally produce more than the 250 shades available in the M303 range:

English Sewing Cotton	Sylko	350 shades
	Trylko	280 shades
J. & P. Coats	Drima	192 shades
	Satinised	364 shades
Molnlycke		209 shades

Compared with the heavier M1003, in which Perivale Gütermann produce 120 shades, J. & P. Coats have only 100 shades in Drima Bold.

Originally the sales effort was concentrated on large accounts such as John Lewis and Debenham. But sales are now made more widely to small haberdasheries which have been traditionally dominated by English Sewing Cotton. The company has avoided extensive magazine advertising but aimed instead to place loaned display cabinets in each shop and keep these supplied with a full range of shades. Cabinets are made in several sizes, starting with 160, 240, or 500 slots for spools, each slot having a capacity for a maximum of 11 spools.

The customers order direct from Perivale Gütermann or wholesalers for the refilling of their cabinets, and deliveries are made through the company van or by post. The representatives also go round to collect the orders. The marketing policy is to deliver within three days for all lines on all occasions. Quick delivery is the important factor to the retail outlet and availability is the key to the final customer sale. If a cabinet is out of stock on any particular line a potential sale is lost as the thread buyer (usually a housewife) has no brand loyalty for accessory items of this type and will simply choose another thread of the right colour from another source.

The demand pattern for some of the M303 lines is shown in Illustration 9.1. The products are sold in boxes of 10 standard plastic spools, the M303 having 110 yards wound on the spool and the M1003 having 33 yards. It gives the history of the number of boxes ordered in each of the twelve months March 1975 to February 1976 together with the total annual demand. The budgeted sales levels for 1976 are prepared by sales at the end of 1975; these are shown in Illustration 9.2. In the view of Mrs Winwood, the materials and production control manager, there is no particular pattern to the sales of the thread shades over time. The total volume of sales has increased as the cabinets have been installed but there is no definite seasonal pattern to guide a stock-building policy. She considers that the carrying of some extra stock is a relatively low risk as the products will eventually be sold. The main cost of holding stock is the limitation on warehouse space and the capital tied up in the completed items.

All M303 and M1003 products are sold at the same retail price of 12p per spool. This includes the traditional 30 per cent mark up by the retailer in this type of trade. Products are costed by a product costing scheme which analyses costs by materials, processing and warehousing with an allocation for overheads. The standard costing breakdown for the M303 and M1003 articles in pence per box of 10 spools are:

	Materials	Variable	Fixed	Total Cost
M303	37	7	2	46
M1003	36	11	3	50

3. Production Facilities and Organisation

Most of the production facilities at Perivale are used for the production of industrial threads in twisting, dyeing, etc. Mara threads however are bought from the German company of the Gütermann group ready twisted and dyed. They are rewound at Perivale on to spools suitable for domestic sale, packaged and despatched.

The conversion of the retail threads into the finished form is undertaken by a small section of staff under Mr John Jones, the foreman of retail products. He was put in charge of the section in August 1975. The layout of the production area is shown in Illustration 9.3 giving the physical routing of the work and the documentation associated with the various tasks. There are five types of worker in the section, fulfilling the required functions:

Printer:	prints two-part spool, puts into magazine and places in appropriate rack.
Service Worker:	repacks the yarn in bins ready for the rewinding machines, checks quantities.
Operator:	sets up and monitors the winding machines.
Controller:	inspects wound spools and boxes them in tens.
Packer:	bands the boxes into groups of ten, stamps and stacks on trolley.

Under conditions of full production, over 20,000 boxes are packed per week. Weekly output in boxes over 1975 is shown in Illustration 9.4. However, in the spring of 1976 demand had fallen off and Mrs Winwood in materials control had agreed with Mr John Jones to set a current target output of 15,000 boxes per week. At this level the number of staff on the section had been reduced by temporary transfers to other sections and only three of the six winding machines were in use. (One operator can handle three winding machines.) A three-shift system was being operated with the following distribution of operators:

	operators	controllers	packer	printer	service worker
Morning shift	2	2	1	1	1
Afternoon shift	2	1	–	1	–
Night shift	1	1	–	–	–

The overall process was kept in balance with this arrangement. The printer can produce 65 to 70 cassettes per shift (250 spools per cassette). The winding machines can wind at 40 cassettes per eight-hour shift, producing 10,000 spools of M303 products on three machines. As the M1003 thread is only one third of the length of M303, the rate of production in spools is three times as fast on the M1003 products. Normally machines are run with two shades concurrently, each shade occupying five of the ten spindles per machine. Each set of spindles winds from a 1-kilogram factory cone (the large spool on which the yarn arrives) on to 250 retail spools, giving 25 boxes, the retail spools being fed into the winding positions automatically and dropping into a magazine. The daily efficiency of the machines is affected by the batch sizes. Overall labour time required to set up the winding machines is five minutes for a batch of the same colour but for a different colour of thread it can take up to fifteen minutes. The sequence of shades influences efficiency; it is desirable to work from light shades to dark as the fluff retained in the atmosphere can affect the finished appearance of the successive items.

All work is undertaken against batches or orders issued by Mrs Winwood's section in materials control. Groups of production orders are issued every week, each having a reference number, and there are usually 200 to 300 orders outstanding for the section. Illustration 9.5 shows some outstanding orders at the beginning of March for the M303 range. This includes only orders for which documentation has passed through the computer section. The orders are written out on a multi-part document set, each part being identical in form but having a different colour. The pink copy goes to the printing section to authorise and record the printing of spools as soon as the order is issued. The white, blue and yellow (after being routed via the computer section for registering the 'replacement' orders as they are called) go to the warehouse to authorise the issue of yarn. Warehouse keep the blue as a record of materials issued. Mr Jones calls forward the yarn after the spools have been printed (known to him through his file of completed pink tickets). The yarn and the spools are matched together by joining the pink and yellow copies in Mr Jones's office and the work with the white copy is given to the winding operator.

The controllers record the quantities actually boxed on the white tickets. Any surplus yarn is sent back to the warehouse and the pink tickets go to materials control section to amend their stock records.

The output from the winder operator and the controller (both of whom are called direct workers) determines the bonus for the section including the printer, packer and service worker, who are regarded as indirects.

Any machine breakdowns (varying between 2 per cent and 7 per cent of running time) are recorded on the daily work sheets and the foreman edits the section daily work sheet for the records section and for bonus calculation.

4. The Planning of Retail Mara Production

Orders for retail Mara come in direct to the sales office at Perivale from the 500 retail outlets. About 10 such orders are placed each day, each order requesting a group of items. The quantity required per item can vary from one box to several hundred but usually only one or two boxes are demanded. The total intake of orders in boxes is shown in Illustration 9.6 for the 52 weeks of 1975 and for the start of 1976.

These customer orders are passed directly to the computer section who enter the relevant facts of the order on to the computer. This creates the despatch documentation which is passed directly to Mr Gordon in the stores, who is responsible for all despatching. Normally despatches are made within three days on all retail items. If an item is not despatched, or if it is not available from stock — and this may be indicated by a W printed by the computer on the despatch note — the despatcher does not put a tick against the order. When copies of the despatch notes are returned to the computer section the missing deliveries (or part-deliveries) are noted and a new order is issued (approximately three days later). A stock check is made every three months to ensure compatibility between the stock records in the computer and the actual stock levels on the shelves.

The authorisation of the orders to replenish finished goods stock comes through Mrs Winwood's materials and production control section. They control the purchasing of the raw material yarn which is bought in bulk from Germany for both industrial and retail Mara. The replacing of supplies orders with Germany takes place weekly but the supplies orders are created continuously. Each time a production order is made out, the supplies position is checked in the supplies book and if necessary a new supplies order is made out. There is a page of the supplies book for each shade. It gives the details of orders placed, their arrival in the warehouse, the issues and the stock balance. Supplies from Germany usually arrive on time in the correct quantities.

If production capacity seems short at Perivale, materials control can order the finished items from the German factory. In the early autumn of 1975 demand appeared to be building up and a bulk order was placed for 180,000 boxes of a few finished colours from Germany to cover the period October 1975–February 1976. (These are shown in Illustration 9.5 by a P marked in the second column.) With the adverse movements in the value of the £ against the Deutschmark there was no profit in this subcontracting as the cost of a box from Germany was nearly £1. Packaging materials are bought in by the purchasing office in bulk in the light of expected sales patterns.

Although a broad picture of needed stocks is indicated by the sales budget, Mrs Winwood has to adopt a flexible procedure for determining the stock levels and production commitments. Once a month a computer printout is produced (see Illustration 9.7) which gives, for each shade: the stock level, the free (i.e. uncommitted) stock, amount on orders, average demand per 20-day month, number of new orders issued this month and the implied number of days' coverage provided by the free stock. Mrs Winwood's aim is to have six weeks of each shade in stock as it takes six weeks to get a new order completely through the system — four weeks for supplies from Germany and two weeks for the cycle time in production.

In order to decide whether a new production order should be placed, one of Mrs Winwood's assistants examines for each shade whether free stock [Illustration 9.7] minus the three highest demands [Illustration 9.1] is a positive or negative quantity. For shades for which this is a negative quantity a 'candidate' order is considered with a batch size set suitably to cover six to eight weeks supply and a multiple of 125 boxes because of the practice of winding from five factory cones at a time. (A loss of 10 per cent is expected in the order during processing for faults detected at inspection and caused by yarn shortages.) At this stage it is assumed that yarn is available for all the orders. The total of all these new candidate orders (plus uncompleted orders from last month) are added up to assess production capacity requirements. If the total implies less than four weeks' production Mrs Winwood may increase order sizes so as to maintain production levels although stocks will rise; if it implies more than six weeks, she may decide to halve the order sizes to ensure that some orders of each shade come through into stock. When a decision on the right set of production orders has been made any yarn shortages are chased up and the order documentation is prepared and issued in weekly bundles, taking any priority orders first and generally sequencing in the order of least 'free stock in relation to average demand'. The orders placed in March 1976 for M303 are shown in Illustration 9.8.

This procedure necessarily has to make trade-offs between stock levels, smoothing production requirements and customer service and it is a difficult task to manage the detailed order placing in relation to a defined production policy. With the advance of the computer system, the company are considering how to automate the re-ordering procedure and use more discriminating formulae for determining the timing and quantities for batch replenishment. 'But, in the end', as Mrs Winwood says, 'you have to be flexible and be able to respond to the changing pressures from different quarters. On the other hand you must not change the output targets downwards more than once every four or five months. You have to exercise continuous discipline over the routine use of paperwork so that you have control to move the production system to a new objective using a picture of the current situation as seen from the materials control office.'

Question for discussion

Assess the procedure for placing replenishment orders in retail Mara.

BY ARTICLE SHADE ANALYSIS
DEMAND PER PERIOD - QUANTITY

03/03/76

Shade No.	March 1975	April	May	June	July	Aug.	Sept.	Oct.	Nov.	Dec.	Jan.'75	Feb.	Annual Demand
0000	3123	1461	2289	2955	4790	1136	2784	5116	4284	1980	3416	1911	35247.7
0001	228	198	292	508	420	204	304	154	53	51	374	154	2943.0
0005	847	938	505	1150	1131	607	738	1000	604	701	588	621	9432.8
0006	198	194	261	312	402	231	212	141	219	59	72	202	2505.0
0008	299	150	164	296	454	72	221	188	245	97	158	174	2520.9
0011	306	209	270	287	463	224	165	165	179	84	253	241	2847.5
0016	178	116	140	181	260	76	191	89	184	80	217	135	1849.5
0017	138	77	76	61	126	70	142	176	183	151	192	149	1543.0
0019	62	41	33	29	67	32	46	98	62	62	43	51	616.5
0021	541	418	340	452	613	240	516	364	536	296	455	575	5350.4
0023	619	423	361	645	699	264	566	362	675	392	710	637	6355.9
0025	410	204	250	517	569	155	459	264	420	160	195	303	3909.4
0026	25	18	30	36	40	41	42	33	56	39	20	35	390.5
0028	160	55	98	133	216	14	171	121	115	80	91	136	1421.4
0040	326	123	185	457	496	113	406	258	288	258	181	279	3374.3
0046	467	278	244	384	531	220	340	273	405	186	446	379	4156.9
0052	395	163	184	391	523	78	385	200	390	192	228	350	3422.4
0064	67	66	64	99	96	85	217	235	312	63	95	140	1670.5
0068	109	109	76	126	127	100	50	86	128	192	100	85	1161.0
0075	220	171	145	208	238	179	200	431	382	370	351	349	3247.4
0080	324	244	273	637	461	221	443	323	409	172	169	237	3916.4
0082	84	74	88	102	110	74	109	113	216	88	66	94	1221.0
0093	100	57	53	59	165	38	109	167	311	96	86	142	1386.4
0095	119	57	77	70	198	50	119	154	157	123	169	137	1413.4
0096	258	38	195	323	341	136	250	200	253	102	155	156	2522.9
0100	82	146	118	106	211	71	70	26	71	78	37	56	968.0
0106	231	40	132	529	510	162	390	216	775	124	160	296	3931.4
0107	429	403	299	569	672	168	551	226	781	168	294	354	4772.9
0108	165	284	117	92	250	84	119	106	106	84	106	121	1389.9
0111	196	62	184	131	313	124	171	114	225	115	246	250	2161.3
0112	721	88	652	923	1342	628	736	681	466	191	335	476	7615.3
0113	121	454	168	121	195	94	196	217	187	115	285	224	2009.0
0130	469	82	277	305	436	209	262	179	392	204	577	471	3979.9
0136	10	195	14	13	7	6	62	57	36	24	17	17	275.5
0139	440	10	371	424	881	118	409	306	517	180	269	331	4560.4
0143	584	312	644	891	1154	472	607	475	1516	298	410	526	8334.9

ILLUSTRATION 9.1   Monthly demand M303 from March '75 to Feb '76

Product Range: Perivale Gütermann

Month	Number of weeks	Weekly sales M303	M1003	Monthly sales M303	M1003
Jan	4	15880	2314	63520	9259
Feb	4	16745	2440	66980	9763
Mar	5	17987	2622	89939	13110
Apr	4	16426	2394	65704	9577
May	4	19235	2803	76940	11215
June	5	17207	2508	80036	12541
July	4	17469	2546	69877	10186
Aug	4	16349	2383	65396	9533
Sep	5	16817	2451	84085	12257
Oct	4	20321	2962	81285	11849
Nov	4	18458	2688	73832	10762
Dec	5	15415	2247	77075	11235
Total				900669	13287

ILLUSTRATION 9.2   Sales budget in boxes for 1976

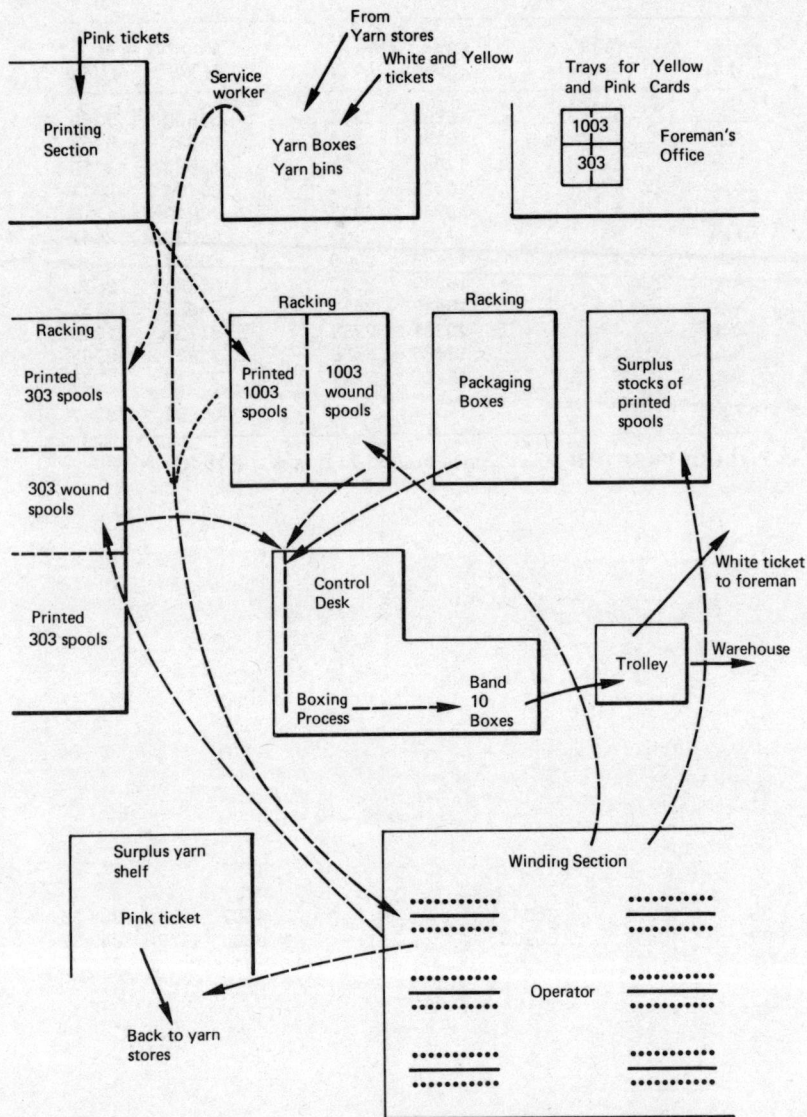

ILLUSTRATION 9.3   Layout and routing of work in retail Mara production

Week No. 1975	M303 weekly	4-week totals	M1003 weekly	4-week totals	Total (weeks nos.)
4	10653	42615	2139	8559	1—4
5	8608	40569.5	2321	8740.25	2—5
6	8608	38524	2321	8921.5	3—6
7	8608	36478.5	2321	9102.75	4—7
8	8608	34433	2321	9284	5—8
9	8382	34206.75	3136	10099	6—9
10	8991	26207.5	3881	7777	7—10
11	13134	39115.25	749	10087	8—11
12	5901	36408	—	7746	9—12
13	6205	34231	—	4630	10—13
14	8771	34011	—	749	11—14
15	10199	31076	—	—	12—15
16	11344	36519	—	—	13—16
17	7634	37948	782	782	14—17
18	16836	46013	386	1168	15—18
19	12843	48657	2253	3421	16—19
20	9542	46855	5529	8950	17—20
21	2345	41566	2090	10258	18—21
22	13466	38196	3567	13439	19—22
23	12824	38177	5047	16233	20—23
24	13825	42460	1783	12487	21—24
25	9162	49277	—	10397	22—25
26	6040	41851	—	6830	23—26
27	14618	43645	247	2030	24—27
28	6750	36570	3122	3369	25—28
29	18532	45940	3305	6674	26—29
30	16859	56759	4534	11208	27—30
31	17978	60119	2043	13004	28—31
32	15905	69274	95	9977	29—32
33	19599	70341	113	6785	30—33
34	10765	64247	2341	4592	31—34
35	16753	63022	1548	4097	32—35
36	18926	66043	—	4002	33—36
37	19456	65900	2911	6800	34—37
38	12872	68007	8153	12612	35—38
39	17326	68580	6593	17657	36—39
40	19669	69323	4141	21798	37—40
41	20852	70719	2497	21384	38—41
42	24557	82404	4160	17391	39—42
43	26539	91617	2375	13173	40—43
44	24601	96549	922	9954	41—44
45	14226	89923	1754	9211	42—45
46	18410	83776	3660	8711	43—46
47	22422	79659	2919	9255	44—47

Week No. 1975	M303 weekly	4-week totals	M1003 weekly	4-week totals	Total (weeks nos.)
48	19241	74299	6685	15018	45—48
49	20909	80982	3773	17037	46—49
50	24172	86744	1897	15274	47—50
51⎱ 52⎰	23472	87794	148	12503	48—52
Total Av.	**719,901**		**116,982**		
wkly.	13844.25		2249.66		
1976 1	17180	85733	7466	13284	
2	20422	85246	4676	14187	
3	15927	77001	10166	22456	
4	21474	75003	4013	26321	1—4
5	8634	66507	6510	25365	2—5
6	13954	60039	7231	27920	3—6
7	16363	60475	5145	22899	4—7

ILLUSTRATION 9.4   Production in boxes 1975/76

ALL REPLACEMENT ORDERS AS AT 03/03/76   PAGE   1 of 4

SRCE	ARTICLE			SHADE	REF	ORDERED	COMPLETED	DELIVERY SCHED	REV	ACT
22 P	M 303	FD	0000		2177	6000.00	0.00	034	094	000
01 M	M 303	FD	0001		6918	250.00	0.00	123	123	000
22 P	M 303	FD	0005		2178	1800.00	0.00	034	094	000
01 M	M 303	FD	0008		6919	250.00	0.00	123	123	000
01 M	M 303	FD	0016		6920	125.00	0.00	123	123	000
22 P	M 303	FD	0021		2179	1000.00	0.00	094	094	000
22 P	M 303	FD	0023		2180	1000.00	0.00	094	094	000
01 M	M 303	FD	0035		6922	125.00	0.00	123	123	000
01 M	M 303	FD	0038		6923	250.00	0.00	123	123	000
01 M	M 303	FD	0040		6924	500.00	0.00	123	123	000
01 M	M 303	FD	0046		6925	250.00	0.00	126	126	000
01 M	M 303	FD	0068		6926	250.00	0.00	123	123	000
01 M	M 303	FD	0080		6927	125.00	0.00	123	123	000
01 M	M 303	FD	0093		4802	250.00	74.00	104	104	077
01 M	M 303	FD	0100		6928	500.00	0.00	123	123	000
01 M	M 303	FD	0107		6929	125.00	0.00	123	123	000
01 M	M 303	FD	0108		6930	250.00	0.00	124	124	000
22 P	M 303	FD	0111		2181	1800.00	0.00	094	094	000
01 M	M 303	FD	0112		6931	250.00	0.00	124	124	000

D = Demand

ILLUSTRATION 9.5   Production orders M303

Week No. 1975	M303 weekly	4-week totals	M1003 weekly	4-week totals	Total (weeks nos.)
4	9018	41869	1773	8616	1—4
5	7767	43158	1166	5856	2—5
6	22393	57530	4311	9590	3—6
7	9947	49125	1648	8898	4—7
8	13867	53969	2327	9452	5—8
9	10418	56620	1504	9790	6—9
10	7555	41782	1641	7120	7—10
11	22403	54238	3235	8707	8—11
12	12939	53315	1860	8240	9—12
13	8587	51484	1038	7774	10—13
14	8244	52173	1829	7962	11—14
15	8107	37877	1199	5926	12—15
16	15875	40813	2010	6076	13—16
17	19365	51591	3005	5038	14—17
18	16236	59583	2553	8767	15—18
19	3858	55334	635	8203	16—19
20	29929	69388	2951	9144	17—20
21	3790	53813	722	6861	18—21
22	9495	47072	2831	7139	19—22
23	15860	59074	2763	9267	20—23
24	16139	45284	1573	7889	21—24
25	8454	49948	1793	10856	22—25
26	30516	70969	3689	9818	23—26
27	15665	70774	2782	9837	24—27
28	7005	61640	704	8968	25—28
29	30684	83870	5621	12796	26—29
30	44452	97806	5546	14653	27—30
31	6918	89059	756	12627	28—31
32	19381	101435	2054	13977	29—32
33	5070	75821	836	9192	30—33
34	6355	37724	1012	4058	31—34
35	38005	68811	5581	9483	32—35
36	17903	67333	3251	10680	33—36
37	7319	69582	1514	10346	34—37
38	4527	67754	913	11259	35—38
39	11231	40980	2620	8298	36—39
40	41116	64193	6927	11974	37—40
41	18890	75764	3914	14374	38—41
42	7096	78333	922	14383	39—42
43	5051	72153	857	12620	40—43
44	6149	57186	1175	6868	41—44
45	67692	85988	10511	13465	42—45
46	3572	82464	591	13134	43—46
47	5717	83130	1141	13418	44—47
48	7203	84184	2019	14262	45—48

Week No. 1975	M303 weekly	4-week totals	M1003 weekly	4-week totals	Total (weeks nos.)
49	8871	25363	1116	4867	46—49
50	31579	53370	6762	11038	47—50
51 52	2813	50466	392	10289	48—52
Total	763,326		124,416		
Wkly. Av.	14679.35		2392.62		
1976 1	1412	44675	1119	9389	
2	15371	51175	3813	12086	
3	23824	43423	2625	7949	
4	14433	55043	1477	9034	1—4
5	8614	62245	1475	9390	2—5
6	23938	70812	3345	8922	3—6
7	13913	60898	1214	5771	4—7

ILLUSTRATION 9.6   Incoming orders 1975/76

Type.Pat.Shade	Stock	Count.	Free Stk.	Un-Order	Av. Dmd.	Issues	Days	L1.	Value	Shade
Product-M. 303 FD.										
1 1 0	9838.00	637.20	9200.80	6000.00	293.3	4.00	66	20	4515.64	0000
1 1 1	1300.70	304.00	996.70	250.00	237.6	1.00	106	20	597.02	0001
1 1 5	4230.00	246.00	3984.00	1800.00	762.9	1.00	107	20	1941.57	0005
1 1 6	832.40	31.00	801.40	0.00	205.3	1.00	79	20	382.07	0006
1 1 8	878.50	21.00	681.60	250.00	226.1	0.00	68	20	322.49	0008
1 1 11	326.10	124.00	754.50	0.00	236.1	1.00	74	20	403.23	0011
1 1 16	412.70	49.00	277.10	125.00	153.3	1.00	42	20	149.67	0016
1 1 18	199.50	43.50	369.20	0.00	132.7	1.00	64	20	189.42	0018
1 1 19	1838.50	2.50	196.50	0.00	51.4	1.00	77	20	91.34	0019
1 1 21	1038.50	153.00	1766.50	1000.00	437.1	1.00	86	20	890.23	0021
1 1 23	1392.80	259.00	1379.00	1000.00	552.2	1.00	61	20	751.34	0023
1 1 25	100.50	42.00	1350.60	0.00	324.4	1.00	85	20	639.32	0025
1 1 35	419.30	12.50	88.00	125.00	12.2	1.00	61	20	46.12	0035
1 1 36	948.00	18.00	401.30	0.00	117.9	1.00	70	20	192.45	0036
1 1 38	853.00	45.00	903.00	250.00	275.5	1.00	67	20	435.13	0038
1 1 40	745.40	236.00	617.00	500.00	344.1	1.00	49	20	391.52	0040
1 1 46	821.90	53.00	692.40	250.00	282.7	1.00	52	20	342.13	0046
1 1 52	325.50	31.50	790.40	0.00	132.0	1.00	118	20	277.25	0051
1 1 64	761.90	146.50	615.90	250.00	206.8	1.00	59	20	453.99	0064
1 1 68	1422.50	48.00	1374.50	0.00	313.3	1.00	54	20	149.72	0068
1 1 75	341.40	19.50	321.90	125.00	99.1	1.00	87	20	652.92	0078
1 1 80	559.50	36.00	523.50	0.00	110.8	1.00	67	20	256.70	0080
1 1 82	221.80	41.00	180.90	176.00	114.0	1.00	37	20	256.31	0082
1 1 93	810.00	38.00	772.60	0.00	208.4	1.00	76	20	101.65	0093
1 1 95	308.00	13.50	294.50	0.00	81.1	1.00	76	20	372.15	0095
1 1 96	1584.10	58.00	1526.10	500.00	309.1	1.00	96	20	141.37	0096
1 1 106	1919.70	132.00	1787.70	0.00	367.0	1.00	96	20	727.10	0104
1 1 107	299.50	43.00	256.50	125.00	113.5	1.00	51	20	861.14	0106
1 1 108	457.30	70.50	386.60	250.00	185.3	1.00	50	20	137.47	0107
1 1 111	5983.00	54.00	5929.00	1000.00	810.4	2.00	185	20	209.90	0108
1 1 112	342.50	93.00	246.50	250.00	159.7	1.00	40	20	2950.55	0111
1 1 130	1318.00	395.00	923.50	0.00	336.4	1.00	79	20	157.20	0112
1 1 132	231.50	16.00	215.50	0.00	21.5	0.00	201	20	604.96	0130
1 1 139	1607.10	280.00	1327.10	0.00	375.2	1.00	64	20	106.25	0132
1 1 143	3040.70	92.00	2940.70	0.00	866.4	1.00	67	20	737.35	0139
									195.68	0143

Notes: Pat. = Demand pattern: High usage = 1. Count. = 1. Count. = Committed stock for forward orders in total.
Free stock = Remainder. On-order = Sum of replacement orders for each shade.
Av. Dmd. = Total Demand - see Illustration 1 - divided by 12. Value = Value of free stock.
Issues = Number of replacement orders issued this month. Days = Number of days at average demand
rate covered by the free stock at 20 days per month. L1. = Lead Time on orders in production (set
by the user).

ILLUSTRATION 9.7   The stocks position, M303

Orders Placed for March at end of February 1976
on all M303 lines

					100m.						
1	250	165	375	276	125	397		595	125	788	250
5		167	125	280		401	125	600		800	
6	375	169	250	283	375	402	250	610		810	375
8	250	170	250	285		406	375	612	250	815	250
11	500	177	125	286		412	125	615		818	125
16	375	180	375	289	(250)	414		616		821	375
18	125	186	250	291	125	415	125	631		824	250
19	125	188	125	292	250	417	375	633	125	827	125
21		189	250	297		432	250	634	250	833	
23	(250)	290	125	300	250	435	1500	639	375	837	375
25	250	192	125	304	125	439		649	250	842	125
35		193	125	307	250	446		650		854	
36	250	194	250	309	375	448	500	656		861	
38	250	195	750	310		469		658	250	868	500
40	375	196	375	311	250	472	875	659	250	869	125
46	375	197	500	312	125	473	625	665	1000	870	250
52		199	125	320	250	474	1000	671		875	
64	125	205	(125)	321		480	125	682		887	250
68	250	210	250	322	625	463	125	685	500	889	625
75	375	211		325		488		689	(125)	890	250
80	125	213	500	327		496	125	694	1000	893	375
82	250	214	500	331		503		696		896	375
93	250	215	500	332	(250)	512		697		903	625
95	250	216	250	334		517	125	701	375	904	250
96	250	218		336	375	519	125	702	625(375)	909	125
100	375	221	750	339		528	125	707	750	913	125
106	250	223	125	340		531		714	375	916	
107	250	226	125	350	125	537	250	715		919	375
108	250	230	500	351	125	542	125	716	125	924	
111		232	750	362	125	545		718		925	250
112	250	234		364		553	125	722	500	929	500(375)
130	500	235	250	367	250	561	125	724	125	931	625
132	250	237	250	368	500	568	250	727		932	
139	(375)	239	125	369	250	575	125	728	500	934	250
143	1000	247	125	375	125	578		730	(125)	965	500
152	500	251	125	382	125	580	125	755	125	967	125
153	250	257	125	384	250	582	250	758	125	968	375
155	500	258		386	125	585	250	759	(250)	979	375
156		259	125	387	250	586	375	761	250	982	500
158	250	265	125	391	125	589	625	764	250	Blk 000	
160	250	269	125	392	125	591		766	375		
163	125	274		396		593		769			
Sub Totals	11,000		10,250		6,500		9,500		9,375		10,000

Note: Orders brought forward from the February schedule are shown in brackets.

ILLUSTRATION 9.8   Production orders placed for March, M303

10 Integrating separate processes: English Steel Plate Mill

1. Performance in the Plate Mill

In the English Steel reorganisation at the beginning of 1973, Dr Ron Vincent took over the responsibility for all production control activities in the Sheffield area. Vincent sets broad guidelines for the operations at each plant, fixes the sources of supply, and puts targets on stock turnover levels, delivery performance, and utilisation, while 'line' (equipment and running) responsibilities remain under individual plant managers. As Ron Vincent put it: 'The plant managers have to keep output up regardless of what it is and the production controllers have to make sure that what comes out is the right stuff at the right time.'

One of the areas for initiative was the plate mill at Woodcote Lane where a new production controller, Paul Snowdon, took over in June 1973. The plate mill rolls stainless steel plate from slabs to specific customer requirements, the customers being individual purchasers or final users and steel stockists.

The required output from the mill is measured in tonnes and defined in the Annual Operating Plan (A.O.P.) prepared one year in advance; this represents the intended capacity of the plant. The A.O.P. assumes a certain mix of customer requirements in terms of types of steel and plate sizes. The plan is updated monthly to provide a Most Recent Forecast (M.R.F.) giving the forward estimates for 12 months ahead. In boom periods the M.R.F. is decided by production control as plant capacity is the limiting factor, and in slack periods Sales decide the M.R.F. as customer demand settles the output expected. Illustration 10.1 shows the weekly tonnage actually delivered from April 1973 to July 1974 against the A.O.P., and Illustration 10.2 shows the actual tonnages rolled on the mill each week. Actual performance depends critically on the weekly shift patterns used, the stoppages occurring on equipment and supplies availability. Illustration 10.2 also shows the shifts worked and the stoppages due to breakdowns, etc., on the two key processes: the mill and descaling. This data is collected from the clock cards and the shift records which give the output.

By October 1973 Ron Vincent and Paul Snowdon had increased the plate mill performance from 65 per cent of potential maximum capacity to nearly 80 per cent, aiming at an ultimate 86 per cent. Much of this improvement in capacity was attributable to the reorganisation of maintenance and some new incentive schemes. The stages of improvement are shown in Illustration 10.1

Delivery performance had also improved. Previously 75 per cent of orders were over four weeks late. The situation had been so chaotic that all the orders were completely replanned one weekend to achieve realistic dates. By November 1973 only 30 per cent of the orders were more than four weeks late and the mill was beginning to roll ahead of plan. Several statements of delivery performance are used. Of the orders packed each week Paul Snowdon records the tonnages, distinguishing between orders overdue, those due in the current week and those packed in advance of their due dates. Some orders are packed from stocks. Illustration 10.3 shows these figures. Paul Snowdon also records by month the percentage of orders delivered more than four weeks late. Between September 73 and August 74 this varied between 31 per cent and 84 per cent. A delivery 'accuracy' statement is also provided by English Steel across their product types and by plant (Illustration 10.4).

2. The Plate Mill

The plate mill is an enormous bay 150 yards by 30 yards which converts slab steel into flat stainless plates through a series of massive equipments. The plants (value £10 million) were installed 10 years ago and handle an annual turnover of £11 million. The products are made to customer orders which specify the number of plates and their size, the delivery date, and precise technical specifications on the steel. Plates typically measure 6 ft. by 12 ft. and need lifting by overhead crane between operations. The tonnage for an order varies from one to 200 tonnes, averaging seven tonnes. Each customer order leads on to several works batches, averaging just under one tonne per works batch. The average batch size is 15 plates although there may be over 100 plates in a customer order. More than 100 works batches are launched each day. There are 450 men in the direct labour force, working a two or three-shift pattern depending on the process. The men earn £40 to £50 per week plus a bonus based on tonnage through the mill in the primary operations and on footage in the secondary finishing processes. Paul Snowdon's 25 production control staff earn an average of around £1200 per annum.

The layout of Woodcote Lane is shown in Illustration 10.5. The initial processes constituting the right-hand side of the diagram are the primary stages and the left-hand side is the sequence of finishing stages. The total operation is divided between Woodcote Lane and Mill Lane (12 miles away). The Mill Lane plant has a variety of different finishing processes and batches are routed to Mill Lane at various stages as indicated in the chart. Jobs which have to be worked at Mill Lane are indicated on the routing card, but where jobs could go to facilities at either site, decisions on routing are made on an *ad hoc* basis as capacity loadings seem to dictate. Batches are despatched to customers from Mill Lane if that is their final process, but they are managed by Woodcote Lane production control. The mill output of 570 tonnes a week is divided between 320 tonnes finished at Woodcote Lane and 250 tonnes finished at Mill Lane. Before rationalisation Mill Lane undertook small orders whereas Woodcote Lane was designed for longer runs on a make-for-stock range of standard sizes of plate. The overall production control is now operated from Woodcote Lane.

The organisation of capacity at each stage varies considerably and it is important in assessing overall capacity to be aware of the different technical operations in some detail. In the following description the stages are operated on an eight-hour day unless the shift pattern is shown. The shift patterns can be changed but three to four weeks' notice is needed for extra shifts although some labour flexibility is available between processes. Normally the shift work as a gang on a process. The plates are moved between stages by overhead gantry cranes which pick up the plates through a pair of electrically operated pads which are lowered on to the plates and adhere magnetically.

(1) The slabbing bay
Slabs of steel produced at other nearby E.S.C. plants are transported to Woodcote Lane mill and stocked in the slabbing bay. There are a large variety of types – up to 50 qualities, 25 ft. long and 3 in. to 10 in. thick in steps of ½ in. From this possible range Woodcote Lane draw on 185 types of slab. They are ground in the slabbing bay on one of two grinders to remove scale and cut to the appropriate sizes for the orders to which they are allocated

(2) The mill and hot shear (10 shifts per week – 2 shifts per day)
Slabs are rolled into plates according to a predetermined daily programme. The mill is operated on a definite technical sequence going from wide to intermediate and then to narrow plates so as to avoid marking. This sequence is further complicated by the desirable requirement to enter thick slabs first as they may need several hours' preliminary heating and this can be done overnight. About one-tenth of the slabs are rolled twice and these can be fitted into the sequence anywhere as any marks will subsequently be removed.

The width required varies from one metre to two metres with the distribution shown:

Wide	>60 in.	(55%)
Medium	48–60 in.	(20%)
Narrow	<48 in.	(25%)

There are two parallel rolling processes on the mill. Steel and iron rollers are used; generally the iron rollers need to be replaced every three days for regrinding whereas the steel rollers can last for four days. There are three sets of steel rolls and two iron rolls. For rolling steel below a certain thickness it is essential to use steel rolls. Current practice is to issue the mill with a three-day programme revised daily and roll six shifts followed by two hours to change the rolls. An objective for the mill operators is to maximise roller utilisation and life by careful use. A new pair of steel rolls costs around £55,000 whereas the iron rolls are less than £20,000. After rolling, the hot shear cuts the plates into appropriate lengths for the order.

(3) Off-loading
After shearing, the plates are stacked in large piles. Some of these plates will go to Mill Lane for further processing. The in-process stocks located there are also useful as a buffer to accommodate imbalances between the flow rates at different process stages and help to cope with breakdowns.

(4) Softening (15 shifts per week - three shifts per day)
This is an annealing stage in which the steel is heated to produce the required finish. The main temperature setting is around $1000°C$ but varies between $800°C$ and $1200°C$. A small proportion (10 per cent) is annealed at $520°$. The time to change the temperature is proportional to the temperature difference required — a change of $100°C$ takes 10 minutes. The annealing process on average takes five minutes per plate but a batch which has gone cold in the pile requires half an hour for pre-heating. The annealing furnace can normally process four to six plates concurrently.

(5) Leveller
The plates are flattened in the levelling process.

(6) Mark and transfer table
The transfer table enables plates to be moved across to the finishing line directly from the leveller to the intermediate stock point. The individual plates are marked up on the table for shearing to their final sizes.

(7) Intermediate stock
Intermediate stock is held to feed the finishing line and for re-routing to Mill Lane where appropriate.

(8) – (14) Continuous finishing processes (10 shifts per week)
These processes form a continuous run from side shear to end shear. The side shear is made with the plates horizontal and thereafter the plate is held vertically. Sometimes after end shear the plates are withdrawn for bench dressing and re-enter the system at de-scaling. The whole length of the system is driven on rollers at 8–12 ft. a minute. The plates are examined on the move by two inspectors who grind out small faults with hand tools. Larger faults require the plate to be recycled (14).

(15) Despatch and packing bay (15 shifts per week)
The despatch bay is essentially a stock-holding area. Often plates have to wait in despatch prior to packing as the full batch does not reach the final stage at the same time. Sometimes a part despatch is made.

3. The Paperwork System

Sales department place customer orders on the plate mill. Each order will be for a variety of steel types and deliveries and these are broken down into the required despatches for particular product types needed in particular months. An order will generate up to 60 works batches on the plate mill approximately four months in advance of the actual due date for the order. Production control department receive the customer orders and process them through the following steps:

Step 1. Break the customer order down into delivery batches and for each of these select a delivery date from the capacity diary. It consists of a list of capacity commitments for each week distributed over the 'hot rolling' categories in a mix consistent with the annual sales plan. Sales and customers are informed of the booked week, which becomes part of the works order number.

When an order arrives, say for 10 tons for delivery in week 23, assuming a four-week cycle time inside the plant from mill to finish, production control look for 10 tons spare capacity both in despatch in week 23 and in hot rolling in week 19. If space is available the order is booked, otherwise successive weeks are inspected and the first available dates are booked.

Step 2: Steel ordering.
Production control now assess steel availability with the properties and
thickness required for that order. The quantity of steel needed is
computed by calculating backwards from the final weight required and
making standard yield allowances on the processes. This quantity gives
the number of slabs to order. The weight is notified to the cost office.
(All costing is done by weight.)
The appropriate quantity of steel may be available as surplus steel stock
but usually a new purchase order for E.S.C. ingots has to be made and
booked against the particular batches. Once a week purchase orders for
steel are placed for four weeks ahead for the variety of types and quantities needed, and normally Woodcote Lane Mill will receive the seven-
tonne ingots to cover the requirements for the group of batches of any
particular quality for the particular week. Any surplus is available for
suitable future orders. Usually steel is supplied within five or six weeks
but the 10 per cent which comes late will often include some special
qualities which may take up to 18 weeks to arrive.

Step 3: Master Record Card.
A unique master record card is prepared for each works batch showing
the exact sequence of operations together with tonnage through at each
stage. Also a set of job tickets are prepared describing, authorising and
recording the work at each stage of the process.
These first three steps in production control can be completed within
48 hours. But in November 1973, with orders being booked for 14 weeks
ahead, the orders were being held simply as order acknowledgements for
four weeks prior to entering them through the first three steps in the
order entry procedure.

Step 4: Mill Programme.
When steel arrives it is entered up into the stock list. It is booked against
batches, not necessarily the original set, and these become candidates for
the mill programme giving the list of batches prepared daily for rolling
for the next two or three days. The details of rolling a particular batch
are given on the back of the job ticket for the mill and used by the mill
controller. When the batch is entered on to the mill programme, all the
job tickets for that batch are released to the various stages on the plant
in readiness for its arrival at the separate processes.

The actual progress of a batch, once launched, depends on pushing from
progress chasers and customers. There is no explicit priority system. Feedback

of information on the status of an order arrives in production control as bundles of filled-in job tickets for each process giving the date and the number of plates passed (and by implication the amount scrapped). The availability of this information has improved significantly under Paul Snowdon: now about 90 per cent is available within a few days, whereas three months before only 70 per cent would ever have been recovered.

When this information is returned it is entered onto the appropriate master record card in the production control office. If a job gets stuck at the bottom of a stack the tickets can be there for many weeks. Sometimes, even if the job moves, the ticket gets lost and the progress of the job will only be identified formally when a later operation is reported by the return of a job ticket.

A new shift recording system was being developed to help to deal with these problems. For each shift at each process the operators will be required to fill in their actual production on batches on a blank work sheet indicating the work order numbers and quantities and the cause of down time. An example is shown in Illustration 10.6 This will require the workforce to present work done and output quite independently of the job ticket system. By collecting these work sheets production control will be able to find out what has actually happened each shift on each process, although many jobs may be only partially processed on the shift. On the basis of these sheets the men will be paid their bonuses and accounts will use them instead of the delayed job tickets for their standard costing system.

The men initially demanded 10p an hour to fill in these new work sheets. The management offered 2½p, and temporarily the matter was settled by agreeing to an experimental period free of charge to see what it involved. Nevertheless in the first week of operation when the foremen asked the men to fill in the new tickets they walked out on strike for a week. Paul Snowdon thought that although the unions had agreed to the scheme it had never been properly put across to the men. 'But', he added, 'it was quite a useful week for me as we got all the work-in-progress sorted out and the floor area cleared to Mill Lane.' The men finally agreed to fill in the forms for an extra 6p per hour.

4. Control Difficulties

Preparing a plan for all this work in the plate mill is difficult enough, but even when a plan is worked out it will be disturbed for a wide variety of reasons.

Firstly, there are materials handling problems. The plates are stacked in piles and it is inevitable that the plate on top gets selected first for the next process. Therefore depending on how the piles are arranged it is a 'last-come-first-served' system for working through the queues at the work stations. A batch can get right through in two days 'if it's lucky'. The problem becomes particularly acute if the piles get high, as generally with one plate stacked directly on top of another it is physically impossible to identify the plates which are at the bottom. The management of the stacking is limited by the availability of four gantry cranes, two on each side of the bay picking up one plate at a time with the magnetic pads for transfer to the next stage.

Secondly, individual batches get split up partly because of the stacking problem, and because some of the plates have flaws which need to be corrected. Some plates in despatch can wait six weeks for the remainder to come through.

Thirdly, the plant design is awkward for the size of the batches being processed. The finishing processes are really a flow line suitable for longer runs of stock items. However the current policy is for Woodcote Lane to make to order entirely. Although the layout of the plant is straightforward the use of space for stacking plates at intermediate stages is not satisfactory. Places are marked on the floor for certain groups of plates (e.g. for Mill Lane), but the plates are not always located correctly. The individual plants are one-off designs and are sometimes difficult to maintain. The end shear Davy—Ashmore machine recently broke down and it took two weeks to get it fitted up again for use. Meanwhile all the work on that operation had to be sub-contracted.

Fourthly, there are conflicts of interest in the sequencing of work at individual processes. The best mill cycle is to run from wide to narrow gauge and within a gauge by thickness. This conserves rollers, helps product quality and reduces set-up times. The feed from the mill to softening should ideally minimise temperature change. For materials handling purposes, the men sequence the work which is available in the order on the piles because they are paid on tonnage or footage through the process. Their incentives can radically affect capacity: in Paul Snowdon's view the initial grinding machines could do double the work with the right incentive scheme. And of course there is the desired sequence from the point of view of customer due dates.

Finally problems occur when faults occur in process. A faulty plate is removed and a new batch is started for the order. The faulty plate is stocked temporarily with the aim of using the steel for a subsequent order. Mistakes may be made as early as the initial cutting of the ground slabs, and Paul

Snowdon estimates that 5 per cent of the ground slab stock is a result of
these errors. If the initial slab is sheared incorrectly it may even mean a new
steel supplies order. Some staff argue that additional plates should be made
against each order to allow for faults. But Paul Snowdon believes that it is
appropriate to make individual replacements and that the surplus plates
which are faulty for one batch will be available for future orders. About
2 per cent of the batches end up at despatch with the wrong identification
having lost their chalk marks during descaling. This can be disastrous if the
customer gets steel with the wrong functional properties. Often detailed
tests are made approving the products for their final destination and these
are stamped on the job tickets.

All these aspects pose problems in managing the orders in the plate mill.
Paul Snowdon's task was to find a way in which he could resolve these
individual problems adequately, so that the whole system could be collectively optimised.

Ron Vincent and Paul Snowdon were both agreed that a useful first step
towards improving control of the current operations was to provide a clearer
and more immediate picture of where all the orders were at a given time.
They believed that this required a much faster and more effective information
system than the one currently in use which required laborious searches
through files, and had no facility for assessing the implications of the current
position. They were considering the possibility of a computer terminal-based
scheduling and order entry system supplied by a time-sharing computer service
in Edinburgh. The system had been investigated by the management services
staff of E.S.C. and it was estimated that the system would cost about 50p per
ton of steel to run.

Ron Vincent expected the payback from the system would come largely
in the form of an improved information system so that the production
control side could become more positive in relations with the commercial
side. As he said, 'It will provide a means of forecasting when an order will be
late. We will be able to pre-empt a customer's irate phone call. We want to
be ahead of the customer. It will also be an education in the use of on-line
production control.

'First we will simply maintain the order book on file and access it. Later
on we will start to use the system for the loading of orders and the improved
utilisation of capacity. At present we don't relate an order intake rate and
mix to mill output, nor to work-in-progress levels, customer service and
cycle times. Perhaps we can't relate these because of the slowness of our
information base; perhaps because of the volume on the plant. We can't
tell—so the system may help on this too. If Paul has more dynamic control
he will be able to influence sales to advise on the order mix in peak times

and get them to recruit business in lower parts of the business cycle. That would be ideal.'

Question for discussion

How can the plate mill's delivery and utilisation objectives be met?

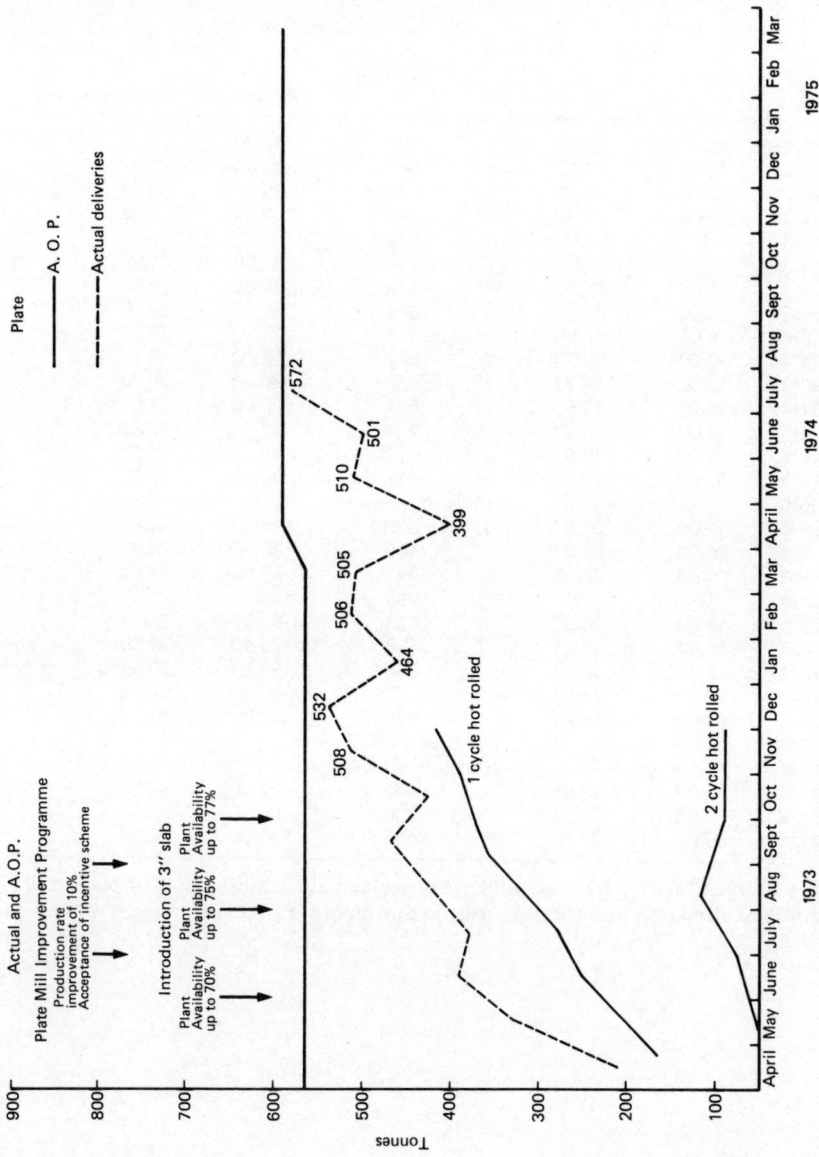

ILLUSTRATION 10.1   The annual operating plan and deliveries achieved

| w/e | Plate mill | | Tonnage rolled | Descaling | |
	Gross hrs	Stoppages (hrs)		Gross hrs	Stoppages (hrs)
9/2/73	80.00	25.46	500	72.00	28.92
16/2	72.00	17.00	649	80.00	35.93
23/2	80.00	21.75	560	80.00	30.58
2/3	80.00	22.40	592	80.00	33.88
9/3	?	?	922	?	?
16/3	?	?	726	87.00	34.08
23/3	72.00	15.52	730	96.00	39.82
30/3	80.00	36.21	396	80.00	32.08
6/4	74.00	23.40	478	72.00	25.50
13/4	80.00	20.18	622	92.00	42.79
20/4	53.00	14.71	488	80.00	29.79
27/4	80.00	17.62	691	96.00	34.02
4/5	80.00	15.17	730	96.00	46.69
11/5	80.00	19.91	677	72.00	36.50
18/5	56.00	17.45	418	80.00	35.15
25/5		Works shut-down			
1/6	80.00	27.84	520	128.00	41.67
8/6	80.00	36.67	480	80.00	34.42
15/6	96.00	26.35	741	80.00	37.57
22/6	?	?	650	?	?
29/6	64.00	16.95	624	80.00	22.17
6/7	80.00	23.81	598	120.00	28.69
13/7	80.00	18.81	655	80.00	20.65
20/7	32.00	14.95	33	80.00	24.85
27/7	48.00	15.75	375	72.00	32.17
3/8		Works shut-down			
10/8		Works shut-down			
17/8	80.00	28.91	460	72.00	44.25
24/8	72.00	31.50	530	80.00	38.48
31/8	56.00	20.06	495	120.00	48.37

ILLUSTRATION 10.2   Sample stoppage and availability data for plate mill
and descaling unit and tonnage rolled from February 1973 to August 1973

Weeks			Process orders				Ex-stock orders	Grand total	Overdue statement tonnes overdue on delivery
			Overdue	Current	Total	Forward			
8	9	73	83	16	99	61	49	209	–
15	9		192	24	216	225	101	542	–
22	9		198	11	209	167	60	436	–
29	9		158	27	185	260	12	457	1407
6	10		192	19	211	225	20	456	1460
13	10		163	16	179	200	48	427	1635
20	10		257	12	269	185	35	489	1536
27	10		180	15	195	183	54	432	1618
3	11		211	15	226	111	71	408	1618
10	11		246	45	291	235	54	580	1775
17	11		271	28	299	233	48	580	1586
24	11		222	15	237	74	42	353	1813
1	12		189	13	202	128	49	379	1443
8	12		275	48	323	174	30	527	–
15	12		278	15	293	260	54	607	–
22	12		–	–	–	–	–	–	–
29	12		hol.	hol.	hol.	hol.	hol.	hol.	hol.
5	1	74	107	8	115	83	5	203	1236
12	1		253	66	319	214	51	584	1249
19	1		192	35	227	170	33	430	1258
26	1		259	58	317	240	38	595	1336
2	2		227	54	281	143	40	464	1350
9	2		270	82	352	127	64	543	1567
16	2		269	63	332	129	54	515	1311
23	2		233	64	297	127	71	495	1364
2	3		215	92	307	190	17	514	1524
9	3		157	117	274	64	31	369	1791
16	3		300	70	370	105	14	489	2029
23	3		295	84	379	131	38	584	2101
30	3		234	35	269	77	36	382	2068
6	4		248	11	259	140	73	472	2023
13	4		281	4	285	173	39	497	1910
20	4		253	30	283	219	18	520	–
27	4		250	37	287	249	35	571	2164
4	5		298	59	357	159	46	562	2138
11	5		296	50	346	109	35	490	1996

ILLUSTRATION 10.3   Plate mill packing performance against overdue statement

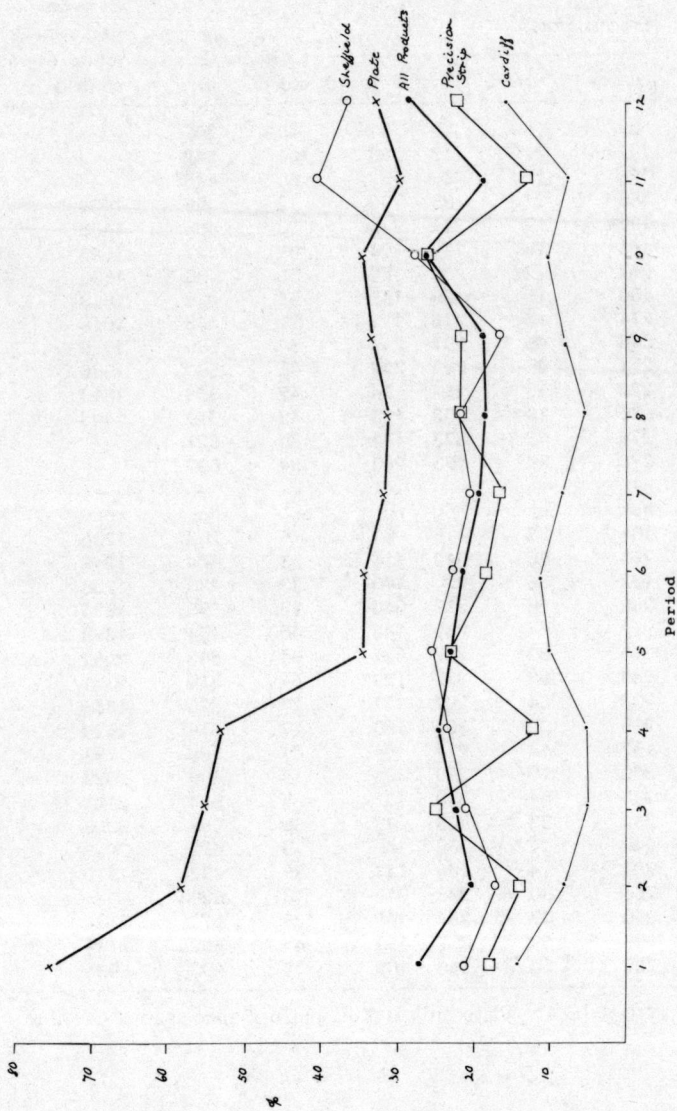

ILLUSTRATION 10.4 Delivery accuracy for various plants, April 1973 to April 1974 (% of items delivered more than 4 weeks after due week)

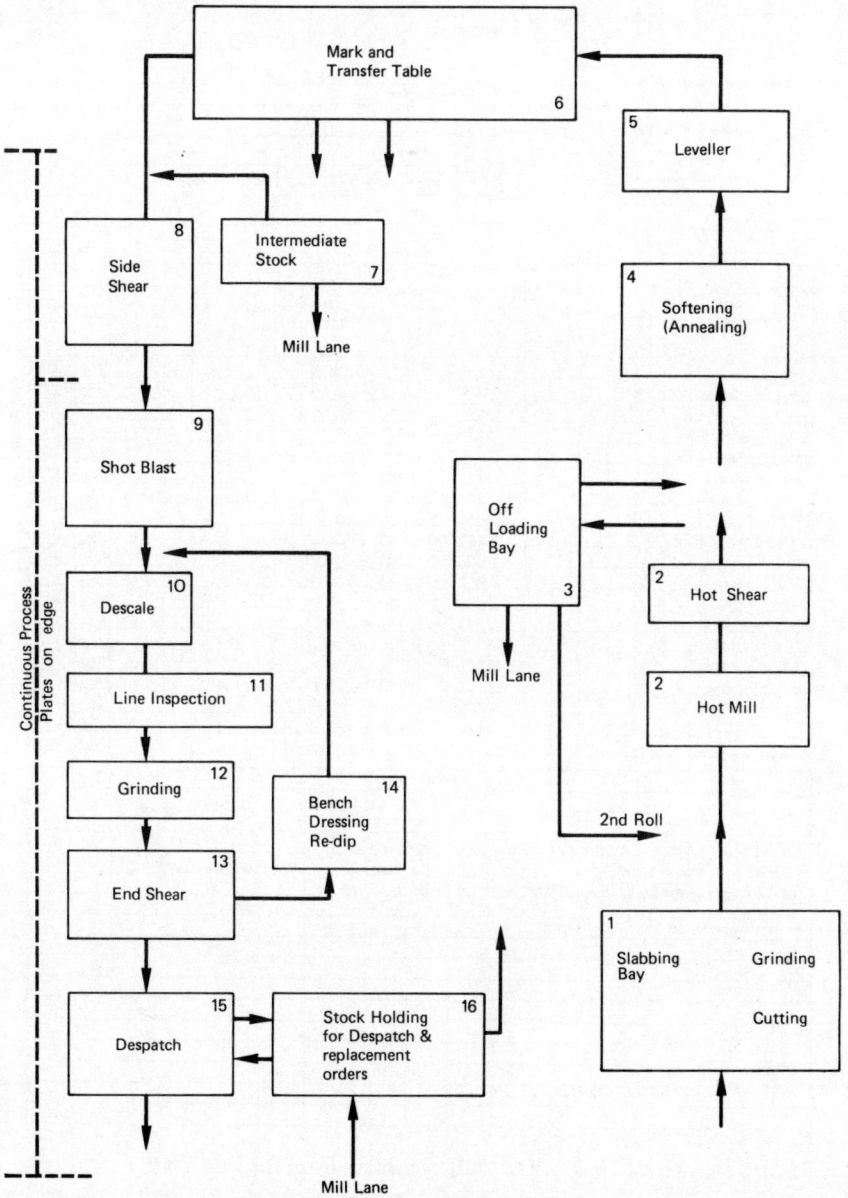

ILLUSTRATION 10.5   Layout of the plate mill

| DATE 18/6/75 | SHIFT 6-2 PM | OPERATION | SHOT BLAST (1 OF 2) | BACK (53) 43,364 | K |
| | | | | REO.R (13) 8,092 | |

SHIFT SUMMARY						
NUMBER OF PLATES PRODUCED	38	ML	MECHANICAL	70	S/E	START/END OF SHIFT
		E	ELECTRICAL		MG	MANNING
TOTAL LENGTH PROCESSED		NW	NO WORK/LINE DEMANNED	90	MS	MEALS	20
		PE	PLANNING ERROR			TOTAL STOPPAGES	3-00
NET HOURS WORKED	5-00	WC	WAITING CRANE			NET STOPPAGES	2-40

PRODUCTION

WORKS ORDER No.	LENGTH (INS)	WEIGHT t kg	WORKS ORDER No.	LENGTH (INS)	WEIGHT t kg
SD/11/A-2442/3	240	580	SD/19/A-5394/6	326	890
SD/28/W-1604/1	325		SD/23/A-6119/3	322	2150
— .. —	320		— .. —	326	
SD/28/W-1608/2	290		— .. —	322	
SD/23/A-6141/1	258	358	SD/27/A-6819/1	326	720
SD/28/W-1608/2	292		SD/33/A-6536/5	322	720
4D/09/K-2696/6	309		SD/27/A-6821/2	334	715
SD/28/W-1608/2	310		SD/27/A-6821/3	325	715
4D/28/K-7369/4	224	1605	SD/33/A-6536/3	330	715
— .. —	230		SD/27/A-6823/2	383308	715
SD/28/W-7422/1	396	540	SD/23/A-6114/3	333	1430
4D/09/K-2696/5	372	1756	— .. —	326	
SD/27/A-6822/3	370	730	SD/23/A-6380/3	335	715
SD/19/A-5361/4	370	1825	SD/27/A-6819/2	163	1040
SD/24/A-6521/2	309	2090	— .. —	306	
— .. —	165		SD/23/A-6113/3	155	1570
SD/23/A-6119/2	306	1045	— .. —	306	
— .. —	163		SD/30/W-1774/2	332	827
SD/24/A-6549/2	164	900	SD/27/A-6821/1	173	400

STOPPAGES AND DELAYS

CODE	REASON FOR DELAY	TIME From	TIME To	Total Time (Mins)	Bonus Ext.	COMMENTS
NW	WAITING ACCUMULATION OF WORK	6 00	7 00	60		
ML	NO 1 SIDE SHEARS.	7 30	9 00	90		← MEAL TIME INCLUDED
NW	WAITING DELIVERY OF PLATES FROM TRANSFER	9 00	9 30	30		
		.	.			
		.	.			
		.	.			
		.	.			
		.	.			
		.	.			
		.	.			

ILLUSTRATION 10.6   The shift recording form for shot blast

11 Managing Sales Variations: Adams Ice Cream

1. The Company

Adams Ice Cream is one of the four well known producers of ice-cream for desserts and confectionery products. Adams and its main national competitors produce approximately 80 per cent of the total ice-cream consumed in the United Kingdom, the remaining 20 per cent being produced by about 200 smaller firms also in the market. The company is part of the International Foods group and is therefore in a strong marketing and financial position. It has two factories, one at Winchester and one at Finchley, and over 30 depots for national distribution. The company headquarters and the main cold store are located at the Winchester site.

The Winchester works has over 400 employees. It is relatively new, having been built in 1959, and highly capitalised, giving a high value of plant on the balance sheet. A profit and loss account and a balance sheet are shown in Illustration 11.1. Total capital employed is therefore high relative to sales levels for this type of business despite the low contribution of debtors to working capital as nearly half the sales are paid for in cash.

For marketing purposes Adams' products are divided into five main product groups by type of eating situation:

Name	Type of customer	Approx % retail value	Approx no. of lines
Confectionery	Individual impulse purchasing	45	45
Entertainment	Cinemas, Theatres	5	10
Desserts	Take home	30	45
Catering	Hotels, etc., using deep freeze	15	40
Other (soft cream, wafers, hot dogs, paper bags)		5	—

Adams aim to provide a full range of ice-cream products to their customers and increasingly in recent years the revenue has become dominated by the accounts of the large multiple stores.

Many lines have a short life cycle. Sales, particularly in the impulse purchasing area, depend on novel shapes and styles of packaging and about 75 per cent of the products are changed in some degree each year. In 1960 there were about 40 lines: by 1970 this figure had reached 140, with 40 or 50 new lines each year replacing approximately the same number of existing lines. Appeal to children has been an important force towards variety. In the spring of 1972 a competitor brought out a special product to catch children's attention called 'King Arthur's Magic Potion'. This product was affecting Adams' sales in this impulse area by 5 per cent and within six weeks Adams brought out a rival product with a similar appeal called 'Frankenstein's Deadly Secret'.

2. Sales Forecasting

The whole of the Adams' operations are based on the sales forecasting scheme. In the autumn of each year the marketing staff prepare a forecast of total sales for each product for the next year so as to achieve an International Foods' Head Office total revenue target. Broadly, Adams expect their turnover to increase at the rate of rise of real incomes in the community. The annual forecast is first split down into product types based on the history of sales over the last year, new product styles, advertising plans and predicted competitors' policies. The estimated annual volume for each product is then phased into monthly requirements. (The monthly forecasts for 1972 for six major products are shown in the fifth column of each section of Illustration 11.4.)

The forecasts are based on a 'de-weatherised' forecasting system which Adams have built up on the basis of weather records over the last thirty years. The monthly sales are forecast assuming normal weather and the expected variation from this pattern is assessed for stock cover. For existing products the de-weatherised sales profiles over the year are known; for new products a profile is built up from the average of similar existing products. In building up the profiles for the next year an attempt is made to make allowances for the effects of new products competing with existing ones.

The demand pattern depends critically on the temperature. The ratio of peak weekly sales occurring during the summer to average weekly sales is about 2.3 to 1, with a ratio of 4 or 5 to 1 for a typical summer week compared with a typical winter week. The ratio of sales between successive summer weeks can often vary by as much as 2 to 1, because of changes in weather conditions. The graphs in Illustration 11.2 show how sales depend on maximum daily temperature and how they have varied during 1971.

Quite apart from the weather problem, marketing staff recognise that their forecasts are only best guesses and the uncertainty varies with the product line. For standard lines Vanilla Choc Bar, Vanilla Gallon and Vanilla Family Sweet, marketing estimate an error of only ±10 per cent in the cumulative total sales over the year (excluding weather effects). For products more in the impulse-purchasing area, however, the error can be much larger: Standard Vanilla Bar forecasts may deviate by 35 per cent and Ice Bangas by as much as 50 per cent. The uncertainty is most extreme for new products such as Strawberry Mousse, which may or may not catch on, and the error here may be as much as ±70 per cent. Of course as the year advances the errors can be reassessed and in April a major revision is made for new product lines.

To some extent the forecasts can be controlled by advertising but the effects are extremely difficult to disentangle. About half the advertising budget goes on special discounts for the shops and the remaining half on advertising directly to the public on television. The former merchandising promotions are conceived as 'come and buy' selling and the second type, on television, as 'go and buy'. But as a marketing manager stated: 'It is very difficult to influence our total annual market share by advertising. We can offer a discount and increase our sales by up to twice their normal level in any one month but this tends to draw off the sales from the surrounding months. The supermarkets may not bother to sell in the previous month because they know they'll sell next month and the consumers buy up in the discount month, store in their deep freezes, and don't buy so much in the following month. Generally we expect to sell at a 25 per cent increase in sales in the campaign month on the advertised lines and we hope to get a 10 per cent average increase above expected sales over the total three months. The effort on a campaign can cost £3000 per product line on the advertising charges alone. Alternatively a sales drop can be counteracted by a price reduction of 1p or 2p, which can stimulate demand by as much as 10 per cent over the next few months.

'Of course we are basically advertising ice-cream and all one may do is increase the purchases from our competitors. Or we may cause people to switch to the advertised line from another of our lines. It's very difficult to tell what's happening. We've been trying to build statistical models of the effects but it's tricky. Anyone who can do it is made! It's a little bit easier to study the effects now that we can apply regional effort through local television stations.'

3. The Production and Distribution Stages

The physical processes at Adams are typical of a large company manufacturing consumer products. Initial storage of food and packaging materials is followed by a machine-intensive mixing and forming stage and finally by a labour-intensive packing stage. The products are then inspected and entered into central cold stores at Winchester before being shipped on in Adams' transport to the 34 depots and ultimately sold to the customer. A large proportion of the costs goes on the materials — a much smaller proportion going into labour and distribution. A breakdown for the costs of the six products mentioned previously is shown in Illustration 11.3.

(1) Supplies
The whole working of the manufacturing system depends on the availability of the raw materials of vegetable oil, butter, milk and sugar which arrive in tankers and are poured directly into materials storage tanks. These food materials can be called off at short notice from a forward schedule given to suppliers and plenty of storage is available for these supplies at Winchester. Occasionally significant discounts can be obtained by the Adams buyer depending on the national market for the food items. Packaging materials for the final product on the other hand are designed specially for Adams and need to be ordered well in advance, the suppliers needing about seven weeks' notice to send the new batches for the individual package designs. This lead time has been increasing throughout 1972 because of the shortage of paper materials and the more novel styles of packaging required, and supplies are often up to four weeks late in arriving.

(2) Mixing and Packing
The production sequence begins by pumping supplies of ingredients into the 'high temperature — short time' pasteurisation equipment and mixing vats on the ground floor of the factory located next to the storage tanks. When the correct quantities have been mixed for a given product in a mixing vat, the liquid cream is pumped to the first floor to one of the production lines. Here it passes through a forming station where it is shaped into the product.

The forming station consists of a freezing tunnel where the product is cooled and shaped by the moulds, often many moulds at a time. Sometimes a stick is inserted when it is partially frozen and the product is automatically wrapped in its appropriate wrapper. The forming processes can generally make a small variety of product types with different moulds inserted. They are costly pieces of equipment. For example, the installed cost of a circular filling machine is about £22,000 and an extrusion machine £31,000: these are two main types of forming station.

As the products emerge from the forming machine on the conveyor belt, the packers for the line collect up the products and pack them in a cardboard or paper 'outer'. At a nearby final station a packer from the packaging team places the appropriate number of outers into the aluminium cans. (The aluminium can measuring 16 in. x 5½ in. x 8 in. is the standard unit for cost and capacity measurements.) The cans arrive at the final packaging stations on a continuous conveyor which starts from the point where empties are washed (delivered by trucks returning from the depots). The filled cans go on to a conveyor which runs parallel to the empty can conveyor right round the factory floor, finishing up at the cold store.

Adams have a large number of these forming and filling lines feeding the overall conveyor. The wide differences in the product requirements mean that the machines are not in use all the time. Average machine utilisation stands at only 300 eight-hour shifts per annum. The lines also require very different crew sizes. The machine types and crew requirements for the six products are shown in the table.

Product	Machine Type	Crew	Output rate (cans per hour)
Vanilla Choc Bar	Extrusion	4	50
Strawberry Mousse	Circular Filling	9	120
Vanilla Gallon	Circular Filling	7	250
Family Sweet	Extrusion	3	150
Vanilla Bar	Extrusion	2	70
Ice Banga	Circular Filling	6	50

Normally four extrusion machines and two circular filling machines are sufficient for the total production of these products, which collectively represent 25 per cent of total sales volume.

The bulk of the direct labour is employed on the forming and filling stations. Labour is paid on a day rate of 75p per hour and £1.00 per hour on the night shift. The operators are generally transferable between the production lines with a few shifts for training and gaining experience. Each line is cleaned at the end of each shift by the shift teams. The line will then be immediately available for use on the next shift unless the line is being switched to a different product or pack size. In this case an allowance of between one and three shifts lost production is made until the new line is operating under full efficiency. The allowance accounts for the reorganisation of materials and the crew's 'learning' time to gain full speed, and depends on the availability of moulds and packaging materials.

(3) Inspection

In the course of production all products are monitored for weight and inherent characteristics of the foodstuffs. Random checks are made of the weight of products and quality controllers also check the temperature of products in process. The ice-cream also passes under an electronic scanner. Samples are taken of all mixes as they enter products, and these products are not released from cold storage for at least two days while a bacteriological check is made and to allow for hardening of the ice-cream in the cold store. The frozen products are assumed to have a 20-week shelf-life in the cold store. When over-runs occur on risky products Adams can be forced to dump up to three weeks' worth of made stock and double that quantity of packaging materials.

(4) Distribution

The distribution chain runs from Winchester and Finchley cold stores (with 600,000 and 150,000 can capacities respectively), through the 34 depots scattered across the U.K. (with a total of 200,000 can storage capacity), through the retailers to the final customers. The cold store at Winchester costs around £150,000 per annum to operate, £37,500 of which is spent on labour for handling and administration. Extra cold storage space can be purchased in the Winchester area at a 10 per cent premium if necessary, and if any surplus space is available at Winchester it can be sub-let to external customers.

The general policy for distribution has been to keep the depot sizes to a minimum for their needs and to try to guarantee a good supply from the Winchester and Finchley cold stores. Each factory generally manufactures its own products but some of the finished stock is transferred between the main cold stores. The depots act as independent customers of the Winchester cold stores, placing their orders in 12, 14 or 18-pallet loads when they wish and receiving their orders one or two days later. The final retailers in turn place their orders (a minimum of two cans) with the depots once or twice a week (or in some cases once a fortnight or once a month) depending on the ratio of sales value per week to size of refrigerator. They are supplied by the depots within one or two days of making the order. This system relies heavily on the effectiveness of the central cold stores operations. The aim of the depot manager is to satisfy his local customers and he will be judged on his customer service in terms of total sales, shortages and customer complaints, and he mainly depends therefore on the speed of service he receives from Winchester and Finchley.

4. Planning of Capacity

From the monthly sales forecasts prepared in November for the year ahead
the production and stocks plans are computed. The planning effort is
distributed right across the organisation. First the sales plan (Illustration 11.4,
column 5) is passed to the company planner who reviews its consistency with
company policy and long-term trends and he tries to detect any special
operating problems. He also establishes the operating guidelines. This is a
written document which states: 'The basic rule is to have a stock level for any
product which, with the normal planned production in the first week, plus
overtime in the second week equal to 20 per cent of a normal week's
production, will meet a two-week 'peak' expectation and provide for normal
sales in the following third week.' The sales plan then goes to the distribution
manager and one of his assistants prepares a desired stock-building position
for each month (Illustration 11.4, column 6) giving the total stock at the end
of each month (at Winchester and the depots). The aim is to have at least one
month's stock at Winchester except during the peak summer months of June,
July and August. This stock requirement implies a production plan and the
figures are now passed over to the factory manager who considers the
implied labour loadings, technical restrictions on the equipment and maintenance schedules of four weeks on each machine.

The planning of the labour requirements is a delicate and vital part of the
procedure. The company factories normally work a variable working week of
36 hours in winter, 44 hours in spring and summer and 40 hours late summer
and autumn. A normal shift lasts eight hours. Normal night shift working is
based on four nights a week. Day shift working is based on four days in winter,
five days in summer and 4½ in the autumn. Overtime working at weekends is
not planned to be used but is available to cover unexpectedly good sales due
to unusually good weather conditions. Weekend working however can cost a
50 per cent premium on day labour rates. Part-time operators are taken on at
short notice and they are given several weeks warning of any lay-offs. Adams
have established good labour relations in the area and the same night staff
return when notices of vacancies are posted locally.

As well as full-time labour, the company employs seasonal labour and
student labour. Seasonal labour can be taken on during February and March,
but it is almost impossible to hire after April and May. Student labour is not
available before June or after September. Although seasonal labour may be
recruited at a little less than the rates for the base load operators the cost of
hiring and training may mean an extra premium on the base labour costs for
both night shift and day shift work. This premium has been increasing

recently with the extra training and skill necessary for the more specialised
new products with more complicated shapes.

The factory manager will alter the planned production to smooth his
labour requirements in the light of these conditions and satisfy his equipment
constraints and at the same time try to keep to the proposed plan. The factory
manager sets the final production figures (Illustration 11.4, column 4) for
each month and he will work out the implied day and night shift workings.
The factory plan may alter the implied stock positions and some renegotiation
will have to take place. Ultimately the agreed plans will be recorded on the
revised company plan as shown for the six products in Illustration 11.4.

But however much effort has been made on the forecasts and the planning
of capacity the actual sales inevitably do not match the forecasts. The actual
sales made, the production and stocks for the first four months of 1972 are
shown in brackets against the plans in Illustration 11.4. The problem is to
know whether to change the production plan and by how much in the light
of the requests of the different interest groups. Distribution staff aim to
keep a balanced load in the cold store to match current usage rates. Production
staff want to keep to the planned labour loadings and hold their budgets. They
have enough of a problem doing this as their actual output can be 15 per cent
below the quantity requested by the production control clerk. Marketing on
the other hand would like to request alterations to the production levels in
the light of their predicted sales changes and to meet their sales value targets.

The changes are managed by a number of exchanges between the interested
parties. Once a month at a review meeting, marketing give the revised forecasts to the factory and distribution managers and hope that these changes
can be accommodated. However, the changes do not always work out
harmoniously, for a mixture of reasons. In 1971 the sales level increased
substantially on one product which had been promoted on T.V., but its
production was limited to one machine and output never caught up with
sales. On another product, on which demand had weakened, marketing
launched a sales campaign but at the same time purchasing cancelled further
packaging materials as production staff had assumed the product was tailing
off. Throughout 1971 Adams marketing staff pushed the 3p products but
the public stuck to the 2p products in impulse purchasing despite the
advertising efforts.

Once a week production staff meet to work out the exact schedule which
they can operate in the light of the materials availability position. They
document any special information for communication to sales and distribution.

Even more immediate changes are made by short-term interventionist
tactics. If sales and distribution shout loud enough (and therefore convey

enough urgency) the production plan is switched to the specific lines they need. An urgent mid-week change can get a batch of product into cold store within 48 hours, and at the peak of the season the quoted 'priority' products can vary from day to day. The reason for switching is nearly always a cold store shortage. The Winchester staff assume that when the total stock position at Winchester and the depots falls to two weeks, Adams must be losing 20 per cent of sales on the product and if it falls to one week the lost sales are assumed to be of the order of 50 per cent.

One of the difficulties is that the stock position as recorded on the data is inevitably rather out of date. The stock control clerks record the intake of batches from production (allowing two days bacteriological clearance) and also respond to orders from depots within two or three days. All this data on inflows and outflows is punched up and entered on to the computer, which once a week on Tuesdays, prints out the state of stocks in cans in the main stores and in the field. The actual state of stocks printed is necessarily slightly out of date owing to the time it takes to prepare and process the information. The information available on the Tuesday when the stock sheet is printed relates to the sales up to the Thursday of the previous week. The Tuesday printout is generally examined by production staff for agreement at a meeting two days later for the proposed production in the following week. These delays in the provision of information about the central cold stores mean that the extra stocks have to be held to cover the uncertainty.

The independence of the depots has also led to uncertainties in the stocks position. As the distribution manager explained: 'The depots sometimes engage in "squirrelling". They hoard certain quantities of the products which they believe will sell well. The problem arises on the minor lines — the major product lines are being produced all the time anyway. But on a minor line, if there is four weeks' worth of stock in the field on a small product, half of it may be at one depot and the other thirty will have to share the rest. The remainder will then call for more of the product and this forces us to remake the line at Winchester when it is not really necessary; that in itself may cause us to lose sales on another line which we cannot produce in time. They do the same if they believe we're getting short of a product at Winchester. They may artificially raise their order by up to 25 per cent above their expectations so as to ensure a good quota. In fact we have been in the absurd situation when, if we want to get rid of a product, we tell the depots that we're short of it!

'But the reverse can happen too. The depots can create a false surplus due to the lags in the information system. If a large customer jerks up his demand for a product and the local depot thinks it is a rise in demand in general he may place a large order on us. This can lead us to make a very large run for a supposed real increase in demand which does not really exist. We may then have to scrap a significant quantity of ice cream.

These planning problems and the oscillations in the supply—demand relationships have caused the Adams board to reconsider the structure of the operational planning responsibilities and the methods for carrying out the required tasks. The intention is to create a new position of 'Operations Planner' spanning the functions with a responsibility for coordination. A management services group have also been examining the feasibility of using linear programming to prepare a manufacturing plan of weekly production for all products to meet the sales forecast and minimise the total expense of machine costs, labour costs and stockholding costs in a collective way.

Question for discussion

How should the stocks levels at Adams Winchester Cold Stores be planned and managed?

Profit and loss account 1972
(£000)s

	Sales	11173	11173
Less	Wages and salaries	2245	
	Ingredients	5556	
	Packaging materials	680	
	Welfare	115	
	Power	207	
	Repairs	313	
	Rent/rates, etc.	164	
	Advertising	417	
	Depreciation	499	
	Administration	448	
	Total costs	10644	10644
	Net profit		529
Add	Miscellaneous income		435
	Total profit		94

Balance sheet

Fixed assets	*Cost*	*Depreciation*	*Net*
Land	326	–	326
Buildings	2936	704	2232
Plant	7476	4150	3325
Others	1178	617	561
	11916	5471	6444

Trade investments		
Loan		204

Working capital		
Stocks	976	
Debtors	901	
Cash	8	
	1885	
Creditors	1371	
Short term loans	379	134

Shareholders' interest (equity)	6782
Shares + retained profits	

ILLUSTRATION 11.1   Annual accounting statements

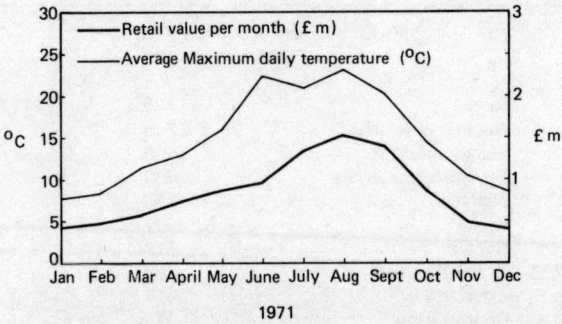

(a) Retail Value and Temperature by month in 1971

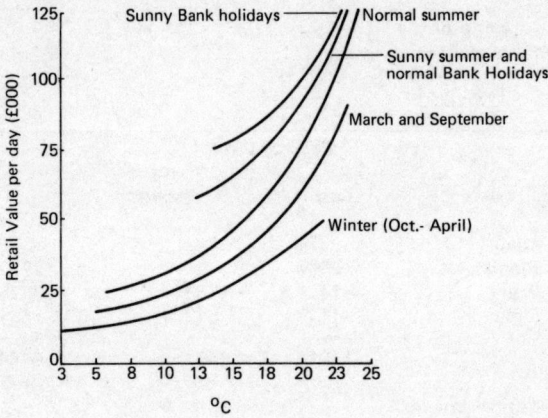

(b) Retail Variation by Daily Temperature

ILLUSTRATION 11.2   Demand variation with temperature

Product and trade group	Vanilla Choc/bar (confectionary)	Strawberry Mousse (dessert)	Standard Vanilla Gallon (catering)	Vanilla Family Sweet (dessert)	Standard Vanilla Bar (confectionary)	Ice Banga (confectionary)
Number of products per can	108	60	2	18	90	120
Wholesale price can (includes tax)	£4.20	£2.20	£1.96	£1.98	£2.80	£1.88
Labour cost (including mixing, can filling and packing)	£0.12	£0.13	£0.04	£0.05	£0.03	£0.18
Variable overhead	£0.10	£0.10	£0.04	£0.04	£0.04	£0.10
Process cost (including raw materials, packing materials and cans)	£1.92	£0.85	£0.62	£0.58	£0.53	£0.50
Cost of distribution	£0.25	£0.25	£0.25	£0.25	£0.25	£0.25
Contribution to overhead	£1.80	£0.87	£1.01	£1.05	£1.95	£0.85

ILLUSTRATION 11.3 Product cost details

735   VAN CHOC BAR x 216 V

WINC.	SHIFTS D	N	PRODN	SALES	END STOCK
B/Fwd					13
Jan	20		8 (7)	6 (6)	15 (14)
Feb	35		14 (12)	5 (8)	24 (18)
Mar	47		19 (49)	13 (17)	30 (27)
Apr	43	44	35 (32)	24 (31)	41 (26)
May	30	70	40	25	56
June	44	45	39	42	53
July	45	44	39	59	33
Aug	30	40	24	39	18
Sept	58		23	24	17
Oct	18		7	5	19
Nov	20		8	8	19
Dec	18		7	7	19
Year			263	259	

844   MOUSSE STRAW x 120

	SHIFTS D	N	PRODN	SALES	END STOCK
B/Fwd					2.2
Jan	2		1.9 (1.9)	1.9 (1.9)	2.2 (2.2)
Feb	2		1.9 (2.0)	1.5 (1.9)	2.6 (2.1)
Mar	1	1	2.4 (2.3)	2.4 (2.2)	2.6 (2.9)
Apr	2	1	3.5 (3.1)	2.6 (2.0)	3.5 (4.4)
May	2	1	3.1	3.0	3.6
June	2	1	3.1	3.5	3.2
July	2	1	3.1	3.5	2.8
Aug	1	1	2.5	2.0	3.3
Sept	1		1.3	2.1	2.5
Oct	1	1	1.9	2.1	2.3
Nov	2		1.9	1.6	2.6
Dec	1		1.3	1.4	2.5
Year			27.9	27.6	

114   GAL STA VANILLA

WINC.	SHIFTS D	N	PRODN	SALES	END STOCK
B/Fdw					48
Jan	30	2	45 (40)	7 (17)	86 (71)
Feb	4	1	29 (25)	12 (8)	103 (97)
Mar	17	17	35 (40)	17 (19)	121 (118)
Apr	7	7	29 (30)	32 (32)	118 (116)
May	2	2	7	27	98
June	10	11	42	34	116
July	13	10	47	53	110
Aug	11	4	30	38	102
Sept	10	4	29	29	102
Oct	10	4	29	29	102
Nov	12	2	29	28	103
Dec	8		17	29	91
Year			378	345	

022   FS VANILLA x 36

	SHIFTS D	N	PRODN	SALES	END STOCK
B/Fdw					21
Jan	11	7	22 (20)	15 (13)	28 (25)
Feb	6	4	11 (15)	11 (6)	28 (34)
Mar	16	15	38 (30)	16 (13)	50 (49)
Apr	20	27	57 (50)	56 (50)	51 (49)
May	20	26	56	45	62
June	20	26	56	55	63
July	26	20	56	73	46
Aug	19	10	35	42	39
Sept	22		27	31	35
Oct	35		30	33	32
Nov	29		35	24	43
Dec	18		22	21	44
Year			445	422	

030   STA VAN BAR x 180 V

WINC.	SHIFTS D	N	PRODN	SALES	END STOCK
B/Fwd					21
Jan	7		4 (2)	4 (4)	21 (19)
Feb	10		6 (8)	5 (6)	22 (21)
Mar	18		11 (10)	8 (9)	25 (22)
Apr	40	5	26 (20)	21 (21)	30 (21)
May	40	20	34	24	40
June	39	30	39	31	48
July	31	27	33	48	33
Aug	20	10	17	29	21
Sept	9		5	14	12
Oct	9		5	13	4
Nov	9		5	4	5
Dec	9		5	4	6
Year			190	205	

738   BANGA x 240

	SHIFTS D	N	PRODN	SALES	END STOCK
B/Fwd					10
Jan	18		7 (6)	2 (2)	15 (14)
Feb	10		4 (6)	3 (3)	16 (17)
Mar	12		5 (6)	6 (5)	15 (19)
Apr	32		14 (12)	10 (10)	19 (20)
May	32		14	13	20
June	30	20	20	16	24
July	30	22	21	24	21
Aug	32	26	23	16	28
Sept	7		3	11	20
Oct	7		3	6	17
Nov	5		2	3	16
Dec	7		3	2	17
Year			119	112	

ILLUSTRATION 11.4   Production, sales and stocks (£) for the six lines for 1972 (000 cans)

Part E: Coordination and Control

The final section studies the connections between the overall company strategies and the operational management tasks. Often there is a wide gap between the future plans as determined at board level and the necessary tactics for the operations management team to carry out the current commitments. The terms of reference are very different. The board thinks in terms of annual profit and market share, whereas the operations managers worry about individual sales, deliveries, shortages and weekly output. The variables which the board consider are new products, new technologies and new sites, whereas the operational staff are concerned with existing products, processes and customers. Yet somehow, to be effective, a company must have a way of translating company policy into the detailed implications for operational planning and control. The company ultimately succeeds by succeeding in current terms and stretching the operational team to the right limits at the right times. Much of the divide between the top and the bottom of companies could be overcome if the operational managers could properly represent their current tasks to the board and interpret the implications of possible company strategies in their own terms.

The connection between company policy and operations management is very individual to each company situation and it would be impossible to provide a general framework for success. (On the other hand the absence of an effective link is usually fairly easily identified in unfulfilled company promises and wasted resources.) The focus for the linkage is through the production planning system, which is the means for relating the daily operations towards the longer-term objectives. If the production planning system is working correctly it can be the main cause of company success; if it is failing then it may require that the whole company strategy be altered.

The first case in this section deals with a situation where the production planning system is working well to achieve the company policy in a large integrated furniture manufacturing company. The second case demonstrates the reverse: the point where the policy of a medium-sized children's clothes manufacturer is beginning to make a great demand on its production planning capability, and the whole system and its performance are beginning to break down. Both these situations are fairly large and the needs of a sophisticated planning system limit the degree of company flexibility which can be accommodated.

The final case is an illustration of a complete contrast: a small company without any planning system outside the mind of one man, the managing director, where total flexibility can be engineered at a moment's notice to almost any extent. Although the company has a main product in aircraft crop sprays it makes almost everything else with every kind of technical and personnel policy. Despite the fact that every rule in the textbook is broken, the single-mindedness of the source of operational authority and company policy provides a guarantee of company performance.

12 Coordinating Sales and Production: Gomme's Furniture

1. The Company

The name of Gomme has been associated with fine furniture for the last 200 years. There is a chest made by James Gomme with a label attached which reads:

> Sold at the original upholstery warehouse of James Gomme, in High Wycombe, where Cabinet Work is done and orders for household furniture of every description executed in the best, and most fashionable manner, 1798.

By the end of the nineteenth century there were about 100 chair manufacturers in High Wycombe. Frequently skilled craftsmen set up on their own. Mr Ebenezer Gomme, who had been apprenticed as a chair-maker and who had worked as a craftsman in several High Wycombe factories, established his own business in 1898 with a capital of £40. From this small beginning the business prospered through hard work and the quality of the products sold. The company went public in 1958 as a holding company and now has an issued capital of 6,448,240 Ordinary Shares at 25p and 500,000 £1, 7 per cent cumulative preference shares. The company stayed in the control of the family and Mr D. L. Gomme is now chairman of the main subsidiary, with Mr D. G. A. Owen as its managing director.

Before the Second World War the company developed a range of dining room, bedroom and upholstered furniture and chairs of outstanding quality and original design. In 1952 the G-Plan theme of 'furniture for the whole home' was launched. This was developed from an earlier range of designs and was nationally advertised with immediate success. Sales multiplied by five times in the next six years. National advertising and the G-Plan brand name have been the basic ingredients of the growth of the company.

The company aims to provide good-value, well-made furniture for the middle and upper-middle income groups and offers a planned choice throughout the house. The range includes 150 models (the upholstered models having various possible coverings) in five groups:

Dining room (sideboards, tables and chairs)	20 models
Wall units (bookcases, cupboards)	39 „
Bedroom units (chests, wardrobes, dressing-tables)	13 „
Upholstered chairs and sofas	59 „
Occasional tables	19 „

The company sells to several hundred main customers and delivers to even more retail outlets in their own vans. Gommes sell their products to the retailer, who will add another 80 per cent mark-up on the wholesale price, inclusive of V.A.T. The total turnover in 1974 was around £15 million and the company has continued to grow at about 15 per cent per annum on volume throughout the last decade. By any financial criterion the company has been extremely successful during this period, usually obtaining a return on capital employed (before tax) in the region of 40 per cent.

Most of the production takes place at the Spring Gardens, High Wycombe, site (established in 1928), which has a full range of modern equipment. The manufacturing processes are fully integrated through buying in timber, drying, cutting, machining, assembling and finishing. A separate line feeds the surfaces of veneers stuck to chipboard into the machining area. In 1959 the company purchased a large cotton mill in Nelson (Lancashire) in order to expand the manufacture of upholstered furniture. Deep upholstered work has now been transferred from Wycombe to Nelson. The total number of employees at High Wycombe is 1200, split between 840 hourly paid, 130 weekly paid and 230 on the monthly payroll. The labour is fully unionised and although the traditional craft skill in the furniture field has been steadily eroded over the previous decades with the advance of machinery, there have been no significant labour relations problems. The payment is based on a piece-rate system and operatives on the day shift can earn up to £3500 per annum, and on the night shift up to 25 per cent more, the bonus amounting to 50 per cent of wages.

The general operating policy has been to hold and gradually increase the labour force and to accommodate fluctuations in sales by lengthening or shortening the order book. The value of the order book has varied from £2 million to £14 million as shown in the table.

	1971	1972	1973	1974	1975
Value of order book (£m.)	2	5	14	8	12
Length of delivery lead time (months)	7	14	18	5	7

Despite the long order book there has been resistance to any form of uncontrolled expansion. In the early 1960s the company invested in an expansion programme which turned out to be excessive, and since that time the board has been cautious about repeating expansionary moves. The long delivery times testify to the attraction of the G-Plan range in the market place.

The company has an integrated and established management team covering the major functional responsibilities. Much of its strength lies in its design team, who aim to maintain the G-Plan image. In recent years Gommes extended their range to include a more traditional style in addition to the Scandinavian image which has proved so popular since the 1960s. In the autumn of 1974 a new 'Arcadia' range was introduced, increasing the number of models by 15 per cent.

Generally the company has no problems with access to supplies, although the adequate supply of timber at economic prices is becoming an increasing problem. Individual deliveries are based on a call-off schedule from the suppliers. As with any furniture operation the yield on original cubic feet of timber runs at approximately 40 per cent. Any saving on material wastage can make a significant contribution as materials costs are four times the direct labour costs — the total direct costs running at around 45 per cent of sales cost.

The starting point of the planning system is the annual budget. The financial budget runs from 1 August to 31 July and is created in the usual way. The annual forecast in total is made; this is broken down into models by week in financial terms; it is then further translated into standard hours on machinery and assembly, which leads to an accounting budgetary control system based on standard costing and cost centres.

The actual planning and control of physical operations and the orders are handled by three teams: sales administration under Doyne North, production administration under Tony Consterdine, and data processing and systems under Ray Southgate and John Keep. All these staff have worked with the company for six or more years. As Doyne North stated: 'In theory the operational planning and control is all straightforward: I get the orders, Tony despatches them, and Ray provides the paperwork in between.' In fact, of course, it is a very complex task with a large number of factors all interacting with one another. However the organisation of operations can be divided into the three sequential but overlapping streams of activities:

Sales Administration
Production Planning
Production Control.

The streams are linked by the overall budget plan and a series of meetings and close personal contact. The whole of the company operations are very much geared up to a strong and effective data processing system which has been specifically and carefully designed by Gomme's staff for their own needs.

2. Orders Management by Sales Administration

The sales administration staff under Doyne North receive incoming orders from the customers. The orders are sorted into 'delivery groups' which are the basic units to be despatched. A customer order will consist of one or more delivery groups and any one delivery group consists of up to five models all belonging to the same major product group: Dining, Bedroom, Wall Units, Occasional and Upholstered.

Usually orders are given a T.B.A. (to be advised) reference for future delivery date quotation. The length of lead time varies as a forward reservations system has to operate for some key customers who take high volumes of orders. They commit their quota of output in advance and arrange for the deliveries of that quota to particular outlets about ten weeks in advance of actual despatch. These commitments appear as orders (delivery groups) much nearer the despatch date. For all orders, the details of each delivery group are prepared on a punching document by sales administration and passed to data processing for entry into the outstanding orders file held on the computer. Each day a computer run prepares an 'acknowledgement set' of documents for sales administration for all orders which have arrived two or three days earlier. These take the form shown in Illustration 12.1.

Orders are assigned a delivery date in due course against a production programme. Every month production control supply a planned assembly schedule for 'one month' six months ahead showing planned model builds by week. (The form of the plan is shown in Illustration 12.2.) Sales administration create a chart displaying the committed reservations and the availability of individual models. The chart is on graph paper divided into sections by model. A dash in a section indicates an availability and an X indicates a reservation. The sales administration assistants book these forthcoming supplies off against customer orders waiting on the T.B.A. list. The total number of bookings made by the four salesgirls each week is 6500. Once a customer's delivery group has received a booking the week number is fed back to data processing, who enter the date on the outstanding orders file. Collecting up all the information on committed orders, data processing produce a weekly statement of the forward load of outstanding orders, showing the quantity and value over the next six months by model (see Illustration 12.3).

The outstanding orders file is later used by data processing to generate further important sets of documents for sales administration activities. Approximately six or seven weeks prior to delivery, data processing scan the outstanding orders file, and produce the 'delivery set' of forms for each delivery group (see Illustration 12.1). These go to sales administration who send them on to the despatch department in readiness for 'tagging' the goods when they actually come through to the despatch area. When the goods are despatched the 'blue copy' of this set comes back to data processing and they produce an 'invoice set' daily. At the same time a multi-copy load list summary of the furniture on each van is printed by the computer for use by sales, production and despatch. One copy is kept in accounts as an audit document. The 'blue copy' of the despatch set is also used by data processing to generate a weekly despatches statement by customer arranged in alphabetical order (see Illustration 12.4).

3. The Production Planning Procedure

The objective of production planning is to create a detailed statement of the manufacturing intentions in the light of the sales forecasts and the individual customer requirements. The decisions on the final assembly outputs have to be made sufficiently far in advance for the organisation of primary manufacture to be correctly coordinated. As explained before, the leading step in the production planning activities is the month-by-month creation of the forward assembly programme six months ahead. The assembly programme for May 1975 (weeks 40, 41, 42, 43) prepared at the end of October 1974 is shown in Illustration 12.2 (one sixth of the total is shown).

The month's assembly programme starts to be 'worked' approximately three months in advance, with about four weeks allowed for actual assembly, although the actual assembly process takes only two or three days. The first two months of the three-month period are needed for the generation of the parts for assembly. Under certain circumstances a machining batch can cover assembly from two to ten weeks.

The initiation of piece-parts manufacture is firmed up on a 'one-week load' at a time basis. Geoff Castle (the production planner working for Tony Consterdine) decides a weekly list of models which he needs to be completed in seven or eight weeks' time for the assembly plan. He fills in a set of 'model batch lead cards' specifying the model number, final week required and quantity. There are up to 30 such cards per week (see Illustration 12.5). Geoff Castle tries to choose the set of cards to satisfy the assembly programme and at the same time to balance the machining facilities by using his knowledge of the machine shop. He also has to bear in mind the problems of congestion both in the mill and the piece parts stores.

This 'model' load for a particular week is analysed by data processing into a detailed piece-part manufacturing requirement. Data processing receive the batch of cards indicating the final machining week, and once a week, using the 'model piece-part file', they 'explode' the model requirements into the 'gross piece-part requirements' needed. The 'model piece-part file' is shown in Illustration 12.6 giving some of the parts needed for Model 1195D. The master parts are indicated down the left-hand column. Some of these are individual components, but others, such as master part 1194010 are called composite masters, referring to a list of component parts which go into the master. Each component has the material 'specie code' shown together with the quantity per component and the dimensions. Finally the master part description is given together with the number per assembly and the 'lead time' or time allowed in the machine shop in weeks for processing the part. The model piece-part file therefore provides the precise details of the parts needed for assembly of the model and the elapsed time for manufacture.

By collecting up all the piece-parts for all the models in the week's intake of model batch cards, the gross piece-part requirements are prepared in master part sequence, combining any common parts in shared lists. This is shown in Illustration 12.7 which is a page of the gross piece-part requirements printout. Geoff Castle receives this list of gross piece-parts and examines the actual physical stock of the items and assesses the quantities of any parts coming forward from his knowledge of launched programmes. He then issues a list of amendments to the gross requirements and sends these to data processing, who amend their list of piece-parts for the appropriate week in the computer file.

This final 'net' set of piece-parts required for approximately six weeks ahead enables the data processing staff to use the material requirements details on lead times and quantities (from the piece part file in Illustration 12.6) to generate material requirements for the manufacture of the parts in the machine shop. These material requirements are expressed as 'cutting lists' placed with the three conversion shops: timber conversion, chipboard conversion and veneer conversion. They are arranged by specie and given to the conversion shops two weeks in advance of the required dates for completion of cutting. Data processing also issue tickets to the conversion shops on which to record the quantities actually supplied to the machine shop. (These tickets later pass through the data processing section.) A part of one page of the timber cutting list is shown in Illustration 12.8. (There are normally 60 such pages issued each week.)

The last step in the production planning procedure is to issue, once a month, a four-week detailed forecast of raw material requirements and machine loading for six to ten weeks ahead, although the initial purchasing cycle is started with a material forecast of requirements five to six months ahead. The detailed forecast has to line up closely with the forward forecast if Gommes are not to run into material supply problems. The forecast of raw materials is made out for timber, chipboard, veneer and ply. (The forecast for timber is shown in Illustration 12.9.) This is needed by purchasing as the conversion shop plans are geared directly to the final assembly programmes and they assume that the necessary raw material requirements will be present when required. Close liaison is maintained between the conversion shops and the staff controlling raw materials supplies. This is particularly important in the case of timber as kilning time can vary between a few days and one month. Data processing also issue a forecast machine loading summary showing the expected loads on the machine groups (Illustration 12.10). This is computed by using the 'component routing file' described in the next section and is needed by production control to advise the works management on the expected loadings on the sections (called production control categories in Illustration 12.10) so that any labour overtime or extra labour recruitment can be planned.

4. Monitoring the Plan

After the planning stage the real test comes in making the plan work. This divides into two activities: the physical issue of instructions by production control to do the work and the monitoring of the actual achievement by data processing staff.

On the assembly side the warehouse (despatch) staff responsible to production control generate a specific weekly programme on the various assembly shops (see Illustration 12.11) aiming to keep the assembly lines busy, balanced and in line with the original programme prepared six months earlier. In preparing this programme, the programmer has to take account of part availability from the machine shop, paperwork availability from sales (despatch notes) and labour availability in assembly. In Illustration 12.11 it can be seen that the model number is listed under two priority numbers giving the machining week number and the assembly week number, e.g. Model 4070 was programmed to be machined in week 43 and assembled in week 48. The difference between the load in standard hours and capacity in Illustration 12.11 is deliberate, to allow for arrears from one programme to another. The assembly programmes are given to the assembly supervisors who request an issue of parts and a block of work tickets. (Normally assembly is done in lots of 50 on the various lines.) When they reach the warehouse they get despatched in delivery groups and the despatch tickets are returned to sales and data processing to trigger invoicing activity.

The success of the assembly programme really depends on the availability of the machine parts according to plan. The physical commitments start irreversibly in the machine shop when production control staff receive a 'week's worth' of job tickets from data processing for the machine shop piece-part manufacturing programme for a particular week several weeks in advance of the time they are needed on the plan. There is one ticket per operation per part (see Illustration 12.12). The progress men (from production control) physically issue the job tickets to the foremen in charge of the various areas in the machine shop when the work-in-progress will allow the extra volume into the machine shop. Material is drawn from the conversion shops and the work is moved in batches on barrows through the operations and is ultimately placed in piece-parts store. The tickets are then returned for payment purposes and acknowledgement of receipt by stores. A copy also reaches the data processing section.

Meanwhile data processing are trying to monitor the execution of the plan in the machine shop and to help production control to have the appropriate information for deciding which activities to chase. This is achieved in two ways: firstly by creating and maintaining a work-in-progress file on the machine shop and secondly by providing information for production meetings.

The work-in-progress file holds details of the status of all outstanding work in the machine shop. Creating this file requires a calculation of the expected flow rates through the machine shop. After the 'net requirements' for a week's machining load has been established, data processing use an 'operations routing file' to calculate an estimated completion date for each operation on each piece-part on each planned machine in the machine shop. The 'routing operations file' (maintained by work study) indicates the machine routing for each of the 6000 piece-parts (see Illustration 12.13). The routing operation file gives the planned machine group (amongst the 140 machines in the machine shop) as well as alternatives and the standard times and bonus times for the work on that machined part. This timing data is used to predict a 'gap' in hours between successive operations in the manufacture of the part as:

$$\text{Gap Hours} = \left[\left(\begin{array}{l} \text{Lead time in week for} \\ \text{manufacture of part} \end{array} \right) \times 40 + \left\{ \begin{array}{l} \text{30 if complicated} \\ \text{part, or 20 if simple} \\ \text{part} \end{array} \right\} \right.$$

$$\left. - \text{ set-up time} - \text{standard time} \right] \div \text{Number of operations}$$

The calculated 'gaps' usually lie between eight and twenty hours, and are used to work back from the due date for the batch and thus estimate the completion dates for each operation. Illustration 12.14 shows these estimated completion dates in column 6 on a small part of the work-in-progress file for batches intended to be completed in week '532', i.e. week 32 of 1975. (There are about 1000 batches in progress at any one time on the shop floor.)

As the work is completed — normally a man will complete two or three batches per day in the machine shop — the tickets go through the payroll system and are passed on to data processing. They input the quantities passed, and record the first and last date on which the batch was worked on on each machine (see Illustration 12.14, columns 7, 8 and 9). Separately 'pink tickets' from production control reach data processing staff and they record the 'completion date' for the work as it is known to production control. This is entered on the top line on each batch on the work-in-progress file. Finally 'advice' is received from stores that the 'complete' batch has arrived. This appears on the bottom line of dates about a batch in Illustration 12.14. All this information is recorded by data processing and used to give the state of progress on all the outstanding work.

Finally, the work-in-progress file is used to prepare weekly action and status reports for production meetings, giving 'work-to-lists' by machine group each week (Illustration 12.15), the outstanding operations by model by week (Illustration 12.16), and the quantities which have gone into stores, by model (Illustration 12.17). Also the information on work done is used to record the day and hours production by machine (Illustration 12.18), so that output and efficiencies can be monitored.

5. The Problem with Deliveries in 1975

Despite this sophisticated and effective operations planning system, Gommes ran into some serious delivery problems in 1975. Deliveries were being made five or six weeks late and some orders were being despatched three to four months later than the date originally promised.

The cause of the problem did not necessarily lie with the planning system itself; both Doyne North and Tony Consterdine attributed the difficulties to the effects of the new Arcadia range on the production schedules and the surprising buoyancy of the market for the existing older lines which had been expected to decline. Doyne North stated the position: 'The manufacturing times for the Arcadia range were underestimated and these uncertainties combined with the larger range were bound to cause extra queueing problems in manufacture. Also the spending boom in consumer durables which had gone on into 1975 despite (or perhaps because of) current inflation levels had made it hard to estimate what demand levels would actually be like.' Doyne also stated that the intention to keep deliveries down to six months' lead time had been impossible 'and the consequential faulty estimates of lead time had probably contributed to the problems.'

Doyne North considered the lateness problem a matter for urgent concern. In the spring of 1975 the managing director set up a special programme committee of the operations managers to meet once a month to monitor this area of potential danger. Doyne had no obvious remedies to hand. It was an extremely difficult job to quote delivery dates a long time in advance. He said: 'In theory you could leave the quotation of dates till much nearer the delivery time and then they would be much more accurate, but the customer wants to know some sort of date as early as possible. And the customer to Gommes is the retail salesman who gets paid on commission when the goods are actually delivered. Although cancellations (running normally at about 8 per cent) have not increased yet, if we lose the retailers' good will we're in real trouble.' Doyne hoped that the coordinated efforts of the programme committee would bring the situation under control.

Tony Consterdine considered that the only remedy was to stretch the order book out for a period until the backlog had been cleared even if this meant fouling up some more current delivery dates. He considered that there were no 'physical remedies' even in the longer run with the current integrated operations and space limitations on the Spring Gardens site. The most obvious possibility for reducing lead times was to uncouple the piece-part manufacturing from the assembly lines by the creation of a piece-part store, re-ordering independently from the machine shop. If this was implemented Tony Consterdine thought it might lead to increases in machine, labour and materials utilisation as longer runs would be possible and more discretion over the mix of parts could be exercised at any time. He had recently estimated that he might get a 10 per cent increase in labour and manpower utilisation if he could double the current run lengths. But the piece-part store idea had not found favour generally. It would cost a lot of extra money as there was no room for it in a single location at the Spring Gardens site, and a systems study prepared by Ray Southgate in 1970 had raised severe doubts as to the economics and effectiveness of an off-site parts store stressing the necessary high calibre staff to run a disciplined parts store properly.

Tony Consterdine concluded: 'As long as the piece-part store remains essentially a work-in-progress store we have to look to the organisation of the machine shop as the key to keeping the whole system in balance. But even here we come up against the shortage of space. We tried introducing the cell system for group-technology ideas into the machine shop but took it out again. The idea was to line up certain machines with specific assembly lines (although the assembly areas are physically on the first floor). But the imbalance on the loads meant that labour had to move about and work-in-progress built up and we have no room for movements around piles of bits in the machine shop. The point should be made that the basic limitations of the site are space — three floors with parts having to go up and down lifts — and a normal general shortage of labour in the area making it very difficult to absorb fluctuations in load.

'I think we will simply have to manage our current policy more honestly. Basically we work to the job ticket plan, go flat out on the day shift, and call in a highly flexible night shift crew (amounting to about 50 per cent of the staff on days) to work on the bottlenecks, the shortages and the delayed items. The night shift have their work list prepared by production control staff during the preceding afternoon. They list the operator's name, his clock number, his machine number, his machine and the work that he is required to perform during the night. He may be asked to do several jobs. Any details of why the work could not be done are recorded. The lists are supplemented by the appropriate job tickets. This night shift scheme provides the essential element of immediate flexibility. We may complain about the shortage of space limiting our production management options, but it forces the kind of coordination on us which may be the secret of our success.'

In some ways Ray Southgate and John Keep in data processing may be in the best position to take an independent view of the means of improving the control of deliveries. They have access to a great deal of the data and instrumentation of the manufacturing operations. As Ray stated: 'Our data processing activities have a responsibility to provide an independent pressure for improved control because they can reveal what is actually happening and not simply what is presumed to be happening. Our objective is to provide production control and sales administration with the relevant information in a quiet perceptive way — to show what is wrong and to give assistance without making demands for a change in their personalised approaches.'

Certainly the information processed by data processing can show that difficulties are occurring in 1975. The delivery promise failures produced for individual weeks of June 1975 show both failures to meet deliveries as well as serious anticipated future failures. For three weeks of June 1975, these were running at

Week	546	547	548
Value of actual failure to deliver	£ 67,412	73,010	69,073
Value of anticipated failures	£967,735	559,646	461,445

The data held in the computer can also show the back record of average lateness of batches completed in the machine shop. An analysis of this has shown that average lateness of batches completed over the period from August 1974 to the end of June 1975, ran constantly at three to five weeks late.

In his position to observe the production system, John Keep suggested four possible reasons for the broken delivery promises:

the sheer complexity of the scheduling job with more than 30,000 delivery groups loaded into the forward assembly programme;
the changes made to the assembly programme inside the final six weeks;
delays in the machine shop prior to the assembly lines;
the difficulty of assessing 'allowance' by sales when making delivery promises.

In his view the route to success is a subtle one: to increase flexibility in one dimension and to reduce it in another. He suggests that the assembly programme should be fixed six to eight weeks prior to delivery and taken as gospel. But, ahead of this six weeks, complete flexibility should remain and the promise of deliveries should be delayed.

Even under that system he thought they would have to go on living with the problems of the machine shop. He had come round to the view that the assembly lines 'behaved' themselves in capacity terms. He calculated the machine shop load in standard hours (prior to assembly) from the hours in the despatches actually made (after assembly) over a month and found a surprisingly steady load::

	Week 1	Week 2	Week 3	Week 4
Despatches in week (number)	37	38	39	40
Machine shop load (hrs)	3,059	3,341	3,239	3,181

This suggested that the delivery quotes should concentrate on ensuring that the machine shop load was in balance without worrying too much about assemblies. As the whole process starts with a financial budget there is a tendency for sales to set the loads by smoothing sales levels or at most model levels and this in turn becomes translated into assembly programmes. One of John Keep's objectives therefore was to develop the concept of loading orders by machine shop standard units, and for this purpose he had computed the capacities and loads from June to December 1975 indicating the implied imbalance (see Illustration 12.19). If a scheme of loading could be established to smooth the demands on the machine shop then reliable and reasonable 'work-to-lists' could be prepared showing which parts should be worked on and at what rate each week as a detailed and effective forward plan.

A major threat remaining to any such scheme of detailed planning would be the reliability of the feedback information itself. Often the data processing department had serious doubts about the accuracy of the work-in-progress information coming from the machine shop — both with regard to times and quantities of completed batches. However, a survey checking back over the last year revealed a steady improvement from 60 per cent to 80 per cent in the correlation between quantities actually coming off individual operations and the quantities which had been planned, which was an encouraging sign. These results confirmed both the viability of the existing control systems and the potential for further improvements.

Question for discussion

Analyse the functions of the reporting in Gomme's production control system.

E. GOMME LTD.
P.O. BOX 27, HIGH WYCOMBE
BUCKS HP13 7AD

DELIVERY ADVICE

deliver to	acknowledge to
CAINES NEWPORT LTD. WHSE EBENEZER TERRACE NEWPORT. MON.	CAINES NEWPORT LTD. 101 COMMERCIAL ST. NEWPORT NPT 1LU

acct. code	Category	Rep. No.	Gomme Order No.	Group	Customer's Ref.	Date
C432	**A1**	16	5 172233 3R	178	PREVIEW/00306/JUNE	21/11/74

1 PREVIEW
2 DELIVER TOGETHER GROUPS
3 3R & 4S
4 DELIVERY REQUESTED ~~JUNE~~ $ SEPT. 75

delivery restrictions	Sales Zone	Batch

Line	Qty.	Model/ Part No.	Cover	Description	D.Wk.	Deliver By	Code	Unit SP Price
1	2	3040 K		BASE UNIT	608	~~545~~ ~~8/08/75~~		
2	2	3042 K		TOP UNIT	608	~~545~~ ~~8/08/75~~		10/10/75
3	1	3043 K		TOP UNIT	608	~~545~~ ~~8/08/75~~		

ILLUSTRATION 12.1   Form of sales acknowledgement and delivery advice note

LONG TERM ASSEMBLY PROGRAM   PERIOD 510

WEEK NOS.	40	41	42	43
MODELS				
4385 D	200	400		
4387 D			450	
4389 D		150	150	160
4388 D	100	100	100	100
4364 D				
4390 R	100	100		
4391 R	100	100		
TOTAL	500	850	700	280
4534 D	450	450	450	450
4535 D				
4540 D	1000	1000	1000	1000
4542 D	200	325	325	325

ILLUSTRATION 12.2   Part of one month's assembly programme determined six months in advance

Product Group Analysis	Model	Qty/Val.	Before	Feb	Mar	Apr	May	June	July	Aug	Sep	Oct	Nov	After	No. Prom.	Total
70	7041	Quantity	1	6	20	20	53	22	1	27	9	24	35	97	15	270
		Value £	47	297	982	987	1637	1071	50	1333	447	1183	1742	2816	698	13,315
70	7041	Quantity	2	9	36	30	17	25	2	28	7	21	29	96	21	315
		Value £	95	438	1783	1494	837	1221	102	976	338	1042	1435	4722	985	15,468
70	7050	Quantity	–	5	5	6	6	–	–	2	2	–	4	3	6	37
		Value £	–	308	300	383	380	–	–	–	128	–	237	186	350	2,272
70	7051	Quantity	–	7	15	6	6	–	–	8	4	–	1	3	6	58
		Value £	–	396	854	471	339	–	–	428	225	–	293	171	305	3,242

ILLUSTRATION 12.3   Forward load of outstanding orders booked by model by month

Company name	Address	Grp	A/C code	Gomme order no.	Qty.	Model	CVR	Date
Brooms	Hoddesdon	000	5879	5 180150 3S	1	3038		24/06
				5 180552 3H	1	4391		25/06
				3H	4	4552	L445	25/06
				3H	2	4553	L445	25/06
				5 181843 1H	4	4540 D	L401	25/06
Brown	Beaconsfield	000	8183	5 320579 1R	1	8790 D		24/06
Brown W. P.	York	000	8304	5 260651 1N	1	8050 D		25/06

ILLUSTRATION 12.4   List of despatches to customer made in a week, 30/6/75

ILLUSTRATION 12.5 Card sent from production planning to data processing to generate piece part machining requirements

```
6/05/75

MODEL PIECE PART FILE EXPLOSION  -  WEEK  548  MACHINE SHOP PROGRAMME  -  SPRING GARDENS

MODEL  1195 D    BATCH QTY    315

MASTER    COMP'NT    SPEC    Q PER    LENGTH    WIDTH    SSM    CU OR SU    DESCRIPTION      NO    LEAD   FACTORY
PART      PART       CODE    MASTR                              PER  1OC                     PER   TIME   TAGS

1186138              1416    01/01    413.0     127.0     1     0.0833     TRAY SIDE LH       2     2     CSS F
1186139   composite  1416    01/01    413.0     127.0     1     0.0833     TRAY SIDE RH       2     2     CSS F
1194010   master     0000    01/01    0.0       0.0       1     0.0000     TOP                1     2     SSS
1194010   1194011    4519    01/01    867.0     576.5     1     49.9818    TOP CORE    right  1     2     SSS
1194010   1194012    1825    02/01    584.5     9.5       1     0.0142     LIPPING            1     3     SSS C
1194010   1194013    1825    01/01    895.5     9.5       1     0.0218     LIPPING     Timber 1     3     SSS C
1194010   1194014    2625    01/01    895.5     17.5      1     0.0396     LIPPING            1     3     SSS C
1194010   1194015    5406    01/01    897.5     600.5     1     53.5121    TOP BACK    veneer 1     3     SSS
1194010   1194016    6606    01/01    897.5     630.5     1     53.5121    TOP FACE           1     3     SSS
1194035              8540    01/01    1622.5    886.0     1     143.7299   BACK PLY           1     1     SSS
1194037              0000    01/01    0.0       0.0       1     0.0000     PLNTH END LH       1     2     SSS
1194037   1194038    1819    01/04    546.5     429.0     1     0.4460     END RL CORE        1     3     SSS P
1194037   1194039    7706    01/04    552.5     435.0     1     24.0619    END RL VEN         1     3     SSS
1194040              0000    01/01    0.0       0.0       1     0.0000     PLNTH END RH       1     2     SSS
1194040   1194038    1819    01/04    546.5     429.0     1     0.4460     END RL CORE        1     3     SSS P
1194040   1194039    7706    01/04    552.5     435.0     1     24.0619    END RL VEN         1     3     SSS
```

ILLUSTRATION 12.6   Piece parts for model 1195D from the piece part file (Page 1 of 2)

```
GROSS PIECE PART REQUIREMENTS  -  WEEK  548  MACHINE SHOP PROGRAMME  - SPRING GARDENS

MODEL/    MASTER     COMP'NT   DESCRIPTION        QTY   REMARKS
SUF/FIN   PART       PART

1195 D    1186138              TRAY SIDE LH       630

1195 D    1186139              TRAY SIDE RH       630

1195 D    1194010              TOP                315

1195 D    1194010    1194011   TOP CORE           315

1195 D    1194010    1194012   LIPPING            630

1195 D    1194037              PLNTH END LH       315   COMBINED BELOW
1196 D    1194037              PLNTH END LH       420   COMBINED BELOW
1196 D    1194037              PLNTH END LH       735   COMBINED RECORD
```

ILLUSTRATION 12.7   Gross requirements for a week's piece parts

TIMBER CUTTING LIST FOR WEEK 540SPECIES 2638 38.00 MM THICK AFRO 38 MM   65 O/O WASTE PAGE 17 WK 540
BATCH   NO PART NO DESCRIPTION   QUANTY +++SAWING SIZES+++   SSM   NET   M ROUTING   TOTAL NET
                                              OF SSM LENGTH   WIDTH   REQUIRED   REQUIRED

543 4070 D 4070 145 STD BAK LEG 4070 147   420   324.0   62.0   1   0.321 SSS FOURCUT
543 4540 D 4540 033 FRT LEG LH   1435   432.0   68.5   2   1.618 SSS FOURCUT
543 4540 D 4540 034 FRT LEG RH   1435   432.0   68.5   2   1.618 SSS FOURCUT
543 4534 D 4534 046 BACK LEG LH   217   851.0   267.0   6   1.873 SSS BANDSAW

ILLUSTRATION 12.8   Timber cutting list for completion by week 540

SPECIE DESCRIPTION		CUTTING WEEK NOS				
CODE		540	541	542	543	TOTAL
5306	TEAK BCKNG R	837.176	17.804	0.000	0.000	854.980
5406	MAHOG BCKNG	5795.467	12513.756	13586.239	6631.809	38527.271
5410	MAHOGANY	0.000	0.000	0.000	0.000	0.000
5530	GABBON	1854.764	1152.926	1498.041	0.000	4505.731
5730	BEECH	448.721	0.000	0.000	0.000	448.721
5806	ROSEWOOD	0.000	0.000	0.000	0.000	0.000

ILLUSTRATION 12.9   Forward timber requirements

7/02/75 MACHINE LOADING SUMMARY FOR WEEKS 540 TO 551

P.C. CATEGORY	WEEKLY CAPACY	540	541	542	543	544	545	546	547	548	549	550	551	REQU'D WEEKLY AVER'G	RECENT WEEKLY ACHV'T
10	343	309	255	185	356		154	285	267	360	149			193	
11	98	73	45	38	87		27	60	47	58	20			38	
12	72	76	26	45	82		60	56	50	52	35	4		41	
13	340	396	378	322	487		590	325	293	352	228	101		285	
14	287	197	303	345	310		113	234	304	86				158	
SUB-TOTAL	1140	1051	957	934	1322		944	959	961	908	432	105		714	

ILLUSTRATION 12.10   Forecast machine loading summary

ASSEMBLY PROGRAMME

SHOP OR GROUP _CABINET_

EXPECTED EFFICIENCY _79/-_

WORKING HRS _46_   NORMAL _40_   OVERTIME _6_

No. OF MEN _18_

EG568   CAPACITY (STD HRS) _650_   LOAD (STD HRS) _387_

DESIGN No.	Priority	ARREARS B/FWD FROM LAST WEEK	NEW WORK PROG.	TOTAL WORK PROG.	STD HRS PROG.	SAT/MONDAY				TUESDAY				WEDNESDAY				THURSDAY				FRIDAY			
						Daily Target	Accum Daily Target	Daily Actual	Accum Daily Actual	Daily Target	Accum Daily Target	Daily Actual	Accum Daily Actual	Daily Target	Accum Daily Target	Daily Actual	Accum Daily Actual	Daily Target	Accum Daily Target	Daily Actual	Accum Daily Actual	Daily Target	Accum Daily Target	Daily Actual	Accum Daily Actual
4070	42/48		75	75	62																				
4071	45/49		50	50	44																				
4072	47/43		100	100	59																				

ILLUSTRATION 12.11   Weekly assembly programme

Batch Number	Part Number	S.U.	S.U.	If Different	T.A.	T.A./100	B.S./100	No Makes	Ticket No.
535 91840	9184 007	250				19.0	19.0	1	
Part Description		Op. No.	Mch. Gp.	Qty.	241		255 8 oF 4		
TOP		35	262	2500	0.0		310 344		

CLOCK NO.	W W D S				JOB TICKET			

	ACTIVITY SEQUENCE NOS.	MCH NO.	TO BE COMPLETED BY OPERATOR				
			QTY PASSED	QTY. REMCH.	QTY. EWA.	EWA. MINS.
1						
2						
3						

DETAILS OF ANY OTHER ALLOWANCES :

For Payment → Payroll input → essential feedback info.

ILLUSTRATION 12.12   Job ticket for a machining operation

```
MCH ROUTING OPERATIONS FILE     NOMAKES   FIRST   LAST   OPER'N DESCR STDY  JIG
                                          CNRD MCH CNRD MCH            NO   NO
                         TIME ALLOWED -MINS/100 PIECES.
    4364 054  END RAIL          BASIC STANDARD - MINS/100 PIECES
  Operation  Machine Comp
III   5 P  100 S   0.0   0.0   1/  1   3709 415 9999 536
     15 P  126 S   0.0   0.0   1/  1   3709 415 9999 536
Planned 15 P  220 S  11.0  10.9   1/  1   3709 415 9999 536
Actual 15 A  222 S  20.7   7.3   1/  1   3709 415 9999 536
     20 P  325 S  59.1  58.2   1/  1   3709 415 9999 536
     25 P  281 S   4.4   4.4   1/  1   3709 415 9999 536
     25 A  289 S   4.4   4.2   1/  1   3709 415 9994 536
     31 P  281 S   0.0  40.6   1/  1   3709 415 9999 536
     31 A  289 S   0.0  40.6   1/  1   3709 415 9999 536
     32 P  370 S   0.0  29.4   1/  1   3709 415 9999 536
     35 A  350 S  17.4  17.4   1/  1   3709 415 9999 536
     35 P  370 S  17.4  17.4   1/  1   3709 415 9999 536
III  40 P  378 S  14.4  14.2   1/  1   3709 415 9999 536
     50 A  500 S  33.6   7.5   1/  1   3709 415 9999 536
     50 A  510 S  33.6   7.5   1/  1   3709 415 9999 536
     50 P  527 S   7.5   7.5   1/  1   3709 415 9999 536
     50 A  540 S   0.0   7.5   1/  1   3709 415 9999 536
```

ILLUSTRATION 12.13   Machine routing file

```
# 18/06/75              SELECTED W.I.P. BATCHES

BATCH      PART PLANNED  OP   PLN   EST    RECORDED TO DATE    COMPLETION
              QTY        NO   MCH   COMP   QTY  FIRST LAST     DATE  TAG
                              GRP   DATE        DATE  DATE
                                    WK 3y      P.C.
                                          P.C. CONVERSION
                                          XXX  XX-X  XX-X
  53201000  0100001  525  CONV        30-5                          TOP
                         MILL         30-5  525  35-4  35-4
                     05  203  30-7   524  35-3  35-3  35-4
                     10  607  31-4   524  35-3  35-3  35-4
                     15  222  31-5   524  35-3  35-3  35-4    P.C.
                     20  285  31-7   520  35-6  35-6  36-5    PINK CARDS.
                     25  310  32-4   520  36-5  36-5  37-5
                     30  375  32-6   520  37-3  37-3  37-5
                     35  540  32-7   520  37-4  37-4  37-5
                         ADV         XXX  XX-X  XX-X  ← STORES MOVEMENT ADVICE
  53201000  0100004  263  CONV        30-5   263  28-7  28-7     TOP FCE VNR

  53201000  0100005  263  CONV        30-5   263  28-7  28-7     TOP BAK VNR

  53201000  0100006  525  CONV        30-5                       RH END
                         MILL               522  34-7  34-7
                     05  203  30-7   540  34-3  34-3  34-4
                     10  283  31-3   540  34-3  34-3  34-4
                     15  203  31-4   536  34-6  34-6  34-7
                     20  607  31-5   536  34-6  34-6  34-7
                     25  222  31-7   522  34-7  34-7  35-4
                     30  285  32-3   535  35-5  35-5  36-5
                     35  381  32-5   504  36-6  36-6  36-7
                     40  400  32-6   494  36-6  36-6  36-7
                     45  540  32-7   520  36-7  36-7  37-5
```

ILLUSTRATION 12.14   The work-in-progress file

PLANNED WORK-LOAD - MACHINE GROUP 564 HARD DRUM SANDER 01 MCHS 88.8 STD HRS/WEEK PAGE 1

← CAPACITY OF MACHINE GROUP.

	BATCH NO	PART NO	OP NO	DESCRIPTION	PLN QTY	COMPLN DATE (WW D HH)	STD HRS	FROM MCH	TO MCH	OUTSTANDING OPS	OUTSTANDING HRS	AVERAGE SLACK	TIME CHANGES T/A	TIME CHANGES SU
ARREARS	539 4542 D	4542 046	75	RHF BACK LEG	2800	38 3 08	37.05	381*	385	03	138.3	530.3-		
	539 4542 D	4542 045	75	LHF BACK LEG	2400	38 4 02	31.76	381*	385	03	120.2	512.2-		
	539 4543 D	4543 048	75	RHF BACK LEG	630	38 5 08	8.34	460*	385	03	40.3	440.3-		
	539 4543 D	4543 047	75	LHF BACK LEG	400	38 6 06	5.29	460*	385	03	30.0	430.0-		
	541 4540 D	4540 033	75		3100	40 6 01	41.02*	350*	560	02	123.5	435.5-		
	541 4540 D	4540 034	75		3100	40 6 01	41.02*	350*	560	02	123.5	435.5-		
	543 4540 D	4540 033	75		2870	41 7 06	37.98*	350*	560	02	114.9	378.9-		
	543 4540 D	4540 034	75		2870	41 7 06	37.99*	350*	560	02	114.9	378.9-		
	545 4534 D	4534 046	60		1300	45 4 07	12.74*	350*	560	02	37.3	229.3-		
	545 4534 D	4534 047	60		800	45 5 02	7.84*	350*	560	02	26.0	218.0-		
	547 4389 D	4389 054	20	GATE FMF ASY	840	47 7 08	2.80*	480	STORES	01	6.8	118.8-		
	549 4544 D	4544 427	75	BACK LEG LH	1330	48 5 05	17.60*	381	385	04	82.0	114.0-		
	549 4544 D	4544 428	75	BACK LEG RH	1330	48 5 05	17.60*	381	385	04	82.0	114.0-		
							299.02 ARREARS							
IN #550	550 4550 K	4550 419	65	BACK LEG LHF	1540	50 5 04	20.38*	580	370	02	40.5	32.5-		
↗	550 4550 K	4550 420	65	BACK LEG RHF	1540	50 5 04	20.38*	580	370	02	40.5	32.5-		
COMING	551 4542 D	4542 045	75	LHF BACK LEG	1690	50 6 03	22.36*	381	385	03	88.3	20.2-		
YEAR & WEEK NO	551 4542 D	4542 046	75	RHF BACK LEG	1690	50 6 03	22.36*	381	385	03	88.3	20.2-		
							384.50 WEEK 550 LOAD							

ILLUSTRATION 12.15 Work-to-list sample

25/6/75

OUTSTANDING OPERATIONS

BATCH	PART	DESC	PLN QTY	DAYS	1 (OP MCH DATE)	2 (OP MCH DATE)	3 (OP MCH DATE)	4 (OP MCH DATE)	5 (OP MCH DATE)	6 (OP MCH DATE)	ADD UPS
548 1195 D	1186138	TRAY SIDE LH	130	7-	20 270 47-3	25 259 47-5	26 580 47-6	30 400 48-3	35 320 48-6	40 560 48-7	
	1194010	TOP	250	0	30 282 48-5	35 520 48-6	40 540 48-7				
	1194011	TOP CORE	250	0							
	1194012	LIPPING	500	10-	CONV 46-5						
	1194013	LIPPING	435	10-	CONV 46-5						
	1194014	LIPPING	250	10-	CONV 46-5						
	1194015	TOP BACK	250	10-	CONV 46-5						
	1194016	TOP FACE	250	10-	CONV 46-5						
	1194025	LH DOOR CORE	315	0							
	1194026	LIPPING	630	0							
	1194027	LIPPING	630	0							
	1194028	LIPPING	315	15-	CONV 45-5						
	1194030	LH DOOR BACK	315	0							
	1194032	RH DOOR CORE	315	0							
	1194033	LIPPING	630	0							
	1194034	LIPPING	315	0							
	1194035	BACK PLY	160	0							
	1194044	RH DOOR BACK	315	0							
	1194047	DOOR LHF	315	6-	30 282 47-4	35 300 47-6	36 522 47-7	40 520 48-4	50 999 48-5	55 540 48-6	1
	1194048	DOOR RHF	315	6-	30 282 47-4	35 300 47-6	40 393 47-7	41 522 48-4	60 999 48-5	65 540 48-6	1
	1194058	SHPE FRT RL	185	12-	25 325 46-3	30 580 46-4	35 560 46-5				
	1194060	BOTTOM CORE	185	0							
	1194061	LIPPING	370	10-	CONV 46-5						
	1194062	BOTTOM FACE	185	10-	CONV 46-5						
	1194063	BOTTOM BACK	185	10-	CONV 46-5						

ILLUSTRATION 12.16 Outstanding operations for week 548's load in the machine shop (Model status report)

```
17/06/75        STORES STATUS REPORT

BATCH    PART    DESCRIPTION      O/S    PLN    ALT
                                  OPS    QTY    QTY

539 4364 D  4362 034  TONGUE             1680   1680
            4362 039  LEG                1680   1656
            4364 015  LEG                1680   1648
            4364 016  END RAIL           840    858
            4364 024  CROSS RAIL         840    744
            4364 025  NICD TRACK         1680   1680
            4364 031  SDE RL DVTAIL      420    451
            4364 032  SDE RL PLAIN       420    300
            4364 033  GUIDE              1680   900
            4364 034  SET LEAVSTOP       420    327
            4364 039  LH LEAF            420
            4364 040  RH LEAF            420
            4364 041  LH FLIP-TOP        420
            4364 042  RH FLIP-TOP        420
```

Balance reject   M/M

ILLUSTRATION 12.17   Stores status report — quantities received in stores from machine shop in week 539's load

```
1/07/75
MACHINE, GROUP, & CATEGORY SUMMARY FOR WEEK  48
```

PRODN CONTL CATY	MCHN NO	MACHINE DESCRIPTION	++++DAY HOURS++++			++++NIGHT HOURS+++++			++++TOTAL HOURS+++++		
			ELAPSD	PRODN	O/O	ELAPSD	PRODN	O/O	ELAPSD	PRODN	O/O
00	1601	SCHWABADISSEN-SHEET SAW	30.6	33.5	109	0.0	0.0	000	30.6	33.5	109
	160	GROUP TOTAL	30.6	33.5	109	0.0	0.0	000	30.6	33.5	109
	1611	SCHWABADISSEN-PANEL SAW	30.6	30.0	098	15.6	18.3	117	46.2	48.3	105
	161	GROUP TOTAL	30.6	30.0	098	15.6	18.3	117	46.2	48.3	105
	5221	HEESEMAN EDGE SANDER UKP11	24.4	23.9	098	0.0	6.4	000	24.4	30.3	124
	522	GROUP TOTAL	24.4	23.9	098	0.0	6.4	000	24.4	30.3	124
	5410	INVALID MACHINE	25.4	29.3	115	0.0	0.0	000	25.4	29.3	115
	541	GROUP TOTAL	25.4	29.3	115	0.0	0.0	000	25.4	29.3	115
00		CATEGORY TOTAL	111.0	116.7	105	15.6	24.7	158	126.6	141.4	112

ILLUSTRATION 12.18   Output and efficiencies by machine (data from payroll system job tickets)'

Spring Gardens Forward Load as at 13.6.75

	Jun	Jul	Aug	Sep	Oct	Nov	Dec	No Prom
Working days in month	10	15	18	20	25	20	18	
Month's capacity (st hrs)	6400	9600	11520	12800	16000	12800	12800	
LOAD—ACTUAL (st. hrs)	5052	12212	8048	13818	7223	5517	165	15377
Unallocated special reserve estimated (st. hrs)	0	0	1168	720	4400	4245		
Total effective load (st. hrs)	5052	12212	9216	14538	11623	9822		
Balance of capacity (st. hrs)	+1348	−2612	+2304	−1738	+4377	+2978		
Running balance	+1348	−1264	+1140	−598	+4377	+6753		
Value (£)	281856	653805	445948	744269	410832	282848	7984	944564
£ per st. hr.	55.7	53.4	55.5	53.8	53.9	50.7	48.4	61.4

ILLUSTRATION 12.19   Total loading on the machine shop

13 Linking Manufacturing Policy and Operational Control: Arnold's Children's Wear

1. The Company

Arnolds make chidren's clothes selling under the brand names Playtime, Childwrap and Babycare. They were established as a family firm in 1933, expanded rapidly with the post-war growth of the children's clothing market, and in the mid-sixties were merged into Pratt Morris. At this time Playtime was the largest children's clothes brand in the U.K., and probably in Europe. They had about 5 per cent of the highly fragmented U.K. market with a turnover of £16m., representing 20 million garments a year. As part of Pratt Morris, Arnolds remained essentially independent with a head office at Stanley, near Durham.

Arnolds' activities cover the whole span of clothing manufacture apart from the production of the original textiles. At Stanley they knit, dye and print most of the cloth that they make up into garments in 10 U.K. factories. They also have knitting factories in Oakham and Portugal. Each making-up factory receives a supply of material from Stanley in accordance with the production plan and returns finished goods to the Stanley warehouse for final packing and distribution. In addition about 25 per cent of manufacturing which requires special skills or equipment is contracted out on a regular basis to companies called merchandisers which supply the finished products direct to the Stanley warehouse. An extra 5 per cent may be commissioned outside when Arnolds themselves are short of capacity, usually at the making-up stage.

Arnolds sell to 3500 retailers in the U.K. through 17 regional agents.

Although it is unusual for a firm of Arnolds' size to use agents in the home market, they have great confidence in the ability of these agents and in the continuity they provide. Arnolds export 15 per cent of their turnover.

The Playtime range covers all ages up to 14, with emphasis on the 4 to 10 range. It contains practically all clothing from underwear to trousers, dresses and swimwear. Considering colour and size variation, they produce nearly 4000 garments each year for their spring and autumn ranges. They draw from 2000 finished fabrics which in turn come from half as many undyed fabrics. Illustration 13.1 gives a layout of the Arnolds' operations with the proportional volume on each route and number of varieties at each stage.

Since the mid-sixties, children have become increasingly fashion-conscious and Arnolds have had to respond with more, and shorter, production runs. They have come under increasing pressure from smaller manufacturers. As Robert Barton, the assistant sales director, remarked, 'a small operator can be in Paris to see the latest fashions on a Monday, and have five hundred garments in a London store by the Saturday.' Arnolds cannot compete on this time scale: their complete production cycle takes about three months. Competition is also expected to increase from the developing countries, who find the labour-intensive making-up operations ideal, and much pressure has already been felt from cheap imports, both of garments and part-finished materials. To counteract this, Arnolds has set up a factory in Portugal.

The move towards fashion-consciousness and increased competition makes it essential that Arnolds' production planning is as accurate and flexible as possible. Since 1972 success in this field has become increasingly important, as the children's clothing market has become more unsettled with the effects of E.E.C. entry, V.A.T. and changes in credit policy still largely unknown.

2. Product and Processes

The products are divided into three classes. Selection 1 consists of the stable products (vests, pyjamas, etc.), Selection 2 of products with an uncertain element in the demand (T-shirts, skirts), and Selection 3 of fashion garments (dresses and swimwear). About 40 per cent of turnover comes from Selection 1 and the rest is approximately evenly divided between Selections 2 and 3. Each of these selections carries a different estimate of error on the sales forecast together with a different profit margin and obsolescence risk as shown in the table. Generally when Arnolds cannot sell products within the season they have to be marked down by a third as discount for sale on redundant stock.

	Selection 1	*Selection 2*	*Selection 3*
Error on initial forecast (%)	10	15	50
Standard profit margin (%)	20–40	20–45	30–55
Average % obsolescence	5	10	25

Each product is manufactured in two main stages: capital-intensive fabric manufacture and processing, followed by labour-intensive making-up. For fabric manufacture the 250 yarns are converted into 'grey fabric' on expensive modern equipment such as circular knitting machines, and on into printed fabric by costly printing machines using dyes. The printed fabric is converted into garments using operator-controlled stitching machines and passing through the series of operations for the making-up process shown below.

Collect fabric → lay → straight cut into blocks → band knife (trimming) → sort bundles into components → pre-sewing → sewing/trim, inspect/fold → bag and box → carton → local warehouse → Stanley warehouse

The products are identified by an eight-digit coding scheme. There are 10 garment groups, each group having a code number which is the first digit in the code for the product: 0–underwear, 1–nightwear, 2–babywear, 3–shirts, 4–knitwear, 5–shorts/trousers, 6–skirts/dresses, 7–swimwear, 8–coats, 9–hosiery and miscellaneous. Each group has a number of sub-groups corresponding to a type of clothing, e.g. a vest which is coded 00, the second digit referring to the sub-group. There are fifty or sixty sub-groups. The next two digits refer to the style of garment (a combination of design and pattern), there being about 400 styles, and the last four digits indicate a colour and size. Illustration 13.2 gives the numbers of product types in the main groups.

Each of the 2500 unique products produced every six months has an exact specification, prepared by design staff and industrial engineering, which is used by production administration for estimating and by technical staff in manufacturing for quality control. The nature of the specifications is shown below.

Product specification

Code:	00	–	08	–	40	–	01
	garment group		style		colour		size

Contents of specification documents

1. Fabric quality : quality spec., finishing process, % yarn content
2. Garment colour and size.
3. Production data (standard quantities)
4. Process sheet (routing)
5. Accessory specs. (zips, etc.)
6. Making up specification
7. Folding and packing spec.

held on data bank in computer and maintained. Used for production reports.

for technical use.

The capacities required for production are determined by engineering staff. Output and stock are measured in lbs. weight which is converted to standard hours for financial purposes up to finished fabric stage, and thereafter the output is measured in dozens and standard hours. Illustration 13.2 gives the volumes for the 1973 season, the number of batches and the batch size used in the make-up operation.

The efficiency of Arnolds' factories varies with location. Generally branch factories can make up garments faster than Stanley as operators train for one job whereas Stanley develops flexibility. External companies are given several months' advance warning and then get the commissioned work a month in advance. The lead times allowed for a batch to get through from launch are five weeks in primary fabric production at Stanley and six weeks for the making-up operations. To these must be added the allowances for the various stockholding stages to get the full cycle time:

one week in grey fabric stock
one week in finished garment stock
three weeks at Stanley warehouse prior to despatch.

This gives an overall cycle time of up to four months from grey fabric to despatch. It is always assumed that grey fabric is in stock and up to 10 weeks' worth of stock is held in fabric stores. The cycle time could be cut if batches were smaller but this would reduce effective capacity by increasing the number of set-ups. Normally at each major stage of production there may be one to five batches of any product or material in progress.

The entire management task from design to delivery is geared to the seasonal concept. The full work for a six-month season extends over 15 months although even nine months before that (i.e. two years before the season ends) sales present a forecast. For example, initial forecasts for the spring 1973 season are made in June 1971, the prime planning work is done from April 1972 onwards, with first orders taken in October 1972, and despatches start on January 1 and continue through to June 1973. The

15-month duration of activity for every six-month season means that there are three seasons of activities overlapping simultaneously as illustrated in the diagram.

Overlap of three seasons activities

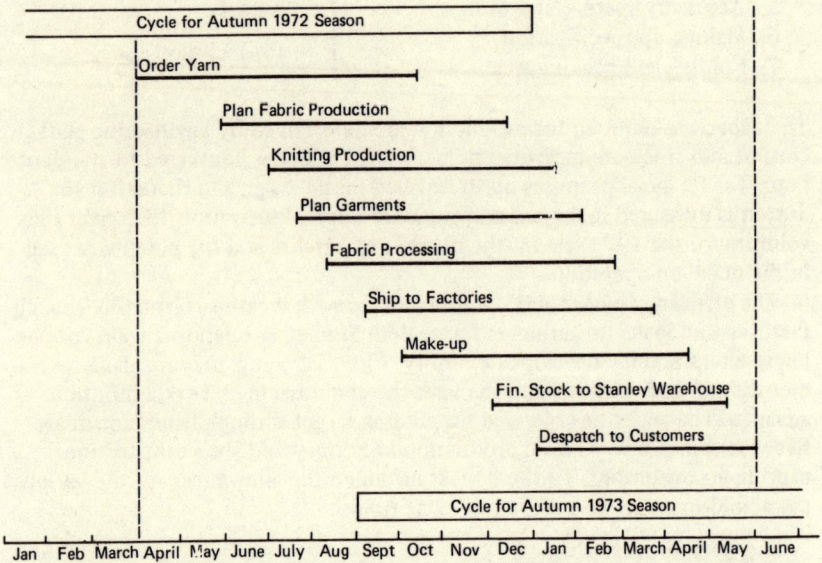

The production steps for the season's work must therefore be integrated with other managerial activities in a complex set of interrelationships. The responsibilities for the right actions at the appropriate times are stated on the company calendar (Illustration 13.3) which is sent round to all senior managers.

Decisions on the most risky selections are postponed as long as possible. The wide range of functions involved in the planning requires effective production coordination and this has been established as a distinct function under a director. The key relationship is between sales and production control.

3. Sales Activities in Planning the Season

The sales department is responsible for forecasting sales, liaising with the agents and managing the warehousing and despatch of finished products. The initial complete range forecast for spring 1973 is produced by the sales department in June 1972. In addition, a time profile of demand for each garment is estimated which builds up over the six-month season to cumulate to 100 per cent as shown:

Cumulative percentage of estimated demand
Sales time profile

	Jan	Feb	Mar	Apr	May	June
Del. dates	2	4	6	8	12	
Cum. %	30	60	80	90	100	
Sales/prodn. periods	1	2	3	4	5	

This sales forecast is used by manufacturing to form a production plan to meet the forecast as well as possible, and to 'promise' deliveries.

After early October, orders start coming in. Most orders come early in the season though requests can be made for any delivery date. A weekly computer output gives the monthly production availability (from the production plan) for each garment on a cumulative basis (for the first four months and end-season) and the percentage of this that has already been ordered. Allowing for orders in the post, mail orders and exports, if any garment's sales for any month are thought to be around the 100 per cent production capacity mark then this is brought to production control's notice. It may be possible to redistribute capacity so that available capacity for that garment is increased. If not, sales instruct the agents to offer only delivery periods after that date.

Orders are forward invoiced as they arrive and despatched from finished goods stores on the appropriate date. (Traditionally, Arnolds only deliver on the 1st and 20th of any month.) Should overselling occur, or production be delayed, there is a priority system for dealing with customers. In allocating stock, account is first taken of the required delivery date; then of the seven customer priority groups and then of the time the order was received.

After about two weeks of receiving orders, sales make the first and most important of their monthly revisions. Both the current sales and the previous like season's sales to each customer are known and, working by priority group, an average estimate of total sales for this season is calculated. (It is planned to use sub-groups and exponential smoothing to weight recent information to improve this estimating procedure.) Finally, the new totals are assessed by sales and production control in the light of budgeted sales and capacity and they are adjusted where necessary. No effort is made to alter the profile, and the new total is sent to manufacturing staff. In due course a revised production plan is issued and the cycle carries on.

To ensure delivery on time the made-up material must reach Stanley early enough for repacking to meet customer requirements. Factories are therefore given dates which are the latest their goods can arrive if they are to be despatched in the correct delivery period. As demand peaks in the second quarter of the season, and the warehouse capability is fairly constant, the peak has to be smoothed out and the bottleneck minimised. This is done by setting the goods-inwards dates immediately in front of the bottleneck earlier than would otherwise be necessary. In this way as much work as possible is cleared through the warehouse before it has to process the peak load.

4. Production Control's Activities in Planning the Season

The organisation of production to meet sales forecasts is spread between a number of managers but rests mainly with the production control manager and the branch factory controller. The various tasks are indicated in Illustration 13.3.

The primary stage of knitting is more or less uncoupled from the remaining operations. At appropriate intervals the overall output levels for grey fabric are set for the next 10 to 12 weeks. Every four weeks the mix combinations of this output are re-established and the stock position is reviewed. All production forward from grey fabric is related to specific garment forecast requirements, and these forecasts will be subject to change. Stocks of printed fabric at Stanley are purely work-in-progress prior to despatch to factories.

The production plan for these primary stages needs to be fixed early before any sales have been made, due to the long lead times and the early peaking of demand. Based on the first forecast, almost all knitting, most printing and even 65 per cent of making-up capacity is committed in the initial production plan. The amount of making-up committed at this stage varies with the selection (Selection 1 has 80 per cent committed, 2 has 70 per cent and 3 only 50 per cent). Taking account of goods already in stock the production for the entire season is called 'the balance to produce'. The uncommitted element of the total required for the season is left unplanned and is called 'the balance to plan'. All committed elements are referred to as being 'planned'.

The actual loading of the make-up factories is done in three stages and at several levels of detail. Based on the totals and profiles, the styles are allocated to appropriate factories. This is agreed through branch factory control at a meeting with the factory managers (the factory managers' seminar). The factory manager assesses the implied commitment of capacity at his factory, his standard hours available and his budgeted costs, then he prepares a broad schedule consistent if possible with the sales profile, and makes his promises to deliver to Stanley warehouse. Finally production control plan the mix in an exact schedule.

The make-up factory capacities are defined in teams of operators, there being 10 to 30 people in a team. For any style there is a standard time to produce a dozen articles, and, making allowance for imperfects and down times, a figure for gross standard hours per dozen per team can be calculated. The allocation of products to factories by teams is distributed to all relevant managers. This document is maintained throughout the season. A page of the spring 1973 plan is shown in Illustration 13.4

This overall plan by team on the factories is further broken down into a schedule by team showing the planned production by garment, colour and style, against the dates on the sales profile. Generally the goods are entered onto the plan three months in advance of the sales date, and the knitting requirements are organised at least four months in advance. Each month the new forecast totals are broken down into quantities and new batches are allocated to the teams forward schedule taking account of the quantity in stock and in the 'pipeline'. These committed allocations are recorded in the Master Ledger. This basic production planning document is the production control 'bible'; it states where all batches are and what is coming forward to the factory teams. It is re-created once a month for all products requiring one week's full-time effort from the production control manager and his chief assistant. Many decisions are made in the creation of this ledger and it requires source information from the following computer printouts:

Forward Planning Report $\begin{cases} -\text{ latest order position} \\[1em] -\text{ orders relative to forecast} \end{cases}$

Forward Remains Report   — undelivered orders to date

A summary of the ledger is passed on to sales and it is against these figures that sales book off the incoming orders from customers.

The plan rolls forward until the entire season is planned. Difficulties arise at the points of sales revision. If, on a sales revision when the total forecast changes, the balance to plan goes negative, then no more of that product need be planned and if possible some should be removed from the plan by altering one of the primary processing stage outputs. If, on the other hand, this (balance to plan) increases, then the extra load needs to be fitted in if possible to meet the profile. Of course, as most of the unplanned work is at the end of the season, it is difficult to avoid a glut of material coming through then, possibly too late.

It has been especially difficult at revision periods the last few seasons as overall demand has been consistently and significantly over-estimated. Also, with new fashion items, a colour mix forecast of 50:50 quite often turns out to be 75:25, so that substantial alterations have to be made to cover the mix effect. The consequences of a forecast change therefore depend critically on the particular products affected, the fabrics they need and the factories at which those products are made. The changes have to be implemented in precise detail on the production plan.

5. The Problem of Variety and Fashion

The production control manager, Mat Bennett, was at the centre of the problem of monitoring plans against production. As he said, 'higher up it's too "broad brush" and lower down you're committed by budgets and detailed plans'. His function in Arnolds carried an unusual mixture of responsibilities: planning garment production, planning and loading and control of fabric and yarn, the materials (fabric) stores, the level of garment stocks and the provision of samples and specials. He had a staff of 21. The production control task had become more hectic over the last five years, as the number of products had gone up, the number of new items per season had increased and the degree of forecast change had become more substantial. As Mat Bennett said, 'the trouble is things develop over time, each decision seeming right on its own but the total leading to a near-impossible situation. With reducing volumes in recent years sales came under pressure and the natural reaction was to introduce new products. Prices were increased, but with the greater control problems of managing the variety, deliveries began to slip. Now in 1973 the pressure is on to cut the number of lines for autumn 1974, to drive up volumes and simplify control. Nearly 90 per cent of our turnover comes from 10 per cent of our products.

'We've tried various devices to help to deal with the situation. First we have considered trying to get the customers to order even earlier to give us more time for planning but there is a limit to how far you can take them. They want to be able to delay their decisions. A second alternative is to build stock but this easily becomes redundant and it costs 15 per cent on the capital tied up. We therefore tend to make in smaller batches with limited commitment to forecast. Thirdly we tried to get more flexibility into the system by pulling a season's production forward by a month. But somehow we never won the extra month. Firm orders for the current selling season are always more commercially acceptable in that extra month than estimates for the next.

'The damage caused by bad delivery is difficult to estimate. Because

Arnolds have a good reputation for quality at reasonable price, some retailers are willing to wait, particularly for the less fashionable items, so Arnolds can modify its demand profile to a small extent without dissatisfying too many customers. But we've certainly lost customers in recent years and this has led to wrong forecasts and failure to meet budgets. What we need to be able to do is to know the real effects all this change is having and the way the various forces are interacting.

'It's so difficult to impress on people how pressurised the production organisation task is. I recently prepared a list of variables to consider when launching a batch of work on to production. The difficulty is to communicate at board level the compounding effects of all these factors. In the end the possibilities for good production control depend on a clear statement of company policy.'

Factors in the decision to launch a batch

making-up factory
sewing team priority
customer priority
fabric stock availability
dyehouse load (batch size)
dyehouse priority
printing run
printing priority
any special making-up instructions
any special packaging instructions
availability of accessory stocks

standard
alternative (reasonable cost + 1 → 15%)
alternative (high cost + 15% & over)

As a start on his analysis Mat Bennett assembled some data. The first discovery was that total standard hours booked for the Playtime production in spring 1971, 1972, 1973 fell from 555,300 to 513,000 to 469,800 despite the fact that available hours in the make-up factories were a steady 130,000 hours per month over the period. This could well be due to the variety and fashion increases; the number of garments for these three seasons which were also in the previous season were 50, 60 and 70 respectively. The detailed data for the spring season's orders and for the changing number of varieties is shown in Illustrations 13.5 and 13.6.

Question for discussion

Assess the effects of variety upon Arnolds' operations.

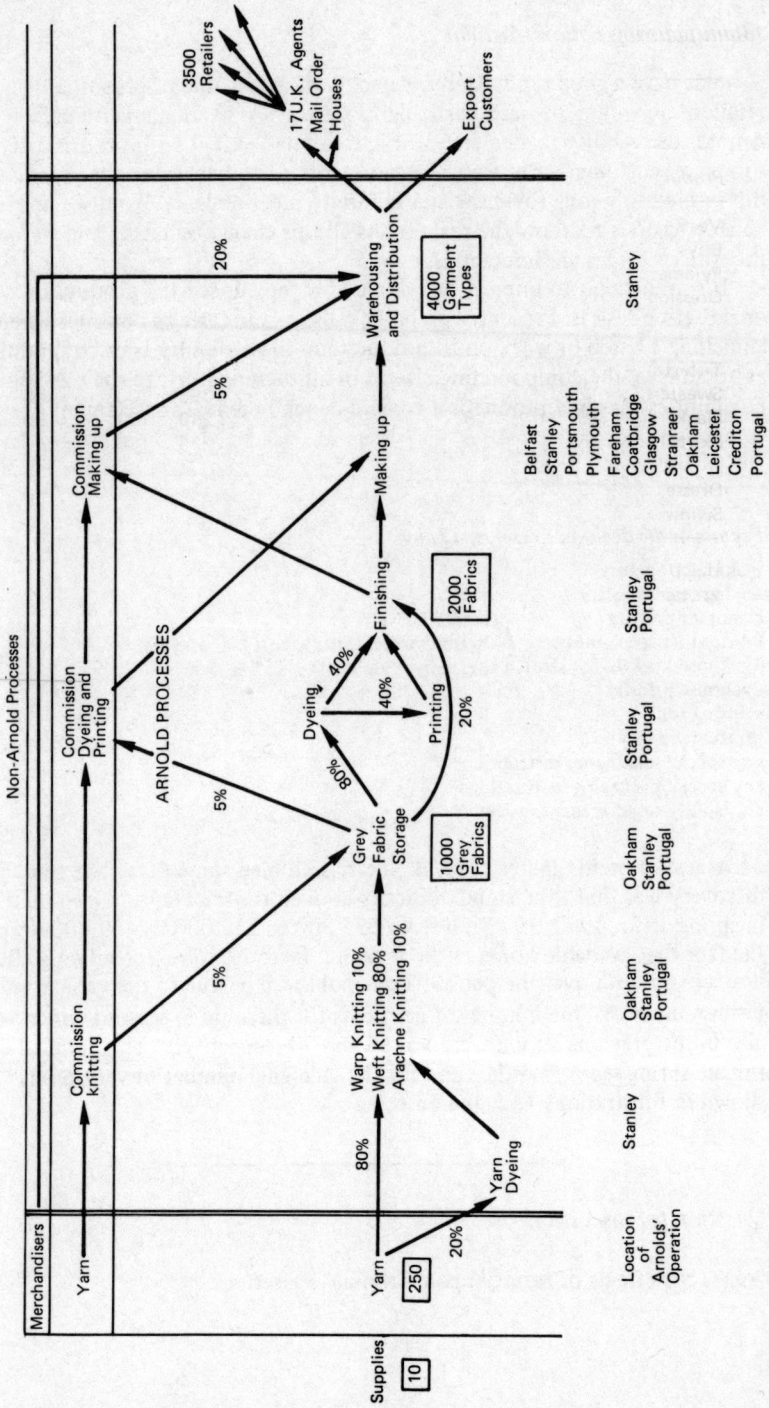

ILLUSTRATION 13.1   Layout of the work flow

Product	No. of garment varieties	Making-up std hrs/doz	Volume '000 doz per season		No of batches per season		Batch size for make-up doz
			aut.	spring	aut.	spring	
Vests	11	0.50	40	47	203	234	180
Boys' Briefs	6	0.75	16	18	18	90	180
Pyjamas	17	2.25	34	19	405	189	90
Dressing Gown	4	3.50	12	2	270	54	45
T-shirts	17	1.0	—	40	—	261	135
Sweaters	12	1.5	20	5	396	108	45
Slacks	18	3.5	29	18	288	180	90
Skirts	15	1.0	12	9	234	180	45
Dresses	39	4.0	21	9	414	198	45
Swimwear	36	1.5	—	50	—	495	90

ILLUSTRATION 13.2   Operating characteristics for the main product groups

204

Selection = ⊕
Selection = ●
Selection = ○
All = +

Event	Responsibility	Mar 7	14	21	28	Apr 7	14	21	28	May 7	14	21	28	Jun 7	14	21	28	Jul 7	14	21	28	Aug 7	14	21	28	Sept 7
Range Selection	Mr. Gray	⊕●																								
Measurement Charts Complete	Mr. Gray				●																					
Merchandise Prices Available	Merchandisers		⊕							○																
G.C.S. List Issue	Mr. Holly			⊕			●				○															
Sales List Sample Requirements	Mr. King				⊕	●						●														
Outside Samples Ordered	Merchandisers					⊕			●						○											
Initial Forecast	Mr. King					⊕		●		●																
Specification Issue	Mr. Holly						⊕			●					●											
Provisional Prices Available	Mr. Loden						⊕				●				●											
Sample Programme Complete	Mr. Bennett						⊕				●					○										
Cloth Requirement to Fabric Buying	Mr. Bennett						⊕			●						○										
Prices Finalised	Mr. Seawright								⊕		●															
Accessory Requirement to Purchasing	Mr. Briden								⊕			●			○											
Fabric Orders Placed	Mr. Lauder								⊕			●			○											
Outside Garments Ordered	Merchandisers								⊕			●				○										
Accessory Orders Placed	Mr. Dunne									⊕			●				○									
Samples Returned to Stanley	Merchandisers/ Mr. Bennett														⊕					●			+			
Last Samples to reach Sample Room	Merchandisers Mr. Briden																								+	
Agents Collect Sample Ranges	Mr. King																								+	
Selling Commences	Mr. King																									+

ILLUSTRATION 13.3   Playtime spring 1973 calendar showing series of tasks

Style	Range	Imp. %	Net bal. firsts to prod.	Gross Std. hrs. to prod.	Team net bal. firsts to prod.	Team gross std. hrs. to produce	Factory	Gross pla target doz day
10/03		5	1053	974	2313	1717	Coatbridge	Inc. in
03/87			1260	543				03/Nylo @ 165
13/09		5	281	529	2716	6336	Belfast	25
10			356	744				
11			1413	3652				
12			666	1423				
14/49		5	437	939	2441	4807	Belfast	22
50			1316	2529				
51			283	558				
52			405	783				
15/21		10	1472	3543	1868	3945	Plymouth	18
22			396	902				
15/19		10	1665	1979	5967	7560	Coatbridge	72
16/52			1031	1586				
53			2013	2723				
55			1648	1071				
58			1349	1826				
59			1287	1827				
60			1480	2279				
16/52		10	1031	1586	4505	5727	Portsmouth	64
53			2013	2723				
55			1648	1071				
58			1349	1826				
59			1287	1827				
60			1480	2279				
17/94			1867	3532	1867	3532	Portsmouth	45
15/27		10	1211	1678	5597	7857	Plymouth	50
28			432	642				
17/88			943	1307				
89			1566	2309				
91			1446	1925				
17/79		10	384	1187	4884	15096	Belfast	45
92			2474	7645				
93			2027	6265				
19/68		10	1633	3637	1773	3950	Plymouth	37
69			140	313				
19/76		5	441	1200	441	1200	Portsmouth	9
24/00		10	2792	4545	6343	11239	Stanley	54
10			1061	2210				
21			606	986				
5/04			315	600				
7/06			1269	2904				
4/11		10	1485	2322	2540	4248	Portsmouth	23
25			1055	1764				
4/52		10	225	394	738	1650	Plymouth (complete early)	13
77			513	1257				

ILLUSTRATION 13.4   Planned production — spring 1973
issue no. 3

Year	Delivery period	cum. 000 doz. (A) ordered	(a) £000 value	cum. 000 doz. (B) overdue	(b) £000 value	000 dozs. Finished goods stock	£000 value	B A	b/a as %
1968	Jan	112	579	20	141	446	1137	17.7	24.3
	Feb	331	1710	72	449	487	1592	26.8	26.2
	Mar	530	3736	115	663	363	1269	21.7	24.2
	Apr	670	3456	128	789	341	957	19.0	22.8
	June	775	3948	55	339	209	443	7.1	8.5
1969	Jan	130	751	30	22	314	1461	22.6	29.6
	Feb	324	2858	81	572	355	1749	25.1	30.7
	Mar	497	2853	89	631	355	1790	17.7	22.1
	Apr	637	3650	80	526	361	1908	12.6	14.3
	June	745	4280	30	198	274	1542	4.1	4.6
1970	Jan	112	710	12	101	443	2198	10.8	14.8
	Feb	339	2170	43	378	598	3146	12.7	17.3
	Mar	507	3242	64	542	472	2578	12.6	16.7
	Apr	590	3776	43	377	430	2352	7.2	9.9
	June	656	4199	14	116	258	1390	2.1	2.7
1971	Jan	104	848	25	225	299	2014	24	27
	Feb	303	2183	71	759	380	2274	24	35
	Mar	458	3709	80	879	348	2319	18	25
	Apr	540	4299	67	701	332	2224	12	16
	June	614	4801	15	151	183	1239	2.5	3.2
1972	Jan	90	769	11	134	301	1883	12	17
	Feb	280	2407	51	575	309	2263	19	25
	Mar	430	3784	72	819	265	2003	17	22
	Apr	487	4382	55	637	249	2116	11	15
	June	541	4682	17	206	209	1251	3.2	4.4
1973	Jan	122	1077	32	364	318	1884	25.7	33.8
	Feb	280	2537	70	864	360	2342	25.0	34.0
	Mar	346	3360	71	872	360	2268	19.3	29.0
	Apr	433	3954	68	790	330	2155	15.8	20.5
	June	504	4280	22	244	281	2237	4.3	5.5

ILLUSTRATION 13.5   Data on Spring season's orders

Year	No. of Playtime gmts.	No. of merchandised gmts.	No. of Arnolds-made gmts.	No. of Miss Playtime gmts. *	No. of unbranded gmts. *	Total no. of Arnolds-made gmts.	Total no. of gmts. in range
1966	209				9†		218
7	234	138	96	—	9†	105 (43%)	243
8	282	172	110	—	9†	119 (40%)	291
9	253	145	108	—	9†	117 (44%)	262
70	284	161	124	11	9†	144 (47%)	304
1	321	106	215	27	9	251 (70%)	357
2	272	88	239	40	6	287 (77%)	372
3	329	93	252	28	19	299 (82%)	375
4	345	88	257	21	30	313 (78%)	400

Year	Total Playtime turnover £000	Merchandise turnover £000	Arnolds-made turnover £000	Arnolds total %
1966	3486	1552	1934	55
7	3338	1522	1815	54
8	3952	1746	2206	56
9	4011	1743	2534	59
70	4207	1679	2527	60
71	4916	1102	3809	77
2	4682	892	3790	80
3	4031	879	3150	80

*All Arnolds-made. †Estimate

ILLUSTRATION 13.6   Summary of garment variety in spring ranges 1966–74

14 Managing without a System: Micronair Aircraft Crop Sprays

1. The initiatives of Jim McMahon

Micronair is essentially a one-man company. It revolves around the personality and initiatives of Jim McMahon, the managing director. He is an example of the possibilities available to the alert entrepreneur. He started his career as an aircraft engineer in New Zealand shortly after the Second World War and became impressed with the possibilities of aerial crop spraying. He came over to England in the early 1950s in the search for a suitable aircraft and appropriate equipment. After a series of difficulties he joined three partners, Frank Mann, John Britten and Desmond Norman, and a world-wide business known as Britten-Norman Aircraft Ltd and Crop Culture (Aerial) Ltd was built up, based at Bembridge airfield on the Isle of Wight. In 1968 because of a difference of opinion in management policy the four partners agreed to an equity separation: McMahon and Mann took the crop spraying business to nearby Bembridge Fort as a manufacturing base while Britten and Norman carried on as owners of the Islander aircraft project. (Unfortunately Britten-Norman went into receivership some three years later.)

Jim McMahon divides his time between the Bembridge works on the Isle of Wight and the overseas crop spraying activities, with the majority of his time spent managing at Bembridge. Bembridge is the engineering arm of the business, manufacturing the crop spraying equipment. He admitted that the Bembridge operation was a struggle as well as a challenge: 'In our other operations, one pilot with one aircraft on a small island in the Caribbean can earn almost as much turnover as the whole of this company put together. Equally a small land deal in the Isle of Wight made in half an hour's telephone conversation can match the annual profit of Micronair without any of the frustrations.'

The establishment of Micronair at Bembridge records an extraordinary series of initiatives, ranging across the choice of site, labour policy and product range. Its continued success, McMahon believes, can be largely attributed to the choice and arrangement of premises. The works is located in an old fort on an isolated hill which formed part of the British defences against Napoleon III. A drawbridge over a moat must be crossed to enter the works. The factory itself consists of 20ft x 40ft bays (ex-ammunition stores buried in the hill) connected by passages (tunnels) surrounding an oval court-yard. This strange site is rented from the National Trust for a few hundred pounds a year.

Micronair has one other site for a related operation, 'Wight Plastics' at Shanklin four miles distant. McMahon commissioned the Council for Small Industries in Rural Areas (COSIRA) to design the complete factory for him for less than £100. The floor area is 14,000 sq. ft. The construction of this factory is being carried out by Micronair staff which, McMahon states, 'ensures a perfect job at half the price'. A further plan is to construct twelve houses nearby to encourage skilled personnel to move over from the mainland.

McMahon also took initiatives in labour policy. He was the first to use cheap local prison labour for simple assemblies but this caused problems and was discontinued. McMahon explained that 'although facilities and equipment were excellent, prisoners sometimes deliberately sabotaged the work.' McMahon has also used locally available skills in design support. A complex metering attachment was developed by a schoolboy electronics enthusiast from Bembridge School.

Perhaps the most surprising aspect of the company is its extraordinary range of products. Besides aerial crop spraying equipment, Micronair make sophisticated wooden rocking horses, 'picked up from a man who sold them over his garden fence'; carpet sweepers for Woolworths, 'taken over from another company'; dehumidifiers for NATO military contracts, 'from a failed enterprise with £100,000 of idle tooling'; Golden Spot fruit machines, 'for a leisure business company'; and then in 1974 plastic moulding activities, complementary to the metal engineering side which can design and manufacture injection moulding dies. The wide range of products is a device to keep the options open if the main crop spraying lines fail.

McMahon has tried to distribute initiative throughout his company with varying degrees of success. He operates through two men: Peter Gatrell in charge of product development and overseeing production and Roy Newnham in charge of finance and administration. Peter Gatrell has worked with McMahon for 20 years and Roy Newnham also for a long period. For a while Gatrell was production manager but his key role and interest has always been product development and watching over the operations in McMahon's absence. Throughout 1973 David Waller was production manager under Peter

Gatrell, but he left in December like many of his predecessors. Although there are only 50 personnel at the fort, the company divides physically and psychologically into four separate groups — the management team (exclusive of production control), production control and foremen, the direct employees and the self-employed. Superficially the personnel structure looks straightforward, but the inner tensions can only be grasped by having a clear idea of McMahon's high aspirations with regard to production organisation and his ideal of 'self-employment' as a motivational force.

The major irony for McMahon is the potential the company has for expansion but the nagging doubts he has about an adequate management team to cope with a larger operation. He is not convinced all his staff appreciate the relentless drive needed to carry on a business continually facing inefficiency and casual suppliers. 'Our customers are not interested in excuses when insects are eating crops: they just want Micronair equipment quickly. Senior staff therefore must be prepared to be on call 24 hours a day seven days a week.' The high-quality engineering at Bembridge has led to the possibility of large contracts, but current capacity will not handle it. McMahon prefers to develop companies as separate entities even if they are partially managed by the same team. Encouragement is given to the heads of different ventures to build up the product and 'run their own show' within the Micronair Company. But this has not always worked out. 'Very quickly an individual's level of initiative is exposed. Excuses plus numerous bad luck stories quickly establish the plateau of the individual who then must be dismissed, otherwise a chain reaction of disorganisation within the company will result.'

McMahon has a distinctive attitude to the role of the director and his relationship with the employees. 'All employees should be cost-conscious and understand the purpose of the company. Apprentices should have an insight into company law, cash flow, the function of a director plus the part the shareholders play. After all, this is where our future managers will come from. I have no time for expense account directors. You have to work — you have a moral obligation to your employees to work. The only real management left is in the small business where both bosses and men can see what's going on. It all comes back to a question of man management: how to set an example and retain a high standard. The manager has got to operate the controls. He has to be able to recruit people and shake them down into the right slots. He's got to be able to keep half-a-dozen balls in the air at one time. He's got to drive the men forward without them knowing they're being driven.' Despite these clear views on leadership McMahon wants an open forum for discussion. 'Everyone is entitled to their own views, and opinions are welcomed provided they are constructive and are not unrealistic.' McMahon's policy is to give two chances to anyone but the third serious mistake means dismissal.

2. Product Policy

All the activities at Micronair divide into five groups distinguished by different companies: the company name, the products and the facilities are indicated below.

Company Name	Products	Facilities for Manufacture
Micronair	Atomisers, brackets and components such as flow-meters and variable restrictor units	Metal cutting and machining equipment, fitting
Wight Engineering	Components for hospital operating tables, temperature gauges	Metal cutting and machining equipment, fitting
Wight Engineering Die and Mould	Tools for plastic injection mouldings	Metal cutting machining equipment spark eroding and die sinking
Burman Engineering	Carpet Sweepers De-humidifiers Rocking Horses Golden Spot Machine	Plastic moulding machines Engineering, fitting, presses
Wight Plastics	Plastic mouldings on sub-contract work at separate site in Shanklin, four miles distant	Plastic moulding machines, dies and tools

The company has no sales force. McMahon believes 'the Micronair product has to sell itself. One salesman travelling world-wide needs £100,000 extra business to cover his costs. As all our potential customers are known we prefer to put extra effort into good service and a refined product with an open door to visit us at any time. In fact most of our sales are spearheaded by technical representatives of major chemical companies. A close relationship has been built up and a very effective indirect sales force is at our service.' By following this policy the sales have become world-wide and considerable new business is now being carried out with the Eastern bloc and Cuba.

Micronair spraying equipment and a large contract with Matburns for hospital bed components contribute 90 per cent of the company's sales turn-over. The demand for spraying equipment has in fact remained remarkably stable, and the new environmentalist lobby has played right into Micronair's hands with demands for ultra low-volume spraying. The main component of the Micronair equipment is the 'atomiser', a rotating cylinder attached to the wings of aircraft by brackets. It draws off chemical from a tank inside the aircraft and breaks it down into fine droplets. The atomiser is supplemented by a restrictor unit, a brake actuator and more than a dozen brackets for different aircraft. Micronair receive a steady supply of orders for the equipment although some of the bracket kits are rare. They can rely on selling more than 1000 atomisers a year. Each atomiser requires about 18 hours of work and each bracket about 2.5 hours.

The Matburn hospital bed equipment consists of head flaps, leg flaps and handles for operating tables. These consist of sub-assemblies of a dozen parts and in 1974 Micronair have secured steady contracts for about 20 of these per week. The production work is 10 hours for a leg flap, seven hours for a head flap, nine hours for the handle.

The die and mould manufacturing business is just being built up as a going concern in 1974, and carpet sweeper production is continuing but will be phased out. The carpet sweeper is under-priced, giving 14p profit on a basic price of £1.40, but it is a contract with Woolworths and McMahon believes in honouring his obligations. The dehumidifier, rocking horses and the Golden Spot machine are nearly in abeyance, although the last two items were very demanding in management and design time during their introduction in 1972. The Golden Spot fruit machine had caused particularly feverish activity, being a product with complicated electronic and mechanical parts which had moved from concept to sale in four months — 'A large company would take 18 months or more to conceive the product.' McMahon justified this effort by stating: 'We have 1½ men in our work force budgeted for development and these products were well worth while if for no other reason than training: they highlight how lucky we are to have a stable product. One day we may come across something which will be a winner. It is better to try and learn by mistakes than do nothing and hope a fairy wand will bring us a new product.' McMahon admits that the marketing of new products is the weakness in the company but considers this to be true of any small company with limited resources. He alone sets the product prices. He has the feel of the market, especially in the Micronair products, which enjoy a world monopoly. His aim was to 'charge what the market will bear', and he aimed at 25 per cent above costs to generate the necessary surplus to plough back into development of new products and avoid the bottomless pit of taxation.

3. Cost Control

Management accounts play a vital role, in McMahon's view, although he believes an unimaginative accountant can put the company out of business as easily as an over-enthusiastic technical engineer. The accounts are used to portray the analysis of product costs and give a monthly report on the viability of each product. At the beginning of the year a budget is prepared by David Milford, breaking down the figures into cost elements by product group. A summary of the total budget and part of the accounts are shown in Illustration 14.1. This presumes a certain sales level across the product range with provision to cut down should movement of the product be slow.

The actual sales and costs are accumulated from the invoices and time cards on a weekly basis. (The invoices from the self-employed may come in a month later than the time at which the work is done and this weakens the accuracy of the accounting system.) A time analysis is used to derive the average labour costs per hour on each product, and once a month the total direct costs are accumulated to give a summary of total labour costs incurred over the year by product (Illustration 14.2). These lead on to the monthly and cumulative cost statement against budget both for a labour cost per hour on each product and a total cost per hour on each product as shown at the bottom of Illustration 14.1.

The costing procedure is rather different for Die and Mould Engineering (in effect a division of Wight Engineering), and for Wight Plastics. Both these activities are handled as self-contained units with seven or eight men. All the work is done on an individual order basis and the group have to win the contracts, organise their own equipment and schedules, and administer their time to include transport of goods, and maintenance of tools and stores. Unlike the atomiser business they always face the task of filling up their order books. They send copies of all invoices and quotes to David Milford, the accountant, who enters the returns and costs for each job and these provide them with information for future estimating and bidding for like work. Milford applauds these self-contained teams, particularly Wight Plastics where 'there is no distinction between men by skill and they all muck in together and clear up collectively. They are paid a group bonus. If they pass the set turnover level they get 1½ per cent of the difference as a bonus and this can amount to £70 for a month. They then share this out on a man-hour basis.' McMahon has concluded that for these self-contained operations it is impossible to make much profit under eight direct workers and a turnover of £50,000 per annum excluding materials.

4. The Organisation of Production

Excluding the Wight Plastics operation all the manufacturing operations for all the products are carried out at the Bembridge fort. The layout of machines and the allocation of operators is shown in Illustration 14.3. The machine types are scattered across the bays and there is often a mixture of self-employed and Micronair staff allocated to a single bay. The die and mould shop, the carpet sweepers and dehumidifiers are run as separate self-contained shops. Although there are up to 30 Micronair staff at the factory many are in supporting roles. The bulk of the output is done by the self-employed, 'where the money is made'.

At the beginning of 1974 a new structure was being added in the forecourt of the fort for new offices and new floor space which will greatly improve the layout. Improvements in the layout are much overdue. Fred Godden, the planner/estimator, said he had never seen a worse layout in all his experience in industry. Ernie Jones, the foreman/chargehand, says he wakes up in the night dreaming about the mess of bits and machines and swarf lying around the gloomy passages.

Despite these layout problems the actual orders get out of the door more or less on time. Incoming orders are received by Roy Newnham and a delivery date is agreed with the customer. The delivery is generally intended to be six to eight weeks from order acceptance. (For the Matburn equipment the load is running on a steady 20 per week requirement.) Recently deliveries have been achieved within a few weeks of target. Data from Mr Newnham's files indicated that the 63 despatches of Micronair equipment made between February and July 1973 averaged 2½ weeks late with only two orders in excess of six weeks late. A few weeks' lateness is usually inevitable for getting letters of credit for the many export orders.

For each order for Micronair equipment Fred Godden places a card on a large chart to indicate visually the forward load pattern. For atomisers, assembly can be carried out continuously as they are in a steady demand of about 100 a month. There is also a fairly even demand for the variable restrictor unit, the brake actuator, and bracket kits for the Pawnee, Agwagon and Agcat aircraft. The demands for the other components in the Micronair set are more erratic.

Two weeks before the due date Fred Godden places an assembly order with the fitting department. Each product is defined by a 'schedule number' and each schedule defines the parts needed for the product. The schedule for the atomiser has 10 pages. For each manufactured part there is a specification giving raw material (or sub-assemblies) and operations. When a new set of parts is to be manufactured or assembled, Fred Godden prepares a shop planning card which will go to one of the machining bays. Parts are drawn from stores and the completed work is returned to stores. The standard times for the operations are held in the production control office on separate cards.

The decision on when to launch the batches depends on Fred Godden

keeping a watchful eye on the number of parts available, in collaboration
with Jack Warren in the stores. Normally for atomiser parts the aim is to
manufacture a batch of 250 parts. Some of the parts are common to a range
of products and these are listed in the common parts register. As the operations progress, Fred Godden racks the cards for the outstanding jobs by their
current operations by milling, auto, fitting, turning, welding groups, although
this functional classification does not correspond to particular areas in the
physical layout of the works. The whole system depends very critically on the
precision of Jack Warren's stock control with more than 1000 different parts
in stores. Often when an assembly order is made shortage lists have to be
issued to get the parts manufactured. The company policy is to manufacture
Micronair equipment for stock but to date this has not been possible, due,
in McMahon's view, 'to increasing business and inability to organise
production'.

5. The Self-employment Policy

Any weaknesses in the physical layout and planning system are secondary
factors in the Micronair operations. The key to the future of Micronair
depends on the success of McMahon's self-employment policy and the finding
of a suitable personality to fill the production management role which links
the self-employment system to the company's production requirements.

One of McMahon's fundamental concerns is worker motivation. Through
observation in his travel he has become convinced that new ideas are
essential in the U.K. 'In America output per man is three times the U.K. level
in the engineering industry; it's a question of good methods, good supervision
and the direct interest of the worker in getting on.' He has therefore introduced the idea of 'self-employment' at Micronair as an experiment to improve
performance.

The basic scheme is that the self-employed man will operate on a personal
contract basis job by job. He can decide when to come in and when to go.
He will not be paid for holidays nor be insured by the company. He makes
out his own accounts and tax returns. The facilities at Micronair are available
to him 24 hours a day.

In McMahon's view the great attraction of this scheme is that it provides
a known volume of output at a price fixed in advance. Also the self-employed
man will often work long hours, increase output per unit time, and double
the machine utilisation. 'The basic incentive is cold hard cash; it gets the
output and there's no leaning on the shovel.'

The idea of self-employment took shape in 1971 when Jim McMahon met a machinist, Roger Barker, and offered to engage him on a self-employed basis. After a short period Barker told McMahon that he could halve the standard times on the atomiser. McMahon took up the idea and offered £1 an hour after deducting one-third from the standard times. When Barker started to make good money a number of the other machinists requested to become self-employed as well and, by the spring of 1973, 14 workers were self-employed. Mainly they machined the longer runs on the atomisers and Matburn work and occupied two distinct bays for turning and welding jobs.

But substantial problems had arisen in the middle of 1973. Barker had formed a group of eight self-employed which he effectively managed on his own. He became 'a factory within a factory' and was forcing David Waller, the production manager, to provide very long runs on the best jobs. The situation became very much out of control when McMahon was away for several months in mid-1973, with the self-employed group threatening to take a stranglehold on the company. Many of them were earning more than £5000 per annum. After a major shake-up on McMahon's return, Barker had to go.

Since then the self-employment scheme settled down again and McMahon intends to extend it where possible. The difficulties which occurred have raised a few questions. 'The trouble with the British working man is that he doesn't know how to be treated as an equal — that is the union's tradition — the confrontation approach. The self-employment idea should get over this. But you still need to be choosey about the men otherwise they will attempt to monopolise the situation. Some men are greedy — you give them £100 a week and they still want more. They always expect work to be available for them. Sometimes this forces pressure back up the pipeline and exposes shortcomings in production control and management — which may be a good thing. If an employed person has no material, incorrect drawings or a machine that does not work, he will sit down and be paid; but not the self-employed individual who sees his income disappearing.'

Certainly the self-employed turned out the volume; they often worked more than 60 hours a week. But they also earned the money and looked for more, to the envy of the employed staff at Micronair. The long runs led to real accounting and control problems of knowing where the work was as a job may go to and fro between Micronair and the self-employed in the course of its operations. The self-employed normally knew the standards (from which 33 per cent time is deducted) for the regular jobs and they bargained at a price per hour. For new jobs the standards have to be agreed, and for welding and brazing work the standard time is reduced by only 20 per cent.

Many of these views are borne out by the self-employed men themselves. One of the earliest 'self-employees' said he went self-employed because the pay at Micronair was so bad. 'To get a reasonable living you have to be self-employed. I can now put in a hundred hours if I want whereas Micronair people work a 46-hour week. You are a foreman in your own right and don't get involved in the politics of the place. The main thing is to ensure the work-load ahead. This has cracked the firm right open on materials and paperwork. I like runs of at least 300 items, so small jobs get left behind. Assemblies have always had shortage lists. Ernie Jones has to get them done in the fitting shop. I shouldn't be tied to fiddling little jobs. I need to make £1.15 an hour at least and I can't get a good price on the short jobs. We're still on 20 per cent less than other contractors, but I work here because I like the company. Mind you, if I was a director I would never bring in self-employed. The company has no control over them. To be complete the self-employed should really own their machines.' Another self-employed machinist suggested that the self-employed system did not imply radical differences from the earlier employee arrangements. 'Really the job's no different now. The job's just as secure. It's simply a glorified bonus scheme.'

6. The Production Management Task

The main pressure point of the self-employment scheme inevitably lay with the production manager organising the work. McMahon saw production management as a key skill involving great ability at man management, an eye for detail and plenty of energy. 'You're either born with it or not.' Obtaining a good production organiser is a selection job not a training task. He considered that you did not have to be a technical man although 'it's a plus if you're an engineer in Micronair.' Ideally he wanted a man who could supervise produc-tion and organise forward planning.

In the struggle to find the right man McMahon had got through ten produc-tion controllers in six years. It was a worrying tale. McMahon related how they had all failed. 'One became frustrated, another had a personality problem, then a hopeful prospect had 'lead in his boots'. One worked himself to death because he couldn't get organised. Then we tried an older man who had done the same sort of work before in a larger company; but he was a disaster. He wanted an assistant and then another assistant for what was half a job anyway. The big job for the production manager is to keep the thing going whatever happens and push down the responsibilities as far as they'll go. Many say I won't delegate but it's really the other way round — I give them so much rope they eventually hang themselves. Only when customers are let down and the bank balance is affected do I move in.'

In David Waller, who occupied the position throughout 1973, McMahon thought he had found the ideal man. 'David was highly practical with great energy and dedication and he had the honesty and courage to face up to anyone. But he wanted to take over everything and thought the job was much too easy. He was erratic. Paperwork and figures were not his thing, and therefore forward planning never got going. He had real problems with the self-employed. Barker, a forceful character, took charge of him, and the quality control went to pieces. It cost us a lot of money in bad work and the back-up team headed by Peter Gatrell had to go in to sort out the mess.'

David Waller had come from a large electronics company where he had been in process planning, converting drawings into operation specifications 'in a very unsatisfactory large-company environment where everyone specialised and watched their own empires'. He had applied for the job of tool-maker at Micronair, but McMahon had detected his enthusiasm for management and offered him the job of production planner at an annual salary of just over £2000.

David Waller's initial weeks in 1973 were hectic. Not only were there no planning staff but the chief foreman was leaving at the end of January and he only had a chargehand to help. He put nominal people in charge of the bays and aimed to feed them the work by getting a good paperwork system going. But it was not easy as he had two new kinds of pressure to deal with; the rising pressure of demand with McMahon shouting for early deliveries and the pressure for special treatment from the self-employed.

David said be never really grasped his relation to the office staff. Roy Newnham constantly fed him with orders under pressure and Peter Gatrell gave him all sorts of extra instructions like 'the clearing of the fort and maintaining the vehicles'. He also had difficulties in relating the work allocation to the costing scheme. 'How do you cost a job when it may or may not be done on a night shift when it's nominally more expensive but when the overhead should fall as the shop's getting higher utilisation? And what happens when you've negotiated a price with the self-employed and they misinterpret the drawing and the factory doesn't have an inspector which you've asked for?' The work volume continued to be a problem. 'They'll take any order and never question whether we have the space or what it will do to the production schedule. We moved heaven and earth to get the first 10 Pawnees out for Easter.' The pressure continued throughout the year. David could not recall any weekend when he was not in at the fort for at least 10 hours. He found a queue of people waiting for him every day, and he seldom got home before 9 at night.

But undoubtedly the major pressure was the self-employed. 'You don't know how to treat them; they're part of you but they're not. Some of them formed into a group with a leader, Roger Barker. He used to set up the machines and then get the men working on the long runs so that there were no real set-up costs and he could take the extra money himself. He wouldn't let me put the times on the cards in case the men saw them. He even asked for a labourer for £1000 and made him into a full-time driller. They worked hard – came at 8 and stayed until 8 at night, often six days a week. They depended on the spare equipment and the work-in-progress to make the money. They were confident and very aggressive. Shortly after I came to Micronair some of the self-employed said, 'Give us extra money in the contracts and you'll be O.K. Otherwise we'll tell Jim your mistakes and you won't last five minutes.' It all blew up to a head in the summer. In facing up to Barker I never got the paperwork sorted out. Perhaps I enabled McMahon to get rid of Barker, but in doing so I wrecked myself.'

After David left at the end of 1973, Fred Godden (who was taken on in the autumn to do the paperwork) continued in the production controller's role looking after the paperwork, but acting as a planner and estimator. He had no intention of going on to the shop floor again and was training a progress chaser to trace the jobs twice a week. 'After 20 years in work study I'm not going into that confrontation scene again. We'll have to get a good foreman – a sergeant-major type to keep the self-employed in check.' Jim McMahon was also intending to invest more money in that function, as each time a production controller goes it leads to a round of traumatic difficulties leading to uncertainties in the management team and further difficulties in the control of operations. On these occasions McMahon formulates a plan, discusses it with his managers and sometimes commits his detailed require-ments to paper. Internal memos (Illustration 14.4), prepared at key moments of production control crises, reflect the agonies.

But McMahon was confident that the future challenges could be taken up: 'There are tremendous opportunities in British industry for anyone willing to train in management expertise. The two positions most difficult to fill are foreman and production manager. After 25 years in England I have not met any high-calibre people in these positions. Those with ability seem to move on to higher positions or own their own firm. The requirements are clear:

an interest in their work;

common sense and organising ability, with strict attention to detail;

integrity;

reasonable personality to mix with and supervise people.

Anyone having these qualities cannot fail in a successful career and I am pleased to see there is at least some movement in training individuals for this role. But the training can only illustrate what the problems are: the reality of management comes when you face men head on and tell them to get the job done.'

Question for discussion

Debate the case for and against the operational policies at Micronair.

Budget (summary)

1973

Value of Saleable   £344,235
Goods Produced

Costs

Labour — direct	46,797	
Labour — indirect	50,386	
Overheads	57,648	
Materials/treatments	107,179	
Sub-contract — R. Barker	13,500	
(45% of £30,000)		
Die Mould	13,500	
(45% of £30,000)		
	£289,010	

Net Profit   £55,225   16.05%

Micronair/Wight Engineering Accounts for 39 Weeks to 29.9.73

	Actual	Budget
Total cost of production	£188092	£216762
Value of goods produced	£197697	£258180
Value of sales invoiced	£220270	£271107

Breakdown by Products

	Labour Rate/hour		Combined Rate/hour	
	Actual	Budget	Actual	Budget
Micronair/Wight Engineering All Products	£0.843	£0.95	£1.972	£2.15
Micronair	0.848	0.86	1.954	1.93
Dehumidifiers	0.702	0.90	1.768	1.97
Carpet Sweepers	0.670	0.79	1.761	1.86
Golden Spot	0.904	0.90	2.133	1.97
Sub-contract	0.852	0.90	2.019	1.97
Die and Mould	0.824	1.00	2.117	2.33
Sub-contract — R. Barker	0.985	1.00	2.036	2.22

ILLUSTRATION 14.1   Budget and accounts for 1973

	Total	Micronair	Carpet Sweepers	Dehumid- ifiers	Die Mould	Sub-contract Wight Eng.	R.Barker Eng.	Rocking Horse	Golden Spot m/c	Plant/ New Tool
Direct Labour Hours										
Micronair/Wight Eng.	60364	39814	4662	2913	7569	1245	2151	–	1035	455
Self-employed at £1/hour.	2793				2793					
	4468						4468			
	69625	39814	4662	2913	10392	1245	8619	–	1535	455
Direct Wages Cost	58715	33760	3125	2046	8553	1061	8490	–	1387	293
Indirect Wages*– wkly	25550	15234	1667	967	3799	420	2659	–	618	186
–*monthly	9810	3569	448	271	3195	268	1834	–	182	43
O/heads + (as per budget)	43212	25212	2972	1847	6437	765	4561	–	1067	301
Total Labour Cost	137287	77785	8212	5151	21984	2514	17544	–	3274	823
Mats/Tmnts	50805	34672	8505	4197	354	400	413	63	2180	21
Total Cost of Production	188092	112457	16717	9348	22338	2914	17957	63	5454	844
Value of goods Produced	197697	126325	14537	10404	21859	3021	18307	–	3571	–
Value of sales invoiced	120470	164607	8623	10291	12489	3429	18938	172	1709	–

* Taken as % of Direct wages cost   + Taken as proportion of Direct Lab. — £ 1974 charged as prop. of Turnover

ILLUSTRATION 14.2   Production Costs and Sales Figures — first 9 months 1973

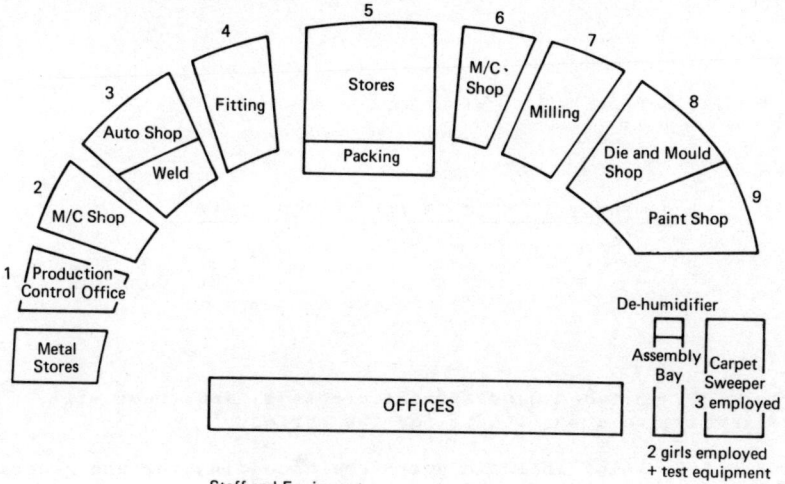

Staff and Equipment

1	Production controller and Assistant Estimator Timekeeper	
2	3 self-employed	2 Drills 1 Lathe 1 Rivetter 1 Router 1 Bandsaw
3	2 Micronair 1 Apprentice 2 Welding (self-employed)	5 Autos
4	3 Self-employed 3 Mincronair	10 Drills + hard tools
5	Jack Warren + Assistant + 2 packing	Racks for parts
6	3 Self-employed 1 Micronair	3 Capstans 3 C/lathes
7	1 Regular (+ Visitors)	2 Milling machines 6 Drills
8	Reg Robinson + 9 (Micronair)	5 Milling Machines 2 Lathes 1 Grinder 1 Drill
9	1 Micronair	Paint Equipment

ILLUSTRATION 14.3   Works layout

ILLUSTRATION 14.4a   Memo no. 1

CONFIDENTIAL MEMO TO ALL SENIOR STAFF

8th January, 1972

During 1971 we faced many serious problems, and these will,
I believe, give a small loss for the period.

These difficulties included out-of-balance disaster and general
rise in costs which we were forced to cover by raising our
prices.

Our new projects - rocking horse and carpet sweeper - are
still not showing signs of being viable.

In 1972 it is therefore obvious we must take stock of the
situation and run our business in such a way as to ensure

(a) It is profitable

(b) Our cash flow is under control

(c) Micronair and Wight Engineering
     are self-supporting.

SALES

Micronair still seems to be coming in at a steady rate at the
usual level and at the present time some 3 months' orders are
outstanding.   The apparent stability of this product is amazing
and in my opinion can lead us into an air of complacency.   Those
who have been with us for some time will recall I have been
striving to get the Company self-supporting and have warned we
may not always have this market which rescues our turnover every
year.

PRODUCTION

It was disturbing last year to discover our profit margin on the
Micronair had disappeared due jointly to rising prices and
inefficient production.   Reluctantly I took the easy way out
by raising prices to the maximum the market would stand but
this gave us only a small profit and it is necessary to improve
future production profitability by at least 20%.

Contd ......

To assist in achieving this the appointment was made of a new Production Manager.

At the same time our balance problem became evident and it has taken until now to get this under control - fortunately it seems without a serious cost.   There is no need for me to comment further on the balance problem - as to how or why it arose - but it is one of the most serious cases of mismanagement I have ever known and it is a miracle the Company has survived.

As Production holds the key to our future prosperity due to labour being the largest variable cost in our product, it is essential that all senior staff continue to give their fullest co-operation and support to G.E. in overcoming present and future problems.

Do not take it that we are out of trouble yet as several hundred potentially unbalanced atomisers are in the field and we must be alert to any tell-tale signs from customers and put them right.

<u>BUDGET</u>

We have now completed a budget for 1972 and the main reason for this memo is to make sure all senior personnel responsible for the following departments:-

Administration	R.W. Newnham
Accounts	J. Munn
Production	G. Erlam
Experimental	R.P. Gatrell

are aware of what is expected of them and necessary if the Company is to be put on a sound basis.

Our overheads at present are such that a turnover of some £200,000 is required.   As we work for 11 months of the year this means each month we must invoice £19,000 or in the region of £4,500 per week.

Having set a budget it is vital the results are checked weekly with our usual monthly graphs showing our achievement to date.

The systems within the organisation, all of which were carefully installed many years ago and let die because of bad organisation, must be put back into service and kept up.

Regular weekly meetings of the four departmental heads have been instituted and these must be carried on to ensure all are working towards the common aim of running a profitable business.

Immediately our turnover starts to fall action must be instituted to raise it or cut our costs, including overheads, to fall in line with the new situation.

One weakness we have is no separate sales organisation or department In the past this has fallen on myself and in the department "General Administration".   There seems to be no way in which this can be changed at present and from the Micronair point of view, will have to continue in the same way leaving G. Erlam and R.P. Gatrell to assist R.W. Newnham on technical matters in my absence.

Contd ....

Concerning sales embracing sub-contract work, carpet sweepers, new products etc., this will have to be a joint effort with production ensuring a simple procedure embracing enquiries, orders, invoicing etc., is set up between departments.

In a small Company such as ours it is essential that all senior staff be broadly au fait with what is happening in the Company and be able to carry out an intelligent conversation with any customer or outsider should the head of a particular department be out. The "don't know" reply "not my responsibility" cannot and will not be tolerated in senior staff or, for that matter, anyone else.

BUYING

To assist in keeping our cash flow in order it is essential all buying is placed under rigid control to ensure cheapest possible purchases are made and also that unnecessary stock is not held in our stores.

All purchases must carry an Order Number and signatures on orders must be limited to one or two senior staff as well as myself. I suggest G. Erlam and R.P. Gatrell with R. Newnham, J. Munn and myself in an emergency.

GENERAL

A purge must be carried out on general efficiency within the Company. This always starts with senior staff demanding a high standard from their department and at the same time keeping an eye on ways and means of improving systems and output. e.g. telephone charges are some £3,000 - £4,000 per annum. By planning calls and restricting the use of the telephones except when necessary this could be cut considerably. Have you ever wondered why many companies do not ring back? In many cases only senior staff are permitted to make long distance calls and even they are instructed to let the other party make the call. We cannot subscribe to this policy, but it shows the ends some organisations go to to reduce costs. Photo-copying, electricity wastage, organisation of transport are all items to be attacked. Have you ever entered a steaming hot office in the morning and wondered how much it cost to keep this temperature up overnight?

Cleanliness and tidy facilities are of the utmost importance not only in workshops, but offices as well. I am often ashamed to take visitors around our premises.

The telephone operator or secretary if often said to be the most important individual in any Company and this has been proved to myself many times. Being helpful and courteous costs nothing and I can recall once when customers used to compliment us on a telephonist we had as it was so unusual in a Company to be warmly received.

Contd ....

The procedure from the switchboard must be as follows:-

1. If the person required is not available, get the party's name, telephone number, purpose of call if applicable and offer to pass on the message.

2. Give the person the option of speaking to someone else before letting him go.

3. Even if someone else takes the call make sure a note is left immediately on the desk of the person concerned, giving name, date, time and, if applicable, what the person wanted, where and when he can be found or any other message.

R.N. Please institute this procedure at once as we have recently had complications because this was not adopted.

Suggest a message pad be obtained for the purpose.

Finally, I want to say this note may appear harsh, but it is not intended to be anything but factual. We have all the ingredients to built a first-class business using the Micronair as a base product and your help is needed to do this. This is why you are all on the pay-roll and by following a few simple rules of business there can be prosperity for all.

Suggestions or proposals for changes will be welcome at any time and if problems exist discuss them among yourselves or with me, but do not keep them hidden. Above all, do not be "Yes Men": bring out any argument you wish to strengthen the Company and remember any discussions on a particular point or subject are not a personal attack on the Head of the Department concerned. This feeling often restricts the smooth running of a Company such as ours by causing friction between Departments.

J.M. McMahon

BRIEF ON REORGANISATION

Serious shortcomings have been evident within our company in
ecent months.   Briefly these can be listed as follows:-

. General lack of enthusiasm coupled with a feeling of
uncertainty and dissatisfaction among shop floor and
indirect personnel.

. On investigation it was found this was due mainly to
shortcomings in our management structure which lacked the
necessary attention to detail and systems to provide a
smooth running organisation:

(a)   No sound planning was in operation and men were given
       incomplete instructions which led to confusion.

(b)   Shop and machine loading was vaguely controlled and
       created shortages in production as priorities became
       confused.   Machines lay idle.

(c)   Schedules were incomplete and times not correctly
       assessed or controlled which created bad feeling.

(d)   Supply of raw materials was erratic due to no forward
       planning and jobs were held up, shelved or changed half
       way through.   Rushed jobs were seen to lay around after
       effort had been put in to finishing them quickly.   There
       is nothing more demoralising to workmen than the above.

(e)   This resulted in our business being run from panic to
       panic to meet orders, which in fairness to those con-
       cerned, were met, but at a cost of human effort and no
       doubt loss of money by the necessity of overtime and
       ineffective use of labour.   Eventually those swept up
       in such a situation lose heart and respect for the
       management - this is exactly what has happened.

(f)   After loss of heart, the classic case is the follow
       on of a general air of dissatisfaction and the more
       pressure that is put on by enthusiastic supervision, the
       more disgruntled people become.   Rumours spread, arguments
       arise, politics grow within the company, forceful char-
       acters stir up trouble, good men leave and the company
       progresses into more confusion than ever.

       These effects eventually reach the customers who become
       dissatisfied, lose confidence also and the company begins
       a downhill slide.   This was starting with us.

       When all this became evident to me, certain action was
       taken to rescue the situation and the following instructions
       given:

(i) Reinstate the planning and systems that had been bypassed or not kept up to date. This means new or revised schedules throughout, proper control over man hours as well as shop loading.

(ii) Ensure proper supervision is installed on the shop floor and new personnel engaged if those amongst us cannot cope with the work. Shop floor supervision is one of the most difficult to fill and thorough conscientious individuals with the ability to organise are required.

(iii) Rework the stores to ensure proper control over all supplies, WIP, jigs and consumable tools is obtained.

(iv) Put in effective quality control.

(v) Provide management capable of running the above with instructions to institute a high degree of efficiency by setting an example and demanding the same high standards from everyone within the company.

It should be appreciated that the above will necessarily place an additional burden on our overhead expenditure and to compensate for this a corresponding increase in our productivity is essential. Furthermore the new administration will be capable of handling a much larger turnover. The immediate opportunities available to us for expansion are:-

1. Auto work

2. Injection Moulding

3. Welding Section (If we can keep the welders)

. ARB approval followed by aircraft work.

. Further sub contract work with possible expansion of Matburn work. However we must get the full confidence of Matburns. At present they are watching our efforts but are not convinced we are on top of our problems.

To put the above into effect, the following management structure has been arranged. It must be stressed that communications between the various sections and personnel concerned is of paramount importance and this must be through the defined channels. Provided simple and straightforward approach is adopted by all concerned and an air of thoroughness injected into the company, we should soon have a smooth running organisation with a cordial atmosphere and until we achieve this our aims will not be fulfilled.

It is vital to point out that those in management have a responsibility to obtain the maximum effort from personnel under them without being aggressive and unreasonable in their demands and above all, no one should be asked to do more than they are capable of doing It should be remembered most personnel are willing to do an honest day's work if they are organised and fed work in a manner to keep them interested and fully occupied. Those who do not respond to this treatment should not be in our employ. If personnel do not t the job or in turn become difficult or disloyal, they must be asked to leave after being given every opportunity to change their outlook. This will also apply to management who do not fit into the pattern of the company.

J.M. McMahon

en by
N RPG RR DW
WB JC FG